Praise for *Beyond Grit*

"*Beyond Grit* is so amazing! Anyone who's ever wanted to reach a new level will absolutely love the powerful tools in this book. Cindra Kamphoff delivers simple, effective strategies for getting the most out of yourself and achieving your goals. While working with Cindra, I have used many of these strategies to not only thrive as a professional runner, but battle cancer at the same time."**–GABRIELE GRUNEWALD, professional runner and U.S.A. Track and Field Indoor Champion**

"I cover world-class athletes and often wonder why, when there are two comparable athletes, one succeeds while the other doesn't. Now I know. Cindra's book gives you real-world examples and strategies you can use to be great in your personal life and career. I am going to read it again." **–JOE SCHMIT, KSTP-TV Sports Director, speaker, and author**

"I have used many of the strategies in this book while working directly with Cindra and have seen a huge improvement in my performance. This is a must-have book for anyone trying to truly unlock their full potential." **–JEFF LOCKE, NFL punter**

"A brilliant and practical guide that extends our knowledge on how to develop grit. Cindra also makes an important point—that there is more to success than grit. The ten practices in *Beyond Grit* will help you thrive under pressure and think and act like the world's best." **–HENDRIE WEISINGER, Ph.D., *New York Times* bestselling author of *Performing Under Pressure: The Science of Doing Your Best When It Matters Most***

"The information in this book just works. I knew there should be an easy way to understand how to improve performance effectively, and this is it!" **–CARRIE TOLLEFSON, 2004 Olympian, TV analyst, motivational speaker, and host of *CTolleRun* and the *Carrie Tollefson Training Camp***

"*Beyond Grit* does an incredible job of presenting powerful mental skills through engaging stories backed by quality research and brought to life through practical exercises. You will feel Cindra's positive energy and brilliance in every chapter. And if you follow her high performance game plan, you will tap into new levels of untapped potential." **–IAN CONNOLE, Kansas State University Athletics Director of Sport Psychology and Vision Pursue, LLC team member**

"This book is an extremely well-written guide for those who want to crush it. Cindra Kamphoff has helped world-class athletes and executives overcome life's obstacles using mental toughness, and she can help you, too." **–GARY HOOGEVEEN, Rocky Mountain Power Chief Commercial Officer**

"*Beyond Grit* has been an extremely valuable resource for our program. Working with Dr. Kamphoff inspires our student-athletes and equips them to better handle pressure, own the moment, and make the choice to be positive. As a coach and teacher striving to serve others while being at my best, the practical wisdom and tools in this book are essential. I'm grateful that Dr. Kamphoff has provided this outstanding work to help us continue to pursue our best in sport and in life for seasons to come." **–TOMMY VALENTINI, Ph.D., Steve Wilkinson Professor of Sport Ethics and Tennis and Gustavus Adolphus College Head Men's Tennis Coach**

"*Beyond Grit* decodes the peak performance tools and techniques employed by top professional athletes and world-class performers and makes them accessible to anybody looking to gain an edge in sports, leadership, business, and life. Cindra Kamphoff bridges the gap between learning and doing by delivering highly practical strategies that can be done daily and weekly to help you master your thoughts and emotions, thrive when challenged, and ultimately 'rule yourself' and discover your 'next level' capabilities." **–BERNIE HOLLIDAY, Ph.D., Director of Mental Conditioning for Pittsburgh Pirates Baseball**

"This is a powerhouse book of strategies, tools, and approaches to help you perform at your best that simply work. Whether you are an athlete, executive, or entrepreneur, Cindra's 'Ten Powerful Practices' are no-nonsense techniques that you can apply immediately. You will refer to this extraordinary book often." **–PAM SOLBERG-TAPPER, executive coach, speaker, 7 Continents Marathoner, at Coach for Success, Inc.**

"Cindra's book is a must-read for anyone who wants to live above their ordinary expectations. Her book is a *Bible of Self-Development* while providing tools that will help you to create an extraordinary life." **–MIKE HAMEL, H & M Contracting partner**

"*Beyond Grit* is a powerful guidebook on how you can become gritty and successful both on and off the field. When Cindra worked with our team, she got us to perform at a high level with these tools and strategies which resulted in our team's most successful season!" **–KAREN HEGGERNES, Hamline University Head Women's Lacrosse Coach**

"Cindra Kamphoff's expertise and passion shine through in this book. So many people fail to reach their true potential. Reading the strategies in *Beyond Grit* will help anyone overcome the fears and doubts that hold them back from true success." **–CARRIE JACKSON CHEADLE, mental skills coach and author of *On Top of Your Game***

"Cindra's book is full of very practical and easy-to-implement strategies and methods to help improve mental performance. I would recommend this for any coach or athlete looking to take their performance to the next level."
–**BRIAN FELL, Mankato West Activities Director**

"Cindra brings tested and effective strategies to coaches and athletes that maximize performance and sharpen focus. These strategies have really helped our players and staff stay focused on the things we can control within the competitive environment and enhance our individual and team performance."
–**PETER HAUGEN, Gustavus Adolphus College Head Football Coach**

"Human performance is about actions, relationships, and the development of a long-term strategy for success. Cindra understands this, and her work offers a compelling look into what it takes to be at your best in all avenues of competition and life." –**BRETT BARTHOLOMEW, strength coach and author of *Conscious Coaching: The Art & Science of Building Buy-In***

"If you have *Beyond Grit*, it's the one book you'll read again and again. Mastering Cindra's practical how-to's will change the trajectory of your life!"
–**BJ HELLYER, Northwestern Mutual Chief Development Officer**

"*Beyond Grit* takes the concepts of resilience and perseverance and gives the reader practical tools and tips to create life-changing habits. Dr. Kamphoff is one of the foremost sport psychology consultants in the world, something that's further evidenced by reading this book. It is a must for those who want to perform at their absolute best." –**JOSHUA LIFRAK, Director of Mental Skills for a Major League Baseball Team**

"Clear, practical, and relevant, *Beyond Grit* reveals the practices that lead to high performance. Kamphoff has made studying high performance her life's work and she will help you reach it." –**DAVID HORSAGER, bestselling author of *The Trust Edge* and CEO of the Trust Edge Leadership Institute**

"*Beyond Grit* is a must-have for any aspiring athlete, coach, or administrator looking to gain a mental edge in today's increasingly competitive landscape. Dr. Kamphoff arms individuals with everything they need to become the best possible version of themselves. The secrets of her success translate equally from the locker room to the boardroom, making this a must-read for young professionals and future community leaders." –**KEVIN BUISMAN, Director of Athletics, Minnesota State University**

BEYOND GRIT

TEN POWERFUL PRACTICES TO GAIN THE HIGH-PERFORMANCE EDGE

By Cindra Kamphoff, Ph.D.

ISBN 13: 978-1-63489-080-9
eISBN: 978-1-63489-081-6

Library of Congress Catalog Number: 2017947423
Printed in the United States of America
First Printing: 2017
21   20   19   5   4

Cover design by Nupoor Gordon
Illustration designed by Nicole Mueller
Interior design by Dan Pitts

Wise Ink Creative Publishing
807 Broadway St. NE, Suite 46
Minneapolis, MN 55413
wiseink.com

To order, visit www.BeyondGrit.com. Reseller discounts available.

To the three most important people in my life,

Dan, Carter, and Blake

Contents

IV: KNOW YOURSELF TO MASTER YOURSELF

V: DOMINATE THE CONTROLLABLES

VI: OWN THE MOMENT

VII: CHOOSE EMPOWERING EMOTIONS

Foreword

My first opportunity to play football for the Minnesota Vikings, I had no contract. I had just graduated from a Division II school. I tried out at a three-day rookie camp that already had a 90-man roster filled. For me to be signed, someone else would have to be cut to open up a slot. If I'd thought for one second about my chances of getting signed, I would not have made it happen. I wouldn't allow thoughts of self-doubt and skepticism to enter my mind. I looked across the field, locked eyes with the guy standing there, and said to myself, *Hey, I'm playing football. And I've got a guy lined up across from me. Let's go beat him.* And I played and played and played.

Against all odds, I got signed. I started out on the practice squad. For a year, I was going up against NFL starters every day, smashing into bodies to get better. I ended each practice bone-tired and filled with discomfort. I went to bed with my muscles screaming. Despite how hard it was, I loved the opportunity that I'd been given. All the aches and pains and sweat were worth it given the incredible growth I was experiencing as a professional football player. I kept my head where it belonged—focused on taking advantage of every opportunity that was given to me. The next year, I made the active roster, and I've been on it ever since. I've now gone from a special teams role to being one of the starting wide receivers for the Minnesota Vikings.

In football, as in anywhere else in life, your goals change as you move along. Outside circumstances can and all too often do adjust your plan. Rather than focusing on all the things I can't control—variables that will change whether or not I want them to—I have to keep my mind on the opportunities I can control. That's how I made it where I am now.

When I first started playing for the Minnesota Vikings, the first thing on my mind was, *Hey, let's get signed and get that opportunity to go to training camp.* Then it was, *Let's at least make the practice squad.* Then, *Get on the active roster.* Last year, my big goal was to contribute heavily to offense and have a really significant role as a receiver. This year, I'll be building newer and bigger goals on that one—and then I'll build even bigger ones on top of those next year. All I can control is how I'm going to improve myself in whatever situation comes along. If I didn't play with that mindset, I never would have gotten to training camp in the first place. That's what the league is all about. You're given chances that you know will never come again, that you have to take advantage of before they disappear forever.

To focus on what truly matters, I have to always be self-aware, conscious of what drives me in what I do. I have to have the mindset of, *Whatever this play is called, I'm gonna do it to the best of my ability.* Power Phrases are important; I always say "*Lock it in*" to myself. I know I'm playing my best when I'm locked into what's immediately in front of me, nothing else. Every time I get in the huddle, I repeat it to myself: "*Lock it in. Lock it in.*"

Your mind can do crazy things—when you're an athlete, you realize how important that is. And that only gets harder when you get to the higher levels of the game. But if you keep control over your thoughts, taking things one play at a time, amazing things can happen.

I remember one game in college—when I was first exposed to the impact of Cindra's mental training and the ten practices in *Beyond Grit*—we were getting crushed by the other team, down 21 points. I could have let that ruin my individual confidence and the confidence of the team. But I approached each drive as a new opportunity to move the ball down the field and score.

Looking around at my huddled teammates, there was no fear or doubt in their faces despite the distance we had to make up. Everybody's eyes said, "Hey, we're gonna do this." And that's what we did. We focused on just that next play, and the next, and the next. We were unstoppable.

When you're that far behind, it's easy to look at the big picture and think, *Dang. There's no way we're gonna win this game.* But you have to take things one play at a time. Don't focus on the outcome of the game, or how many catches you have, or how many yards you need. Block out the distractions and say to yourself, *"Hey, I gotta beat this guy across from me. I don't care if the ball's coming to me or not—I gotta beat this guy. The rest of things will play out."*

We ended up beating the other team in overtime, but that didn't ultimately matter. What mattered was that each of us played his heart out, to the best of his ability, regardless of what happened.

At the end of the day, I play because I have a blast doing it— that's part of my why. I tell my wife all the time: I wake up at five a.m. ready to go to work because I've got the best job in the world. The beauty of football is you're never going to be perfect. You're always striving for that perfection, but you won't make it every time. If you don't have that love for the game, if you can't embrace failure as valuable because it makes you a better player, you're not ever going to be the best you can be.

It won't always feel good. People don't understand; they watch what you do on Sundays and think that's all there is to it. But there's so much more that goes into your performance on game days. There will be a lot of nights where you've had a rough practice that leaves you feeling crushed. Or there will be times you're just in a lot of pain; *Man, my body doesn't feel that great.* But grit is such an important thing. You have to fight through the hurt, you have to persevere. Your best self is the one at the other end of that trail of grit. It would be a shame if you never knew that person.

Ultimately, that's what it comes down to, not just in football but in every area of life: Know yourself. Know what gets you to your best, highest level. What keeps you motivated even when the struggle and discomfort make you wish you could curl into a ball. There will be a lot of trial and error, and you'll have to stay committed—that's why I still see Cindra each week. If you don't keep your why in mind, you'll have to start from square one again and again. But if you can keep building on your why as a foundation—if you never stop searching for what makes you the best version of yourself—you'll take off beyond boundaries you never even knew were there. That's what *Beyond Grit* is all about.

—ADAM THIELEN, wide receiver for the Minnesota Vikings

Introduction

April 15, 2013: the date I completed my third Boston Marathon. The Boston Marathon is my favorite because it's so challenging. The first thirteen miles, all downhill, tear at your quads and cause serious discomfort. The second thirteen miles include five big hills, most notably Heartbreak Hill around mile 21. Those are 26.2 tough miles.

But on April 15, 2013, I crushed it. I owned the course. I pushed up Heartbreak Hill steady and strong, passing more than 100 people. I finished with my personal best time. As I walked back to my hotel, two blocks from the finish on Boylston Street, I had a huge, shiny smile plastered on my face.

Then, suddenly, the significance of the race faded into the background. I heard sirens. Then I learned why: two bombs exploded near the finish line, killing three people and injuring an estimated 264 others, including fourteen who required amputations. From my hotel room window, I could see the terror of the bombs. Hadn't I just crossed the same finish line—the same spot where the bombs were detonated—only fifty-five minutes earlier? It didn't seem real.

I crowded around the hotel TV with my husband and our closest running friends to watch the news. We heard there might be more bombs along the course. We wondered if there could be bombs near us, or even in our hotel. We were only a few blocks from where the explosions had occurred. I forced myself to take several deep breaths and not go to the worst-case scenario. It was hard.

In that hotel room, as I sat watching news reports on that terrorist attack and the manhunt that followed, I went to some deep places. I found myself asking three pivotal questions:

- Why am I here?
- What difference am I making in this world?
- Why do I do what I do?

I sat in the hotel room and thought about my "why," questioning if I was truly following my calling and wondering about my purpose on this earth.

That day was a turning point in my life. After it, I started making different decisions with my time, energy, and mindset. I started living, thinking, and performing intentionally. I started owning my why.

This book would not exist had I not been in the middle of a terrorist attack that April afternoon. I would not be a leading sport psychology professional working with one of the top teams in the National Football League, nor would I have sought opportunities to work with some of the nation's leading companies. Sitting in that hotel room forced me to think about mindset. When the worst things are happening around you, what do you do? When you suffer a deep, gut-wrenching loss or are forced to change direction either at work or at home, how do you remain resilient, strong, and in control? When you find yourself in the middle of change and conflict, do you have the power to see problems as gifts? This is the secret of the world's top performers. Ask any gold medalist, top entrepreneur, or game changer how they overcome the impossible and defeat the unthinkable, and they will tell you that it's all in their approach. It's all about mindset.

WHAT IS THE HIGH PERFORMANCE MINDSET AND WHY IT IS IMPORTANT?

I call this mindset the High Performance Mindset. Others sometimes call high performance "greatness" or "mastery." We "perform" every single day, in each role we hold in life. Every day, I perform as a professor, leader, speaker, writer, coach, friend, athlete, wife, and mom. You likely perform in some of the same or in entirely different—and often challenging—roles, too. In every role, your mind is essential to your success.

In this book, you'll discover the 52 life-altering strategies of the world's most successful executives, athletes, and entrepreneurs. In my research as a professor, I have found that top performers—Oprah Winfrey, Lebron James, Bill Gates—all practice the same mental habits. For these individuals and for us, the High Performance Mindset is a purposeful, daily pursuit of excellence. In other words, great minds *do* think alike.

To live a High Performance Life, we must be fully present, engaged, in control, and confident. When we live in this way, we become more consistent and succeed above and beyond the standard. We become gritty.

As you live the High Performance Life, you'll become practiced at being mentally strong, meaning you take control of your thoughts, your actions, and your destiny. You can grab hold of the goals in front of you no matter how beyond reach they may seem. Whether you're seeking to own your dream business, triple your income, become the best in your field, or merely achieve a higher level of personal satisfaction, your mental strength is key. Here's the deal: When you live a life of high performance, you tackle difficulties with gratitude, recognizing that struggle is necessary. Problems are puzzles that can be understood and solved. With a High Performance Mindset, nothing is too hard or impossible.

But what about the times our own psychology or mindset get in the way? What about the times we get in our own heads, overthinking our decisions and doubting ourselves? How often do your limiting beliefs hold you back? How often have you allowed "paralysis by analysis," irrational thinking patterns, and blame to keep you from living the life you deserve?

In my work, I've seen how fear can take over our bodies when we don't take command of our emotions. Working with some of the world's best athletes and top business executives, I can tell you that even they experience anxiety and nervousness that can shake them. Just like the rest of us, they can overthink their decisions or doubt themselves. But the world's best have ten powerful practices that they undertake deliberately and continually. You may think that mastering your mindset is like riding a bike—once you learn it, you can always do it—but actually living a High Performance Life requires ongoing attention. The world's best know this is true.

HOW TO USE THIS BOOK

Beyond Grit is organized around these ten practices, practices that represent a psychological profile leading to the greatness and mastery we all want in our own lives. These practices are supported by scientific research in sport and performance psychology, positive psychology, and neuroscience. I conducted some of this research in my role as a professor; other studies I read and applied to my consulting practice.

High performers in sports, in business, and in life have mastered the ten practices at the core of this book. These practices are what differentiate the world's best from average performers. I have seen evidence of this in my clients, ranging from NFL pro-bowlers to Olympics champions to CEOs and entrepreneurs. By cultivating these ten practices, my clients are able to compete against the world's best and thrive. Imagine the impact these ten traits could have on your performance and everyday life!

Many people start with grit as the foundation for how to excel in life, but that's only the start. (The title of the book is *Beyond Grit* for a reason!) It's not enough to just be gritty. The key is to master your grit, and to continue developing other powerful practices (nine, to be exact) to truly get where you want to go. These practices get you out of your own way so you can show up as yourself and be ready to move out of your comfort zone.

It's beyond the grit that leads you to take on the High Performance Mindset and to think like the world's best.

The Top 10 Practices of the World's Best are:

1. The world's best *are gritty.*

2. The world's best *are clear on their purpose.*

3. The world's best *are a master of their thoughts.*

4. The world's best *know themselves to master themselves.*

5. The world's best *dominate the controllables.*

6. The world's best *own the moment.*

7. The world's best *choose empowering emotions.*

8. The world's best *own who they are.*

9. The world's best *live and let go.*

10. The world's best *choose their courage zone.*

Knowing about these ten practices is important, but the next step is to understand how to develop them in your own life. The *how* is foundational because I want you to master your mindset and improve your performance. The how is the secret sauce. So this book includes strategies that you can string together to create a high performance habit. These are the same strategies that I teach my clients.

And what is the result?

I have witnessed with my own eyes not only an increase in performance, but also an increase in happiness, confidence, and gratitude in clients who have committed to mastering these strategies. A few years ago I started working with a NFL athlete who the coach said was in a slump. Within eight weeks of implementing the strategies, we witnessed a 18 percent improvement in performance. He also told me he felt happier, more confident, and ready to take on any challenge.

Mastering your mindset is the ultimate game changer.

Those that live the ten practices by implementing the 52 strategies outlined in this book can persevere and overcome unimaginable obstacles. They can remain focused on where they are going and why. They can also feel more consistent, and remain motivated even in the face of obstacles. Most importantly, they can take command over their fears. You can think and act like the world's best.

Mastering your mindset can mean the difference between being cut from or thriving on your team, losing your job or earning that bonus, playing it safe and remaining stagnant or taking a monster risk and having it pay off. Your relationships, career, health, dreams, and life's purpose can flourish if you're prepared to do the work.

APPLYING THIS BOOK

The book focuses on 52 life-altering strategies that you can put in your High Performance Toolbox to use in your daily life. Each chapter describes one strategy. Each chapter also ends with a High Performance Game Plan as well as a Power Phrase to help you develop the High Performance Mindset. You can print the power phrase out or write it on your mirror with a dry erase marker to make it a focus for your day or week.

As you move forward, consider the three ways you can read this book:

High Performance Level 1
Read and Learn.

- You can read this book and learn the strategies and tools needed to improve your life and performance.

- This level would have the lowest level of impact.

High Performance Level 2
Apply and Do.

- You can take the strategies and tools presented and implement them in your life.

- To improve your performance and life, you must *apply and do*, not only *read and learn*.

High Performance Level 3
Live and Teach.

- Living the principles of a High Performance Life and then teaching others how to adopt the High Performance Mindset has the most impact.

- This leads to *your* consistent performance, happiness, and motivation.

- It is my hope that you choose to *live and teach* the principles presented.

For maximum impact, you will need to make developing the High Performance Mindset and using the toolbox a priority in your life. As you read each chapter, consider how you can apply the tools to make your life and performance stronger. Think about how this book can best work for you.

- You could read one chapter each week and implement the strategies during the next seven days for one year.

- You could focus on reading and developing one practice each month for ten months.

- You could read the book all the way through, and then go back and commit a deliberate focus on implementing the strategies and tools.

- If working with a team as a coach, leader, or manager, you could assign weekly readings and then organize regular meetings to discuss how to apply the concepts and strategies as individuals and a team.

- You can also purchase the *Beyond Grit Workbook* to help you in your journey in developing the High Performance Mindset. Visit beyondgrit.com to learn more.

Imagine the impact of continuously working on mastering your mindset. Imagine what you could do and be if you gathered these 52 strategies into your High Performance Toolbox and put them to work. Imagine the impact you could make on your team, within your family, and in this world.

ADDITIONAL RESOURCES

As you go through this book, I hope you *live and teach*. I would love to hear from you about the topic, example, or strategy that helped you.

Hearing from you helps me stay on purpose! Send me a tweet @Mentally_Strong or an email at cindra@ cindrakamphoff.com. I cannot wait to hear about your journey to High Performance.

Additional resources to help you on this journey of high performance are available at beyondgrit.com/bonus.

Take the Beyond Grit Questionnaire to find out how you score on the Top 10 Practices as you proceed on your journey to develop the High Performance Mindset. You can find information about the Beyond Grit Workbook at beyondgrit.com.

Decide on a new level of you today. Go after what you want with passion, energy, and excitement. Your mind is a beautiful thing, and when you are thinking in a productive way, you can do beautiful things with it.

My friends, you have everything you need inside you. Now it's time to be mentally strong and get gritty!

1

Get Gritty

*The world's best
know what they want and
they know why they want it.
In the face of adversity and setbacks,
they go after their goals with
deep commitment.*

Chapter 1

Grit Over Gift

An UnderArmour commercial titled "Rule Yourself" demonstrates the physical sacrifices that Olympian Michael Phelps made in order to compete in Rio in 2016. Phelps does not speak in the commercial. Instead, you see him swimming alone, training hard-core in the weight room, carbo-loading, and undergoing cupping therapy and ice baths. You see him swimming repeats with a parachute dragging through the water behind him. You witness his frustration as he slams his fists in the water after a repeat that doesn't reach his personal standard. The commercial documents his journey to the Olympics without ever showing the destination. It shows the process, the sacrifices and struggles, the relentless commitment to sculpting and taking care of his body.

A tagline appears at the end of the commercial: "It is what you do in the dark that puts you in the light. Rule yourself." I love the "rule yourself" tagline. To me, it reinforces the importance of taking control and responsibility of your destiny. Phelps, a 23-time Olympic World Champion and the most decorated Olympian of all time, was not born the world's greatest swimmer. Instead, he developed himself into the world's greatest swimmer. Legacies like Phelps' are built over a lifetime of sacrifices, commitment, and grit.

Your legacy can be built over a lifetime of the same.

GET PURPOSE

MASTER THOUGHTS

KNOW SELF

DOMINATE CONTROLLABLES

OWN THE MOMENT

CHOOSE EMOTIONS

OWN WHO YOU ARE

LIVE AND LET GO

COURAGE ZONE

I first started deeply thinking on and studying grit after watching Dr. Angela Duckworth's TED Talk several years ago. She defines grit as having passion and perseverance toward your very long-term goals.

It got me thinking about the successful athletes, leaders, and entrepreneurs that I work with and how I see them developing grit over time. The leaders I see kill it know their goals, know why they are pursuing their goals, and keep going despite setbacks and adversity. Without understanding why you want to achieve your goals, it is almost impossible to stay devoted in your pursuit. Being gritty means you do not give up. You don't switch gears when you get bored or tired. Your drive keeps you focused on your goals. You keep going despite setbacks, failures, or difficulties. When you are gritty, you have the inner strength and motivation to keep going when it is difficult. You go the extra mile because you know it will make a difference. You stay focused on your goals. To me:

Grit is knowing your long-term goals, knowing why you are pursuing them, and sticking with your goals despite adversity and setbacks.

If you think about who you most admire, I guarantee that person had grit. Michael Phelps is a great example of someone with grit, but there are many other powerful examples, too. Steve Jobs had a goal of *"getting a computer in the hands of everyday people."* Steph Curry had a goal of *"being the best player in the NBA,"* and Sara Blakley wanted to help *"women feel great about themselves and their potential"* as she was developing her company Spanx. I had the goal of working with "my dream team." It took over thirty connections before it became a reality. The connections included calls, emails, meetings, and networking. I stayed gritty. If you want to play bigger, grow your business, or serve more people, get clear on your destination and then prepare to fight—and keep fighting—against the tide.

Grit applies to all areas of our lives—our careers, our sport performance, our education, our relationships, and our happiness.

When we are gritty, we are happier. Working toward our goals and dreams provides satisfaction. In a study published in 2014 in *Frontiers in Psychology*, Dr. Duckworth and her colleagues worked to predict retention in four places: the military, workplace sales, high school, and marriage. They found that:

- Grittier soldiers were more likely to finish a grueling Army section course.

- Grittier sales employees were more likely to keep their jobs.

- Grittier high school students were more likely to graduate.

- Grittier men were more likely to remain in their marriage.

Grit has also been connected to sport performance. My colleague Jeff Martin along with his research team found that athletes with the highest levels of grit and resilience have the most engagement in their sport. More engagement means more heart, passion, energy, and enthusiasm for what you are doing and those you are around.

Grit—knowing your long-term goals, knowing why you are pursuing them, and sticking with them—creates success over and beyond talent. It is a key part of the High Performance Mindset. When you have two people with equal talent, the grittier person performs better. If you have grit, you'll have more energy—an energy that will sustain you over years and even decades. Grit is why leaders can work over long stretches before seeing any results and not throw in the towel, or why an athlete can train decades for a single competition and not change directions.

Grit isn't just innate—it can be developed.

Although the assumption is that grit is something you are born with, the truth is that grit can be developed. It takes practice. If you know your long-term goals and keep them as your focus, the easier it will be to continue taking the steps necessary to get where you want to go. Success is about sustained performance: the world's best know this. To be great, they choose to work hard every day. They analyze their playbooks on the weekend and they study performances of professionals they want to emulate. They go the extra mile, over and over.

Exercise: Get Ready to Make a Grit Board

To help you get gritty and develop the High Performance Mindset, develop a Grit Board. All you need to get started is an 11 x 17 poster board.

Keep it handy as you read, as you'll use this board to record things for each practice in this book. When your Grit Board is complete, you can frame it and hang it in your home, office, or locker room. My grit board is posted right above my computer. It was in my view as I wrote this book!

You can find instructions and examples of Grit Boards at beyondgrit.com.

GET GRITTY

GET PURPOSE

MASTER THOUGHTS

KNOW SELF

DOMINATE CONTROLLABLES

OWN THE MOMENT

CHOOSE EMOTIONS

OWN WHO YOU ARE

LIVE AND LET GO

COURAGE ZONE

My High Performance Game Plan
GRIT OVER GIFT

1. I choose to raise my game to a new level at work, at practice, and with my family. This level looks like

   _____.

2. I take time to consider my gritty future. What do I want? *Really* want?

3. In order to achieve my long-term goals, I need to make some sacrifices. What do I need to change in my life to make it to where I want to be?

4. I am passionate about _____.

   I need to _____ so that I can

   achieve _____.

My High Performance Power Phrase
**I rule myself. I am focused on my goals and
I keep going despite obstacles in my way.
I am passionate about my future.**

Chapter 2

No Grit, No Pearl

"Grit is not just having resilience in the face of failure, but also having deep commitments that you remain loyal to over many years." —ANGELA LEE DUCKWORTH

No matter how many championships athletes win or how many goals high performers meet, there's typically no gain without struggle. Period. When you think about your life and where you're going, remember that losses, failures, setbacks, and challenges are often required to reach your destination.

Think of your life as a pearl. The price of a single pearl on a necklace or ring can range from the low hundreds to tens of thousands of dollars. Pearls are valuable in part because they take years to develop. Did you know that while a small pearl takes around two or three years to grow, it can take a large pearl up to ten years? A pearl starts with a single irritation—a piece of sand, grit, or shell that serves as a parasite inside the oyster. Because of that irritation, the oyster builds layers and layers of calcium carbonate around the piece of grit or sand. The result? A valuable pearl.

You are the oyster. The pearl is the powerful life you create.

You can sit back and let life happen to you. That is your choice. But to create a pearl, you need to be intentional and purposeful with your vision, determination, and grit.

You must keep going even when things get difficult.

If you think about it, everything magnificent that you've likely accomplished required or even perhaps demanded difficulty, struggle, and grit. You can't develop pearls without sacrifices, tough calls, and pushing past your comfort zone. This relentless focus is grit.

What are the pearls you want to create? Perhaps you seek a gold medal, a Pro Bowl honor, a growing business, a team championship, or a thriving marriage. Creating those pearls will require hours of discipline and sacrifice and a relentless focus on that one goal over the long haul. It will also require saying no to things that distract you from your goal. You might need to devote hours each day to your craft, go back to school, seek out investors, or hire a coach. Your pearls will require effort and grit.

When we look at athletes, leaders, entrepreneurs, and other high performers who we most admire, the common thread is their ability to push through barriers. They know that resistance to the struggle is what stops progress, development, creativity, and productivity. We honor the struggle when we stop fighting it and accept that it's part of how we improve. There are no genetic markers that predict Olympic or World Champions. These high performers are regular people who have talent and have conditioned themselves to be extraordinary. They have conditioned themselves to be gritty. They have conditioned themselves to become the world's best.

Without grit, a pearl is not possible.

In the book *Outliers: The Story of Success*, Malcolm Gladwell outlined the journey of some of the world's most successful people. He discussed scientific studies conducted by K. Anders Ericsson and his colleagues which demonstrated that it takes at least 10,000 hours of deliberate practice to reach mastery or greatness. That means it takes someone at least 10,000 hours (or ten years of commitment and relentless focus) to be the best in a field. Gladwell provided examples of what is called the "10-Year or 10,000 Rule" by describing the journeys of the Beatles, Mozart, and Bill Gates to greatness or mastery.

This 10,000-hour rule doesn't just apply to musicians and computer geniuses. In study after study, scientists have found that to be a master at anything, 10,000 hours of deliberate practice is key. This includes mastering basketball, ice skating, field goal kicking, fiction writing, chess playing, computer programming, or product development. Mastery rarely comes more quickly.

The lesson? You have to put in time to reach your goals and live the life of your dreams. More time means you'll reach your destination faster. And while you are putting in your time, it's important to be deliberate with your practice. Dr. Ericsson, writing in the *Harvard Business Review*, argued that excellence is not based just on practice, but deliberate practice with the intent to better yourself. He said that deliberate practice is "improving the skills you already have and extending the reach and range of those skills." Deliberate practice is working on you—your skills and techniques—in a planned and focused way, asking for constant and critical feedback, and focusing on addressing your weaknesses.

Average performers tend not to do what they think is boring or uninspiring. They're also less likely to be honest about where they went wrong and self-correct. Improving your skills with the focus of mastery takes practice, observation, understanding, refinement, and more practice. It takes time to be great.

So are you ready to develop your pearls? Are you making a dent in your 10,000 hours? What distractions are robbing you of precious time that could be used toward your 10,000 hours?

GET GRITTY

GET PURPOSE

MASTER THOUGHTS

KNOW SELF

DOMINATE CONTROLLABLES

OWN THE MOMENT

CHOOSE EMOTIONS

OWN WHO YOU ARE

LIVE AND LET GO

COURAGE ZONE

My High Performance Game Plan
NO GRIT, NO PEARL

1. Where am I in my journey to 10,000 hours of
    deliberate practice?

2. If I'm going to get to 10,000 hours, I'll need
    to make some changes. What are some things
    I can do to make my journey clearer?

3. I can create a plan to reduce the distractions that
    are getting in the way of me and my goals. What
    things distract me the most? How can I make sure
    they're not obstacles?

4. This week, I will find two people to support me
    in my 10,000 hour journey. I'll tell them how and
    why they specifically can help me get to where I
    need to be.

My High Performance Power Phrase
**I am gritty. I do all the things that others are not
willing to do to reach my dreams and goals.
I put in the hours necessary for success.**

Chapter 3

Difficulties Happen for You

"All the adversity I've had in my life, all my troubles and obstacles, have strengthened me. . . . You may not realize it when it happens, but a kick in the teeth may be the best thing in the world for you." —WALT DISNEY

A couple of years ago, I ran the Twin Cities Marathon. I was on track for a personal best time through mile 17 and felt great. Until I didn't. Miles 17 to 20 were miserable! My legs started to ache and my hands started to swell. Quickly, I realized I forgot salt tablets. I usually take salt tablets several times in the marathon to avoid cramping and stay hydrated. I beat myself up for three miles: "You are such an idiot, Cindra! I can't believe you forgot your salt tablets." (On a side note: I find it way more difficult to control my self-talk when I am physically pushing myself.)

As we were turning to climb Summit Hill, I heard the pacer say, "Embrace the suck!" I laughed to myself. He was right. It did suck! And his comment helped me get unstuck. I looked around. Everyone was struggling. Struggling is part of it! A marathon is supposed to be difficult! I started to embrace the difficulty. I started counting the number of people I passed up Summit Hill. It kept me energized and focused on embracing the struggle. By the finish, I passed 90 people. I finished just over 40 seconds from my personal best time over 26.2 miles. At the finish, I was jacked. As I posed for picture at the finish line, my eyes swelled up with joyful tears. "You are glowing," the event photographer said to me. "You're the happiest person I have seen all day!"

This experience made me realize something very important about high performance: there can be joy in the struggle. Though I did not beat my personal best time, I learned so much about my power to push through difficulties. I've applied what I learned that day to my running, my work, and my life. The way I see it, the difficulties in that race happened *for* me, not *to* me. I proved to myself that I can get through an immense amount of mental and physical discomfort as I push forward toward my goals.

Oh, and I also never again forgot my salt tablets.

Most people don't reach their goals and vision because they give up too easily. They experience difficulties, discomfort, or adversity and decide to throw in the towel. If you've been trying to achieve a goal and haven't yet experienced success, maybe you have said to yourself, "I guess that just isn't for me" or "I can't do it." But people who accomplish their goals not only push through, they also adapt when difficulties arise. They even *expect* things to go wrong. The world's best prepare in advance for the "what ifs" so that they are not sidelined when—or if—they happen.

You need to recognize that it will take time, effort, perseverance, and planning to reach even the simplest of goals. If you underestimate how difficult it will be to achieve something, it's easy give up. Thinking things will come easy will leave you ill prepared. It's easier to tap into your grit if you anticipate difficulty in advance. We do not thrive when we expect ease and perfection.

For example, psychologist Gabriele Oettingen found that women who imagined themselves easily losing weight lost an average of 24 pounds *less* than those that imagined having a hard time resisting temptation. She found similar results with students looking for high-paying jobs, seniors recovering from hip replacement surgery, and single people in search for a lasting romantic relationship. Believing it will be easy is a recipe for failure.

Expect that your journey to reach your goals will be difficult and you will have more confidence to get there!

Consider these examples of famous people who kept their focus on their goals and dreams despite the obstacles that emerged:

- Oprah Winfrey was told she wouldn't make it in television and she was fired from her television job as an anchor in Baltimore. She didn't let that stop her. *The Oprah Winfrey Show* revolutionized daytime talk shows; Oprah now owns her own network and, according to *Forbes*, is worth $2.9 billion.

- An editor fired Walt Disney because he "lacked imagination and had no good ideas." Several of his businesses failed before his breakthrough film, *Snow White*, was produced. The Walt Disney brand is now the most valuable brand in the world with a market cap at $179.5 billion, according to *Forbes*.

- Colonel Harland David Sanders was fired from over 12 jobs. After traveling across the U.S. looking for someone to sell his fried chicken, he finally got a business deal in Utah for Kentucky Fried Chicken (KFC). KFC has now over 18,000 locations and is one of the most recognizable franchises in the world.

- J.K. Rowling was a single mom and supported by welfare. 12 publishers rejected her first Harry Potter novel. She is now internationally known for her *Harry Potter* series, which has sold over 450 million copies. She became the first billionaire author in 2004.

- Michael Jordan did not make the varsity basketball team as a sophomore in high school. He turned the cut into motivation

GET GRITTY

GET PURPOSE

MASTER THOUGHTS

KNOW SELF

DOMINATE CONTROLLABLES

OWN THE MOMENT

CHOOSE EMOTIONS

OWN WHO YOU ARE

LIVE AND LET GO

COURAGE ZONE

and became a McDonald's All-American. He is now considered one of the greatest basketball players to ever play the game. Jordan earned six NBA championships and five NBA MVP titles, and scored 32,292 points in his career.

I could fill this whole book with examples of people who were persistent enough to overcome adversity and accomplish their goals. These stories are not rare. In fact, every successful person has some version of stories like this.

The great news for you is that persistence is learnable. The first step in becoming more persistent is to see the difficulties you experience not as having happened to destroy you, but in order to show you how persistent you are. As author Bryon Katie said, "Everything happens for you, not to you." The world's best see that the difficulties that occur can lead them on a course necessary for success. Difficulties show you how strong you are, how persistent you are. They help you understand your true potential and power.

The second step to becoming more persistent is to see the situation, adversity, or problem as a puzzle to solve. If you see the situation as a puzzle, it is something you can figure out. You will be creative in your ability to be successful instead of giving in because you are mentally, emotionally, or physically fatigued. You will have more energy, have a fresh perspective, and be ready to take on the challenge.

For example:

- Perhaps your business is not generating the profits you would like . . .

- Or you might be playing less on your current team than you would like to . . .

- Maybe you keep making the same mistake in practice or the game . . .

- Or you are having difficulty losing weight . . .

- Maybe you are telling yourself you don't have time to do the extra things that will lead you down the path of success . . .

Turning these into puzzles challenges you to figure out what isn't working, and what might work better.

A third step to become more persistent is to believe you *are* persistent. If you say things to yourself such as, "I have never continued with anything," "I just can't follow through," or "I am just not persistent," you will probably listen to yourself and just give up. When the urge to quit arises, the best response is to believe that quitting is not who you are. Say instead, "I stay the course," "I always deliver," and "I am committed to my goals and dreams." Know that you can get it done.

GET
GRITTY

GET
PURPOSE

MASTER
THOUGHTS

KNOW
SELF

DOMINATE
CONTROLLABLES

OWN THE
MOMENT

CHOOSE
EMOTIONS

OWN WHO
YOU ARE

LIVE AND
LET GO

COURAGE
ZONE

DIFFICULTIES HAPPEN FOR YOU

1. I'm going to decide what I'll do this week to get one step closer to achieving my dreams. Specifically, what do I want to accomplish?

2. How did a problem or difficulty I experienced in the past happen *for* me, not to me?

3. I will take at least one problem I'm experiencing right now and choose to view it as a puzzle. How does this change my perception?

4. I can reflect on my past and consider the difficulties I've persevered through. These are evidence of my persistence.

My High Performance Power Phrase

I am persistent. I see difficulties as happening for me, not to me. I solve my problems like puzzles.

Chapter 4

Dream for a Living

---

*"If your dreams don't scare you,
they aren't big enough."* —DONNA WILLIAMS

Actor and comedian Jim Carrey was born to entertain. When he grew up, his teachers would allow him to perform for his classmates at the end of class as a reward for staying quiet throughout the day. He was only ten years old when he mailed his resume to *The Carol Burnett Show*.

But Jim Carrey's family struggled financially. His dad lost his job and, for a time, his family lived in a Volkswagen van on a relative's lawn. Despite the difficulties, Jim kept dreaming of acting. At the age of 19, he made his way to Los Angeles. Every night he would drive his old Toyota up to Mulholland Drive to look over the city. He said in an interview with Oprah Winfrey, "I visualized directors that were interested in me and people that I respected seeing my work . . . I would visualize the things coming to me that I wanted . . . even though I had nothing at the time."

In 1990, after performing in a show where he made about $100, he returned to that usual spot and wrote himself a $10 million check. He dated the check Thanksgiving 1995, added "for acting services rendered" in the memo line, and put the check in his wallet. The check was concrete evidence of his dream: he didn't just think about it, he wrote it down. He saw the check and was reminded of his dream every time he opened his wallet.

Meanwhile, he made movies. Then, after box office hits like *Ace Ventura: Pet Detective* and *The Mask*, Jim Carrey was offered $10 million for his role in the movie *Dumb and Dumber*. Jim received the offer before Thanksgiving 1995, just as he had envisioned. According to the film's director, it was the highest salary ever paid to a comedian at that time. Eventually, he became known as Hollywood's $20 Million Dollar Man because you couldn't get him in a movie for anything less.

Jim Carrey used the power of his mind to create his future. To experience success in your field, sport, or business, you can follow his lead. We all need a vision for our future, and once we get clear on our vision, we can make intentional decisions every day. We know what to say "yes" to and what to say "no" to. We can align our daily decisions with our vision. When we're clear on our vision, we know which opportunities to pursue, which people we need in our midst, and which ideas deserve more attention. But we can't make our vision a reality without clarity.

So how do we get a clear vision? First, it needs to be compelling. Our vision has to excite us to jump out of bed each day, ready to take on any adversity we experience. It also must be specific. A clear vision isn't vague or ambiguous. Finally, a clear vision is not a little thing. Dream big. Anyone who has ever left a mark in the world had a big dream, a dream that might have seemed too big to the average person. Steven Spielberg, the award-winning movie director and producer of movies such as *Jaws*, *E.T. the Extra-Terrestrial*, and *Schindler's List*, once said, "I dream for a living."

As we age, we can lose the ability to dream. Perhaps we hear too often that our dreams are too grandiose and that there is no way we can accomplish them, and we start to believe those messages. Or maybe we start following what other people want us to do instead of what we know we must do. But it doesn't have to be that way. Age, experience, and responsibilities don't have to diminish your dreams.

It became clear to me how we can lose our ability to dream big after I spent some time in a fifth-grade classroom. I had a great time introducing fifth graders to the power of our minds. During my presentation, one of the teachers asked me my favorite quote. I didn't hesitate. I said boldly, "If your dreams don't scare you, they aren't big enough." She looked shocked.

"They should be scary?" she asked.

"Yes," I said. "Because if you limit yourself to what seems possible right now, you will not grow into what you can become. You will not grow every day to your true potential if you don't have a big dream."

The teacher was stunned. I thought I would shock the students with that quote, but instead, I shocked the adult. The kids hadn't yet forgotten to dream that big.

As Michelangelo, an Italian sculptor, architect, and poet, is reported to have said, "The greatest danger for most of us is not that our aim is too high and we miss it, but that it is too low and we reach it." Are you setting your bar too low? Are you running fewer miles every day than your actual potential? Are you talking about your dream business instead of working toward it? Are you envisioning a future that you feel comfortable achieving versus a future that scares the holy heck out of you?

Most people's dreams are too small. We often let our minds and limiting beliefs get in our way. But when we dream one step more than we normally would, we grow. We are forced to push ourselves. Dreaming above your comfort zone requires you to consider all the possibilities and to choose your courage zone. It opens your mind so you are thinking like the world's best.

Today, instead of dreaming small, take your dreams and vision for your future up a notch. Dream a big dream and get clear on that vision. Pick a date five, ten, or twenty years from now. What does your future look like? Who is with you? What are you doing? What have you accomplished? How are your relationships? How do you feel? Your compelling vision can include career, sport, finances, health and

GET GRITTY

GET PURPOSE

MASTER THOUGHTS

KNOW SELF

DOMINATE CONTROLLABLES

OWN THE MOMENT

CHOOSE EMOTIONS

OWN WHO YOU ARE

LIVE AND LET GO

COURAGE ZONE

fitness, relationships, and/or your contribution to your community. I want you to think holistically here and not hold back. Picture your life in detail. Go big.

Yes, it can be scary to dream big. But when you feel fear, take command of your response. Take a deep breath and remind yourself that you are growing and that your dream is possible.

Remember, you will always hear that your dreams are unrealistic, impossible, or ill timed. Choose not to listen. The world's best don't pay attention to these bits of advice, but instead are gritty and stay the course. As Jim Carrey did, keep dreaming those scary dreams that challenge what you think is possible.

My High Performance Game Plan
DREAM FOR A LIVING

1. I will write down my vision with details and make sure I dream big. I will put it on my Grit Board so I will see it often (see end of Practice 1).

2. I can decide on a practice I can use daily to "dream for a living." I might review the vision I posted or write my dream on my mirror and then look at it as part of my morning routine.

3. I will use my vision as a filter to help me say "yes" to what I want, and "no" to what does not fit with my vision.

4. I'll share my vision with two people this week who support me in my journey. Secrets rarely come true, so I don't plan to keep my vision a secret!

My High Performance Power Phrase
**I dream big. I have everything I need inside me.
I will turn it on!**

Chapter 5

Plan Your Destiny

"You must have dreams and goals if you are ever going to achieve anything in the world."—LOU HOLTZ

Carrie Tollefson is from a small town in northern Minnesota. She grew up dominating distance running in the state and was one of the best in the country while in high school. She received a scholarship to run at Villanova University, where she went on to win five national championships in the 3,000 and 5,000 meters.

In 2004, she had a chance to make it on the U.S. Olympic team. She entered the Olympic Trials in the both the 1,500 and 5,000 meter races. She was a favorite in the 5,000 meters, which was considered "her race." Though she ran hard, she finished in sixth place. She was devastated. She told me on the *High Performance Mindset Podcast*, "That was probably the lowest point in my career at that moment and one of the biggest disappointments in my life."

Her desire to make the Olympic Team was bigger than her disappointment. "I had to suck it up real fast and turn it around fast," she explained. She moved on to the 1500-meter run. No one expected her to qualify in that race, but she was gritty and hungry to be an Olympian. She raced her heart out, qualifying for the Olympics Games in Athens, Greece.

During that race, Carrie became an Olympian, a label she will have for the rest of her life because of an intentional decision she made.

She knew what she wanted; when it didn't happen the first time, she regained her focus, taking her future into her own hands. Despite the obstacles that got in her way, she remained gritty.

You have already created your compelling vision, and it should make you want to excitedly get out of bed each morning. You dreamed big. Now, let's go one step further and turn your vision and big dreams into goals. While a vision inspires you and provides life-changing passion, goals are a vision with deadlines. Goals turn your vision into actions so you can make your vision a reality. You'll notice immediately after outlining your goals that your performance will increase because you are more focused.

One of the most consistent research findings in performance psychology is that clear and consistent goals facilitate top performance. Professors Edwin Locke and Gary Latham spent years examining the power of goals. Their findings? According to these pioneering researchers, "The beneficial effect of goal setting on performance is one of the most robust and replicable findings in the psychological literature." Their research suggests that successful people are goal-oriented—they have a vision for themselves and their future. They know what they want to accomplish each day, each meeting, each workout, each game. They know how their daily goals connect to their long-term vision, plans, and dreams.

Goals direct your focus and help you remain persistent in the face of adversity. Goals increase self-confidence and fuel desire. Goals help you train smarter and harder. The bottom line is that when you set effective goals, they help you perform up to your potential. Most people think about vague goals, but few know how to set goals that sustain motivation and provide direction. You need to write your goals down so you have direction in your performance and in your life. The world's best have their goals written down.

So, how do we set goals that sustain our motivation and provide us clear direction? You follow the Six Gritty Goal Guidelines.

GET GRITTY

GET PURPOSE

MASTER THOUGHTS

KNOW SELF

DOMINATE CONTROLLABLES

OWN THE MOMENT

CHOOSE EMOTIONS

OWN WHO YOU ARE

LIVE AND LET GO

COURAGE ZONE

Six Gritty Goal Guidelines

1. Write your goals down to make the most impact. "Ink it, don't just think it."

2. Write down what you want to do, not what you don't want to do.

3. Be specific. Use detailed language.

4. Record goals for multiple time periods, such as 1, 3, 5, 10, and 20 years from now.

5. Set outcome, performance, and process goals, but put the most emphasis on the process.

6. Plan out your activities daily and weekly with your goals in mind. Take actions that help accomplish your goals.

Gritty Goal Guideline One

When it comes to goal setting, "Ink it, don't just think it." To manifest the true power of goal setting, write your goals down or type them up. Out of sight, out of mind: if you don't get them down on paper, goals can be forgotten. When we write our goals down, we are also documenting our commitment. We can then go back and review them to make adjustments when needed.

Gritty Goal Guideline Two

Don't write what you don't want to do; write what you want to do. Our goals should be stated positively. For example, instead of "I don't want to drop out of the next half marathon I run," write "I will complete a half marathon this year." Writing your goals in a positive way has a dramatic impact on your focus and motivation.

Gritty Goal Guideline Three

Be **specific** with your goals—make them detailed and measurable. Include as many specifics as you can. Thousands of research studies have found that when you spell out exactly what you want, strong performance results.

Gritty Goal Guideline Four

The world's best have goals for various stages, including 1, 3, 5, 10, and 20 year goals, and they review them regularly and reset them when needed. Ideally, you would set three or four goals for each stage. Avoid setting too many goals; that can make it hard to focus.

Gritty Goal Guideline Five

High performers set outcome, performance, and process goals, but put almost all of their emphasis on the process.

- Outcome goals focus on a desired result. For example, you may be an athlete who would like to win the state championship or make it to the pros, or a leader who wants a promotion. Outcome goals often depend on outside factors you can't control. You might play your best game or have the best interview of your life and still not reach the goal. Outcome goals can create motivation and can be exciting, but can also create anxiety and doubt if focused on at the wrong time; only set a few outcome goals and be flexible about achieving them. This is a really important guideline I see a lot of people get wrong without realizing it.

- Performance goals focus on improving your standard. You might be a college student who wants to improve last year's GPA, a basketball player who wants to improve your free throw percentage, or a business executive who wants to improve your performance evaluation next year. Performance goals typically include ways to measure your success. Because they focus on your performance, they are more within your control than outcome goals.

GET GRITTY

GET PURPOSE

MASTER THOUGHTS

KNOW SELF

DOMINATE CONTROLLABLES

OWN THE MOMENT

CHOOSE EMOTIONS

OWN WHO YOU ARE

LIVE AND LET GO

COURAGE ZONE

- Process goals are the actions that you need to take daily to perform well. They are the small steps needed to reach your performance and outcome goals. For example, if I am training for a marathon that is four months from now, my process goals will include weekly training goals, how I run the miles, and my mindset while I run. Process goals are important for improving confidence and decreasing anxiety.

As important as setting goals is how you use them. To explain, let me take you back to 1994. I was a senior in high school and I dreamed of winning the mile in track and field at the Iowa High School State Championship. I wanted to go out on top. I had a mantra—*State Champ, New Car*—to get me out of bed early each morning to train. I was dedicated to run two-a-days (once in the morning and once at practice) to get the edge. My dad told me he would buy me a new car to replace my old, blue station wagon that smoked if I won the state meet.

I used the outcome goal to stay gritty and to keep pushing when I was tired. It helped me get out of bed when I didn't want to go and pushed me during those early morning training runs. But I never thought about the outcome goal before a race. That would have created anxiety. Instead, then (and most of the time) I focused on my process goals. I aimed to implement excellence. I focused on the outcome goal 5 percent of the time, and process goals the other 95 percent.

The world's best follow the 95/5 Rule.
They focus on their process goals 95 percent of the time.

In my professional work, I have come to understand this as the 95/5 Rule. The World's Best focus on their process goals 95 percent of the time. Then they focus on their outcome goals at the right times to stay motivated and gritty—but that's only about 5 percent of the time. To know if you are focused on your outcome goals at the right times, pay attention to how your body is reacting. If you feel anxiety or pressure, it is not the right time and you should instead stay focused on the process.

Gritty Goal Guideline Six

The world's best plan out their activities daily and weekly to accomplish their goals. This planning is an incredibly important step that most people miss. Keep your goals where you can see them and plan your weekly activities with them in mind.

Be like Jim Carrey: Put your goals in your wallet, put them inside your planner, write them on your bathroom mirror with a dry erase marker, or have them framed by your bed. Remind yourself of what you are aiming for every day. This will increase your chance for success and keep you motivated and focused.

GET GRITTY

GET PURPOSE

MASTER THOUGHTS

KNOW SELF

DOMINATE CONTROLLABLES

OWN THE MOMENT

CHOOSE EMOTIONS

OWN WHO YOU ARE

LIVE AND LET GO

COURAGE ZONE

My High Performance Game Plan
PLAN YOUR DESTINY

1. What do I want to accomplish, have, contribute, or give to others in the next 20 years? Write or type it out.

2. Next to each goal from the list above, I'll indicate if that goal is a 1-, 3-, 5-, 10-, or 20-year goal. Then I'll pick three or four goals to focus on this year. I'll write them down specifically and put them somewhere that I can see them.

3. I will outline the kind of person I need to be in order to reach my goals. What habits, attributes, or characteristics do I need to develop? How will I do so?

4. I can place my 1-year goals where I can see them every day (like on my Grit Board).

My High Performance Power Phrase

I go after my goals with passion and excitement. I know what I want, and every day I work toward my goals. I stay focused and gritty.

Chapter 6

Rule Your Day

"My greatest fear as a professional athlete is the fear of losing. The only way you get over it is by working harder and training harder than anyone else." —Usain Bolt, Jamaican sprinter

---

Usain St. Leo Bolt is the World's Fastest Man. He holds the current world record in both the 100 meters and 200 meters, and is the first man in modern times to hold both records at the same time. He is also the first man to win nine gold medals in sprinting in the modern Olympics, and is an eleven-time world champion in track and field.

Bolt came from humble beginnings. He was born in a small town in Trelany, Jamaica. He grew up playing cricket and soccer in the streets with his brother while his parents worked at the local grocery store.

In his autobiography *Faster than Lightning*, Bolt wrote about what he sacrificed so he could experience success. When he was younger, he would skip training to play video games and go to parties. But then he realized to be the best, he needed to train like the best, and that included diligent, daily training to build his strength and speed.

Although Bolt was born with speed, he had challenges to overcome. At 6'5", his height made it difficult to start fast out of the blocks—a weakness he overcame by powering through the second half of the race. He was born with scoliosis, a spinal condition that created weaknesses in his abs and back. Early in his career, the scoliosis caused repeated injuries until he learned how to keep his core strong.

With daily practice, self-control, and intention, he trained himself to complete the 100 meters in 41 steps instead of the usual 44 or 45 steps, and he overcame obstacles that may have held him back.

Without the daily desire, commitment, and hunger to be the World's Best, Bolt wouldn't be the fastest man. Without sacrifices, grit, and discipline, Bolt would not dominate on the world stage. "For me, I'm focused on what I want to do," he said. "I know what I need to do to be a champion, so I'm working on it daily."

Like Bolt, to reach high performance in your field or sport, you have to concentrate every day on what it takes to become your very best and then exert the discipline and self-control necessary to do what you need to do. The only way to live out your planned destiny and perform at your best is to rule your day: to get organized and disciplined with your actions and habits.

But how? You can use the following strategies to rule your day.

Start your day with a Grit Focus Session: Take five minutes each morning to reflect on your daily goals and how those goals relate to your long-term goals. This daily habit reminds you of where you are going and why, building your grit and inspiring you to live in an intentional way. Remember to remind yourself of why you want to achieve those goals and dreams to keep you fueled and passionate. You could couple this exercise with mindfulness meditation to make it even more powerful.

Implement the daily activities you need to thrive: It is possible to be so focused on your goals and dreams that you lose touch with the here and now, with your body, spirit, and health. As you plan your day, consider the activities you need to take care of yourself. These activities could include daily meditation, exercise, healthy eating at regular meals, drinking enough water, and sleeping 6-8 hours. If you are not taking care of yourself, you cannot do the work you are meant to do. You cannot live your purpose if you are exhausted and burned out.

Take time to plan to accomplish your goals: Consider what you need to do each day to accomplish your goal and dreams. Take the time to plan those things into your day, week, and month. What do you need to accomplish? When will you get what you need done, done?

Ask for support: You need people around you who support your goals and dreams. Choose at least one person to be an accountability buddy in your efforts to rule your day. Think carefully about who you will choose: select someone who will be honest with you when the going gets tough. Ask your accountability buddy to inquire about your goals weekly or every other week, and to push you when you are making excuses or lacking self-control or discipline.

In 1972, professor Walter Mischel conducted a classic study on delayed gratification and self-control. Mischel offered participants in his study, all children between the ages of four and six years old, a marshmallow. He told participants that if they waited 15 minutes to eat it, they would get a second marshmallow. What did he find? Only one third of the children waited long enough for the additional treat.

In the first follow-up study 16 years later, Mischel and his colleagues found a positive correlation between the results of the marshmallow test and the success of the children as they became young adults. The children who waited for the second marshmallow were considered significantly more competent than children their same age. In a second follow-up study, research indicated that delayed gratification was related to higher SAT scores and a lower body mass index. The so-called "Marshmallow Test" demonstrated that discipline, self-control, willpower, and grit are essential for success.

Self-control is like a muscle: the more you train it, the stronger it becomes. The key is to give your self-control daily workouts. We all encounter marshmallows that can impede our daily performance. Each day, you need to resist the things that take you from your goals and vision for your life. You can do this by implementing the strategies for ruling your day and by reflecting on the marshmallows in your daily life.

Ask yourself:

- What are the marshmallows that may get in my way of success?

- How do I plan to react to those temptations?

- How can I be more disciplined to reach my goals and dreams?

- How can I start implementing the five strategies in my life right now?

Remember, greatness and high performance take intention and daily dedication. The world's best didn't get there overnight. Respect the struggle and expect hard work as you keep pushing and rule your day, day after day.

My High Performance Game Plan
RULE YOUR DAY

1. Today, I'll rule my day. I'll take command of my time with discipline and focus.

2. I will write down the steps of my Grit Focus Session as a reminder of how to start my day.

3. Then I'll implement my Grit Focus Session each morning to keep my passion and excitement alive.

4. I can identify and record the health and wellness practices I need to implement every day to show up as my best self, and will add them to my Grit Board.

My High Performance Power Phrase

I rule my day. I am disciplined with my time and daily activities. Each day I live intentionally and fully engaged.

Practice 1

CONCLUDING THOUGHTS

Look! You are on your way to reaching your goals and dreams. Here are the things you learned from Get Gritty:

- Your grit is a key factor in your success, and your grit can be developed.

- Reminding yourself that your difficulties have happened to you helps you stay gritty.

- Writing down your vision, goals, and daily activities is the key to your success.

Now, take a moment to record the following on your Grit Board:

- Your vision for the future (pick either your 5, 10, or 20-year vision to record).

- Your 1-year goals.

- The Grit Focus Session steps you will use to start your day.

2

Get Clear on Your Purpose

The world's best own why they do what they do. They keep their why front and center. This purpose keeps them motivated and hungry when the going gets tough.

Chapter 7

Own Your Why

"Working hard for something we don't care about is called stress; working hard for something we love is called passion." —Simon Sinek

Your why is your purpose, your cause, or your belief that inspires you to do what you do. When you know your why, you have the push you need to keep going.

Every single person knows *what* they do. Your what is your role or title: athlete, executive, CEO, coach, parent, spouse, friend. Your *why* is different. It is what ignites your desire and passion, lights the fire in your belly, and keeps you passionate and excited.

The truth is that few people think extensively about why they do what they do. Instead, often our focus is only on results like making more money or winning a championship. But results aren't a why. Results are not the same as passion, purpose, or cause. What do you enjoy most about the work you do or want to do? What is most exciting and gratifying about what you do? What would you like to do more of? These are important questions. Without a clear connection to your why, you can get off track, burn out, and forget to make your why a priority.

Simon Sinek, the author of the bestselling book *What's Your Why?*, made the case that most people communicate from the outside in. They communicate what they do first, and then why they do it. Simon argued that inspired people—athletes, leaders, coaches, organizations, and entrepreneurs—communicate from the inside out. They work to understand why they do what they do, and then they communicate from their why. They tell others about their why to keep themselves and others inspired.

I know this from experience. After working with hundreds of business owners, elite athletes, and championship teams, I know that the number one thing motivating successful individuals is their why. Everyone has a unique why. Sometimes it is to provide the best future for a family. Sometimes it is to be the greatest wide receiver in a franchise. It can be to earn enough money to retire in ten years, or contribute to a community by mentoring others. No matter what it is, the world's best are all clear on their why, and that why inspires their actions.

When you know your why, things start changing for you. You attract the right people to your business and team, and you get the support you need. You stay fueled and energized, and find more inspiration and a stronger sense of purpose for what you do. You recognize you can get through any difficulty or adversity because of what drives you. Tough days get easier.

So in order to think like the world's best, you need to plug into your bigger purpose. Consider how what you do and want to do helps, inspires, or provides for the people and places that are important to you. It is easier to stay fueled when you know how you contribute to the lives of others.

When I work with teams, I start the discussion with this question: When you look deep in your soul, what is the reason you do what you do? Then, to go deeper into their whys and the good that comes from what they do, I have them complete what I call the "So That" exercise. You can do it, too.

GET GRITTY

GET PURPOSE

MASTER THOUGHTS

KNOW SELF

DOMINATE CONTROLLABLES

OWN THE MOMENT

CHOOSE EMOTIONS

OWN WHO YOU ARE

LIVE AND LET GO

COURAGE ZONE

"So That" Exercise

Begin by writing what you do (or what you want to do) at the top of a sheet of paper. This might say Vice President of Company X, or professional basketball player for X team, or business owner of Company Y. Then, write your answer to the prompt "So that . . ." Write six responses. Your six "so that's" get to the heart of your why.

Want to see how this looks for me?

What I do: I speak to and coach leaders, entrepreneurs, professional athletes, and championship teams so they can master their mindset and play bigger.

So that . . .

1. *I can help others show the talent and skill that can sometimes be hidden by overthinking, lack of confidence, or heightened anxiety.*

2. *I can help others own their why and live an intentional life going after their big dreams.*

3. *I can learn from game changers and the world's best and share what they know.*

4. *I can be a role model for my two boys and show them that there are no limits to what they can be.*

5. *I can inspire other women working in the field of performance psychology.*

6. *I can positively impact the world, one person or team at a time.*

Completing this exercise can be a first step in owning your why, in considering fully why you do what you do. Owning your why helps you stay motivated, passionate, and engaged in your career, sport, and life. It is an important step toward figuring out *how* you *will* achieve your goals and dreams.

Your how can and will change as you encounter adversity, setbacks, and opportunities, but your why remains the same. My why gives me a spark when I want to give up. When I face failure or a lack of motivation, I remind myself of my why to stay fueled and gritty.

Owning your why is one step above knowing your why. When you own your why, you can—and should—share it. Shout it from the rooftops! Tell your teammates, your leadership, your family, and your clients!

Communicating your why helps others identify with and connect to you. It builds trust. Post your why on your refrigerator, in your locker, above your desk, or on your Grit Board. Put your why on your website and in your email signature. Make a big deal about your why, because it makes all the difference.

GET
GRITTY

GET
PURPOSE

MASTER
THOUGHTS

KNOW
SELF

DOMINATE
CONTROLLABLES

OWN THE
MOMENT

CHOOSE
EMOTIONS

OWN WHO
YOU ARE

LIVE AND
LET GO

COURAGE
ZONE

My High Performance Game Plan
OWN YOUR WHY

1. I will complete the "So That" exercise, circling one or two of the answers that seem most important to me.

2. I'll use my answers to the "So That" exercise to write my "why" in a single sentence.

3. I'll post that "why" somewhere I'll see it every day.

4. I can share my "why" with someone new each day this week.

My High Performance Power Phrase

I own my why. I keep my why front and center each day. I communicate my why to keep myself and others inspired.

Chapter 8

Find Your Fight

*"Have the courage to follow your heart and intuition.
They somehow already know what you truly want to become.
Everything else is secondary. . . . Stay hungry. Stay foolish."*
—STEVE JOBS IN A 2005 STANFORD COMMENCEMENT ADDRESS

In 2005, Steve Jobs, the Apple co-founder who has been called the Thomas Edison of his time, provided a powerful commencement address. He explained why he dropped out of Reed College—an unusual topic for such a speech—after only six months. He said he struggled because he felt like he was wasting his working-class parents' savings when he wasn't sure what he wanted to do. After he officially dropped out, he continued taking classes, but only those that fascinated him. Only then did he follow his purpose and passion.

One of the courses he took after dropping out was on calligraphy. Reed's course was widely regarded as one of the best in the country. Ten years later, when Jobs and his co-founder were designing the first Macintosh computer, the course proved to be essential to their product: they designed the first computer to have beautiful typography. Had he not dropped out of college and taken courses related to his interests, personal computers might not have the typography options they do today.

"You've got to find what you love," Jobs said. "And the only way to be truly satisfied is to do what you believe is great work. And the only way to do great work is to love what you do. If you haven't found it yet, keep looking. Don't settle."

One way that Jobs made sure he did not settle was to ask himself this bold question in the mirror every morning: "If today were the last day of my life, would I want to do what I am about to do today?" He said if the answer was "no" several days in a row, he knew he needed to change something.

Jobs started Apple in his parents' garage at the age of 20. Apple has revolutionized technology around the world by introducing the Macintosh, iPhone, iPad, Apple Watch, and Apple TV. In 2015, Apple's net income was $53 billion. By not settling, Jobs created something amazing.

The world's best find and follow their purpose to stay gritty, live a fulfilling life, and sustain a high level of performance. But how do they find it? There are strategies that can help.

1. Ask yourself "What am I fighting for?" As an athlete, you might be fighting for that championship your team has never had or that scholarship or contract that you know you deserve. As a parent, you might be fighting to provide opportunities for your kids that you didn't have. As a teacher, you might be fighting for innovative education. As a business leader or entrepreneur, you might be fighting for the kind of business that you have always dreamed of. Knowing what you are fighting for will keep your head in the game.

I've asked myself this same question, and I've discovered two answers. First, I am fighting for the relevance and growth of the field of sport and performance psychology. I am also fighting for the women in my field, demonstrating that working with professional athletes, even predominantly male sports teams, and speaking on the world's biggest stages are within our reach.

These two things fuel me every day as I travel the country as a speaker, as I write this book, and as I work one-on-one with clients. Knowing what I'm fighting for helps me live and perform more purposefully.

2. Remind yourself of what you are fighting for every day.
When I present this strategy to my clients, I see athletes become more passionate about their sport, their team, and their goals. It reflects in their facial expression and in their body language. As you are walking to practice, driving to work, or entering your home, take a moment to remind yourself what you are fighting for in what you do.

What you focus on grows. If you are focused on the difficulties at practice, at work, or with your family, that negativity will expand and will impact your life and your performance. If you are focused on what you are fighting for, you will show up to what you do in a different way.

You are way too important to just be going throughout your day and life without passion, purpose, and full engagement. Today, dig deep and consider your desires and what you are fighting for.

GET GRITTY

GET PURPOSE

MASTER THOUGHTS

KNOW SELF

DOMINATE CONTROLLABLES

OWN THE MOMENT

CHOOSE EMOTIONS

OWN WHO YOU ARE

LIVE AND LET GO

COURAGE ZONE

My High Performance Game Plan
FIND YOUR FIGHT

1. I'll write about what I'm fighting for on a notecard and keep it close to me during my day.

2. What are the three or four times I've felt most alive? What was I doing, thinking, and feeling? How is that connected to what I'm fighting for?

3. What if I found out that I had only had six months to live? What would be in my plans? Are they the same or different from what I'm planning right now? If not, I need to decide to make changes today.

4. I can review the goals I set earlier as I worked through this book, making sure they reflect what I'm fighting for. If not, I'll adjust my goals with my fight in mind.

My High Performance Power Phrase

I find my fight. I remind myself every day what I am fighting for. I stay purposeful and passionate about my life, work, and family.

Chapter 9

Live and Play with Purpose

"The two most important days in your life are the day you were born, and the day you find out why." —MARK TWAIN

We've all met people in our lives that inspire us. We remember them. They stood out because they were committed to something bigger. They genuinely cared about what they were fighting for, and it showed. They were not just going through the motions. They acted with passion and purpose.

Finding your purpose can create powerful change. It's amazing to see this change first-hand in my clients. For example, I work with an NFL athlete who wants to continue to perform at his highest level. When I met him, he was focused on things he couldn't control and dreaming small about his future. Writing his purpose statement gave him a different level of intentionality. It changed the way he viewed his free time and money, and helped him see the important role he played on his team. He started a trust fund to enable his family to go to college, increased the time he spent in a community program each week, and saw his impact on his team's performance and their ability to win when he showed up at his best.

What is his purpose statement?

My life's purpose is to be driven and kind, have a growth mindset, enjoy my quest for flow, and create powerful ripples for my teammates, friends, family, and community.

I believe that we all have a purpose, and that our purpose gives us a reason to persevere. It gives us courage and reminds us of our significance. Verbalizing our purpose gives us power.

Psychologist Abraham Maslow arranged our human needs in a hierarchy with needs like air, food, and shelter at the base. He said those were our most basic human needs. He identified our middle needs as the desire to feel safe and secure daily, as well as to have connection and recognition. At the highest level, Maslow put our need to operate with purpose. He said, "A musician must make music, an artist must paint, a writer must write if he is to be ultimately at peace with himself. What a [person] can be, [he or she] must be. This need we call self-actualization."

What we can be, we must be. When we reach self-actualization, we thrive and perform at our best more consistently.

Our worlds are incomplete until we understand our purpose. Our purpose takes our why one step further. Our purpose takes us deeper into the meaning of our lives and why we are here.

As Richard Leider wrote in *The Power of Purpose*, only when our purpose is larger than just ourselves can we see that we are becoming the best version of ourselves. In other words, we all want to contribute to the world and make it a better place. We flourish when we contribute to the world outside of ourselves.

Our purpose isn't constrained to only our work or just our sport. It can be expressed in all parts of our lives. You can live your purpose even as your job or sport changes. The world's best take time to figure out their purpose so they can live intentionally and in a passionate way all throughout their lives. Researchers have found that people with a purpose are more likely to report being happy and describe that they are living the good life. People who can state their purpose report feeling like they can focus on the most important things in their day and have a vision for their future.

To get to the next level of your performance,
you need to get clear on your purpose.

Your purpose is what makes you unique. No one else has the same mix of experiences, knowledge, values, gifts, and dreams as you. No one else can offer the world, your community, or your team what you can, done in the way that you can. Your purpose is unique to you. Finding your purpose helps you understand you are a unique person with a special motivation.

Knowing your purpose is like driving your car with a full tank of gas. You can't get anywhere in your car without gas! You can't be gritty without purpose and energy!

Your purpose is something that is uncovered by looking inward. You discover it through a process of self-reflection, by considering (among other things) why you get out of bed each day.

To discover your purpose, answer the following four purpose questions:

1. What words describe me at my best? (List between 5-10 words; then circle the 2 or 3 that are most important to you.)

2. What do I want to create or do for myself and others?

3. What is the result or value I provide?

4. Who do I want to help, guide, or inspire in this world?

GET GRITTY

GET PURPOSE

MASTER THOUGHTS

KNOW SELF

DOMINATE CONTROLLABLES

OWN THE MOMENT

CHOOSE EMOTIONS

OWN WHO YOU ARE

LIVE AND LET GO

COURAGE ZONE

Take some time to answer these questions. Then, use your answers to craft your purpose statement. Purpose statements are exciting and powerful! As you are writing your purpose statement, remember that it should:

- Energize you every time you read it, say it, or share it.

- Be a purpose you can experience daily.

- Include gritty words that are powerful and big.

- Focus on what you *do* want, not on what you *don't* want.

- Impact others beyond yourself.

- Be simple enough to memorize.

- Be specific and avoid words that are universal like "always" and "never."

When I help clients write their purpose statement, I provide a structure to fill in. You can use this structure if it is helpful, or modify it if it feels too constrained. Either way, use your answers to the four purpose questions. Below is a way to structure your purpose statements.

> ### The purpose of my life is to _____
>
> _____,
> (use your answer to the first purpose question here)
>
> **to** _____,
> (use your answer to the second purpose question here)
>
> **and to** _____,
> (use your answer to the third purpose question here)
>
> **for** _____.
> (use your answer to the fourth purpose question here)

Look at the purpose statement you created and ask yourself if, deep down, you know this is why you do what you do. If it is, yippy! You have an incredible first draft of your purpose statement. If it isn't, play with the words or structure until it is. Replace words that don't get you stoked with ones that do. It may take some time. Don't rush the process. In addition, expect your purpose to evolve over time. It's good to revisit it yearly.

Completing this exercise changed my life. Before writing my purpose statement, I was struggling to explain what I was doing. I felt frustrated and defeated. Now I have my version framed by my bed on my Grit Board. I say it out loud each morning as part of my routine so it can get in my body and I can show up as my best self. I read it before every workshop, speaking event, and client session. I live, play, and perform more intentionally because I know what that means to me.

The purpose of my life is to be authentic and passionate, live with a service mindset, and help others PLAY BIG so they can be their best self.

Living on purpose is a choice we make each day. Your purpose statement is your inner guide that helps you choose how to act and think. When you live on purpose, you know who you are and you bring your whole self to your life intentionally. Identifying your purpose today and then honoring your purpose is perhaps the most important step that you will make toward high performance!

GET GRITTY

GET PURPOSE

MASTER THOUGHTS

KNOW SELF

DOMINATE CONTROLLABLES

OWN THE MOMENT

CHOOSE EMOTIONS

OWN WHO YOU ARE

LIVE AND LET GO

COURAGE ZONE

My High Performance Game Plan:
LIVE AND PLAY
ON PURPOSE

1. Who is someone I know who lives or plays on purpose? What attributes and actions of theirs could I emulate?

2. I will take the time to put my purpose statement on paper, and place it somewhere I can see it every day (like on my Grit Board).

3. As part of my morning routine, I'll say my purpose statement out loud.

4. I will use my purpose statement to inform my choices in sports, business, and all other areas of my life.

My High Performance Power Phrase:

I live and play on purpose. No one else has the same experiences, knowledge, and gifts as I do. I have a unique purpose and live that purpose.

Chapter 10

Connect with Your Uniqueness

"Hard work doesn't feel like hard work when you are doing what you love." —UNKNOWN

I was on the beautiful beaches of Punta Cana, Dominican Republic, when I read Dr. Gay Hendricks' book *The Big Leap*. Hendricks doesn't talk about high performance or the world's best in the book, but they are all I could think about as I was reading it. I sat in the sunshine taking it all in.

In the book, Hendricks describes the activities in our lives as taking place in four zones. The first zone, called the *Zone of Incompetence*, consists of activities that we are just not good at. Other people can do these activities so much better than us. He says that, if possible, we should avoid activities in this zone because it doesn't fulfill us; avoiding it leaves more energy and passion for what we are meant to do. Activities in this zone might include the tasks in our work life that someone else could do a lot better than we can. In sport, it may include positions on the team played better by others, or sports we just aren't good at.

The next zone, the *Zone of Competence*, includes activities that we do well but others can do just as well. We can spend too much time here because while these activities do not necessarily drain our energy, they don't ultimately provide fulfillment. We can survive, not thrive, in this zone. You might be good, but not great, at the activities in this zone. For example, you might be good, but not great, in a specific position on your team, or at certain roles (like managing social media) in your business.

The third zone, the *Zone of Excellence*, includes activities you do extremely well. Even though you do these things very well, this zone can trap you. You can stay here instead of getting outside your comfort zone where you flourish. This might be playing third base on your baseball team when you should be pitching because you are unstoppable, or competently doing payroll in your business when your real gift is strategic planning. If you stay in the Zone of Excellence, you won't be completely fueled because you are not yet where you are meant to be. And you are meant to be in the *Zone of Genius*. The world's best live in their Zone of Genius.

The only zone in which you thrive consistently is your Zone of Genius. Your Zone of Genius includes the activities that you were uniquely designed to do. They are the things that you do the best and love. Throughout our lives we get glimpses of our Zone of Genius activities; there are real consequences if we don't pay attention to what we learn. If we ignore these urges, we can experience depression, a loss of direction, and relationship conflicts. We can fail to thrive.

I used to ignore signs of my Zone of Genius, putting these activities on the backburner because other tasks kept me busy. But, after that day reading on the beach, I now spend more time on the activities that I was made to do. I focus on speaking, teaching, podcasting, writing, and consulting, things that reflect my purpose and the difference I can uniquely make in this world. I outsource budgeting, designing, and editing my podcast, all activities that belong in my Zones of Incompetence, Competence, and Excellence.

The world's best pay attention and know to stay in their Zone of Genius. They do this because they understand the importance of following their purpose and engaging in activities that they are fulfilled by. They know when they love what they do and it doesn't feel like hard work. High performers say "yes" to their Zone of Genius activities and "no thanks" to the activities outside that zone.

I've seen this play out in powerful ways. One of my clients, a high-level manager at a Fortune 500 company, was having difficulty planning her day and being disciplined with her time. She felt overwhelmed by too many tasks. She was burnt out and needed to take control of her time quickly. We outlined the activities in each of her zones and found her Zone of Genius activities included implementing the long-term vision of her division, making connections with other divisions, and strengthening relationships with high-level clients. Several of the tasks she had on her daily to-do list were outside of her Zone of Genius, but she could delegate them to others who could do them well. And she did! She felt calmer and motivated immediately.

To help us think about what is in—and out of —our Zone of Genius, Hendricks provides a few questions:

1. What do you most love to do? (You love it so much you can do it for long stretches of time without getting tired or bored.)

2. What activities do you do that don't seem like work? (Again, you can do it for long stretches of time without getting tired or bored.)

3. What are your unique abilities? What is the special skill you were gifted with?

GET GRITTY

GET PURPOSE

MASTER THOUGHTS

KNOW SELF

DOMINATE CONTROLLABLES

OWN THE MOMENT

CHOOSE EMOTIONS

OWN WHO YOU ARE

LIVE AND LET GO

COURAGE ZONE

Many of us have gifts that we are not expressing to their fullest. We may not have reflected about what is unique about us, or we might have taken our own unique gifts for granted. We may have even overlooked or downplayed them. But when you name your gifts and work to find your Zone of Genius, you gain more excitement and energy to live your life on purpose.

What is in your Zone of Genius? How can you spend more time in that zone? When you make the choice to do just that, you thrive. You spend more time doing what you love and what you were uniquely designed to do.

My High Performance Game Plan
CONNECT WITH YOUR UNIQUENESS

1. I commit to live more frequently or fully in my Zone of Genius.

2. I will list the activities that are part of my Zones of Incompetence, Competence, and Excellence so I know what I should spend less time doing. How do I make that happen?

3. What activities are in my Zone of Genius?

4. What is an action I can take right now to get closer to living in my Zone of Genius?

My High Performance Power Phrase

I own my unique skills and talents. I engage in the activities I love, which keeps me fueled and excited about my work, sport, and life.

Practice 2
CONCLUDING THOUGHTS

Congratulations, my friend—you are one step closer to living and playing with purpose, on purpose. Here are the things you learned from Get Clear on Your Purpose:

- How owning your why is a game changer.

- How your purpose statement is your inner guide that helps you choose how to act and think.

- And how your Zone of Genius includes the activities that you were uniquely designed to do.

Now, take a moment to record the following on your Grit Board:

- Your why in a single sentence.

- What you are fighting for.

- Your purpose statement.

- And a few of your Zone of Genius activities.

3

Master Your Thoughts

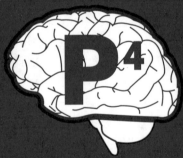

The world's best

*are intentional with their self-talk.
They exhibit powerful, positive, and
possibility-oriented thinking patterns
focused on process.*

Chapter 11

Choose an Optimistic Perspective

"A pessimist sees the difficulty in every opportunity. An optimist sees the opportunity in every difficulty." —Sir Winston Churchill

Not long ago, I delivered a workshop on mindset for a construction company in upstate New York. The night before the workshop, I had dinner with one of the owners, Mike. Over dinner, Mike disclosed that a former employee had recently stolen $270,000 from their company. It drastically impacted the company's bottom line, and yet, as he shared the story, I noticed how Mike mentioned the amount stolen with no obvious discouragement or discontent in his tone. In fact, you'd have thought only $2.70 was stolen from his business based on how calm and even light-hearted he was as he told the story. I was amazed. When I asked him why he was not pulling his hair out over this, he told me, "Since this happened, we continuously ask ourselves, 'What's our opportunity here?'" He smiled as he shared, "I could be upset, but what would that solve? I know our company is fine and that we'll learn from what happened."

Mike was practicing what I call the Three OPP Strategy: in other words, when presented with a difficulty, you identify three opportunities. And it's a good thing that he was! Instead of dwelling on the financial hit his company experienced, taking the issue personally, and feeling overrun with anger, Mike chose to seek the silver lining. In fact, he even believed his business would be better, not worse, as a result of this setback.

Research conducted by Martin Seligman, a professor at the University of Pennsylvania, suggested that leaders, entrepreneurs, and athletes who practice optimism are more likely to experience:

- A longer life. Optimists live longer than pessimists. They experience fewer infectious diseases, are less likely to have cancer, and have overall better health habits than pessimists.

- Better performance, consistently. Optimists perform better under pressure and have more consistent results than pessimists.

- Less stress, and more self-confidence and resilience. Optimism decreases the bad and increases the good.

That night, Mike asked me how I would define optimism. To answer, I told him about Martin Seligman's work on explanatory style, which gives us powerful insight on this topic of optimism. Seligman argues that our explanatory style determines if we are an optimist or pessimist and that there are three parts of our explanatory style (permanence, pervasiveness, and personalization).

Parts of Our Explanatory Styles

* Permanence: An optimist believes that successes and positive events will continue and are not a fluke, and that bad events or setbacks are rare and will not continue. A pessimist believes that when bad events occur, they will persist.

* Pervasiveness: An optimist believes that good events in one area—sports, business, relationships—positively affect other areas. A pessimist believes that a difficulty in one area will spread. In addition, a pessimist makes universal explanations for their failures. For example, they might say, "All coaches/ teachers are unfair" or "I am never good at anything!"

GET GRITTY
GET PURPOSE
MASTER THOUGHTS
KNOW SELF
DOMINATE CONTROLLABLES
OWN THE MOMENT
CHOOSE EMOTIONS
OWN WHO YOU ARE
LIVE AND LET GO
COURAGE ZONE

> * Personalization: An optimist believes they are the cause of good events. They take credit for their success, see success as a result of their hard work, and protect their confidence even when they fail. A pessimist sees success as a result of luck or circumstances outside of their control.

Over time, we've all developed an explanatory style based on our experiences and on those around us. But we can change our explanatory style by shifting how we explain events in our lives. We can change how we see difficulties, obstacles, and setbacks, and in turn, we can maintain our optimism and confidence.

Mike presented the Three OPP Strategy to his team, applying the optimistic explanatory style. As a result, I spent the next day with his team outlining three opportunities that emerged from the theft. Their responses?

> * The opportunity to better assign duties to set the company up for future success.

> * The opportunity for the management team to work smarter and more closely together.

> * The opportunity for team unity as everyone rallied together to fix what went wrong.

Mike's company came to understand, just as Mike did, that opportunities come from difficulties. And difficulties are not unique to that company! We all experience challenging situations. In fact, obstacles and setbacks are a given. It's how we respond to them that matters.

How would your life change if you saw failures and obstacles as opportunities? Think about it by using the Three OPP Strategy.

- First, think of a difficulty you are experiencing right now. Maybe you lack focus during your game, your company is not positioned to meet its financial goals this year, or your kid is misbehaving at home.

- Second, consider at least three opportunities that come from this difficulty. Perhaps this difficulty provides an opportunity for you to learn techniques to improve your focus, to hire additional staff, to spend more time with your child, or to simply focus on the things that are going well instead of dwelling on the things that aren't.

- Finally, write these three opportunities down on paper or on your Grit Board. Writing them down makes them stick.

When you use the Three OPP Strategy, you are more creative and excited about possibilities. You have an energized perspective on what you are experiencing right now instead of dwelling in anxiety or focusing on worst-case scenarios. The Three OPP Strategy helps you expect that something good will come from everything. It helps you develop an optimistic explanatory style as you begin to see challenges leading you to something better.

The next time you experience a difficulty, take the optimistic perspective and find the opportunity.

GET
GRITTY

GET
PURPOSE

MASTER
THOUGHTS

KNOW
SELF

DOMINATE
CONTROLLABLES

OWN THE
MOMENT

CHOOSE
EMOTIONS

OWN WHO
YOU ARE

LIVE AND
LET GO

COURAGE
ZONE

My High Performance Game Plan

CHOOSE AN OPTIMISTIC PERSPECTIVE

1. I commit to developing an optimistic explanatory style like the world's best.

2. Next time I'm faced with a difficulty, setback, or obstacle, I'll use the Three OPP Strategy to explore the opportunities in the situation.

3. When I experience a success this week, I'll believe that the success will continue and spread to other areas, and is within my control.

4. When I experience difficult events this week, I'll believe that setbacks are rare and will not continue.

My High Performance Power Phrase

I am an optimist. I see the opportunity in every difficulty. I believe I determine the success that I experience. I make it happen!

Chapter 12

Don't Let Your Negativity Grow

"Negativity spreads faster than any Justin Bieber song."
—Vanilla Ice

I had a terrible game against that team a few months ago . . .

It's gonna happen again tomorrow . . .

I have to bounce back . . .

Am I playing well enough to stay? . . .

What if I get traded, or worse, cut from the team? . . .

Those were the exact thoughts of one of my clients, a pro athlete. Though he never said these things out loud, he said them in his head. They were his self-talk. As you might have guessed, he wasn't playing well, not because he had the negative thoughts, but because he believed them.

We all have negative thoughts. They are called automatic negative thoughts, or ANTs for short. I first read about ANTs in Dr. Daniel Amen's book, *Change Your Brain, Change Your Life*. This was many years ago, and the concept was life-changing for me. I wish I would have read and understood it as a college athlete! Back then, I struggled to compete at my best consistently and always seemed to get in my own way. Understanding ANTs would have prevented a lot of suffering.

The problem is that we don't always choose our thoughts. Thoughts have a habit of creeping in and making themselves at home before we realize they're even there. The crazy thing is that our thoughts drive everything we do. Everything. Our thoughts determine how we interact with others, how we feel about ourselves, and how we act. Thoughts become emotions that lead to actions and then become habits. Simply put, our thoughts determine our destiny.

Our thoughts are the most important factor in our success or our failure.

I know, that's a bold statement. But I see its truth all the time in my clients, and in myself. What we think about determines everything we do. Our thoughts have physical properties that impact every cell in our body. Our thoughts are so powerful that research presented by neuroscientist Caroline Leaf has found that between 75 and 98 percent of mental, behavioral, and physical illnesses can come from thoughts.

Too many negative thoughts lead to toxicity, a downward spiral into moodiness, depression, and irritability. Our thoughts inform our feelings and actions; therefore, if a person's mind is filled with toxic thoughts, they will act with toxicity. Too many ANTs deteriorate our ability to perform under pressure and show up as our authentic self. They don't allow us to function at our full potential.

Some Common Automatic Negative Thoughts/ ANTS

- **"Always/Never" Thinking.** This occurs when we think things will always happen the way that they happened once before, or that things never happen because once they did not. We use words like *no one, everyone, every time, everything, never,* and *always* out loud or in our minds. For example, your coach yells at you once in a while, and you think, "She/he always yells at me." Or after a conflict with your children, you think, "My kids never listen to me." This thinking leads us to assumptions that are simply not accurate.

- **Focusing on the Negative in a Situation.** This happens when we see only the bad in a situation and not the good. For example, you receive feedback from your boss and only focus on the one or two comments that were negative, not the many comments that were positive. Or you don't win the game and only focus on what went wrong instead of what went right. This type of thinking doesn't give us the energy to tackle tough situations or allow us to thrive.

- **Fortune Telling.** When we fortune tell, we can predict the worst possible outcome of a situation. You apply for a job and predict you won't even get an interview. Or you predict you will get crushed by your rival in an upcoming game. The problem is that when you predict that things will be bad, you can make those bad things happen. Fortune telling hurts our chances of feeling good and enjoying the moment.

- **Mind Reading.** We mind read when we believe we know what other people are thinking. We think, "My teammate doesn't like me," or "Those people are talking about me," or "The coach doesn't believe in me." Of course, we have no idea what people are thinking unless we ask them. We can't read other people's minds. Plus, the majority of the time, they are not thinking about us at all!

- **Guilt Tripping.** Guilt can result from using words like

GET GRITTY

GET PURPOSE

MASTER THOUGHTS

KNOW SELF

DOMINATE CONTROLLABLES

OWN THE MOMENT

CHOOSE EMOTIONS

OWN WHO YOU ARE

LIVE AND LET GO

COURAGE ZONE

should, must, have to, or *ought to*. It can happen when we tell ourselves, "I ought to spend more time at the office," or "I should spend more time on my homework." Guilt can be counterproductive because it creates a resistance to do what we need to do.

- **Personalization.** We personalize when we believe negative events have personal meaning. Our boss or coach doesn't acknowledge us while passing us in the hall and we think, "She/he is mad at me." Or we see our teammates talking across the field and we assume they are talking about us. It's important to remember that there are many other reasons people do what they do, and we never fully know why they do it.

- **Labeling.** This happens when we attach a negative label to others or ourselves, saying things like, "I am such a terrible shortstop," or "I am miserable at speaking in front of others." The problem with this is that we lump others or ourselves into categories and start generalizing, and then start acting according to those generalizations. There have been lots of times that you have been a terrific shortstop or talked comfortably in front of others. The key is to remember those times.

- **Blaming.** This happens when you blame someone else for your problems or the situation. This is the most dangerous and poisonous ANT. In fact, it is a red fire ant. We say, "It's your fault that . . ." or "This wouldn't have happened if . . ." When we blame others for our situation, we become powerless to change it.

If you see ants in your kitchen—real, live ants—would you let them grow and multiply? When I see an ant in my kitchen, I do something about it. My guess is that you do, too. We have to, otherwise they take over our whole kitchen.

The same thing can happen in your mind. Your ANTs grow and grow until the negativity takes over your emotions, body, and actions. ANTs can grow until they take over your future. You don't need to let the negative thoughts impact you or remain in your mind for a long time. You can debug your performance and your life.

An important part of reaching your greater potential is recognizing that you shouldn't believe everything you hear—especially in your own mind.

The world's best athletes, leaders, business people, and entrepreneurs don't believe everything they think. You, my friend, should not believe everything you think either! You can control your reactions, and you do have a choice on how you will address your ANTs. Noticing your ANTs is the first step in controlling your mind before it controls you.

GET GRITTY

GET PURPOSE

MASTER THOUGHTS

KNOW SELF

DOMINATE CONTROLLABLES

OWN THE MOMENT

CHOOSE EMOTIONS

OWN WHO YOU ARE

LIVE AND LET GO

COURAGE ZONE

My High Performance Game Plan
DON'T LET YOUR NEGATIVITY GROW

1. Starting today, I'm going to reduce my negativity so that I can thrive and reach my best more often.

2. I will increase my self-awareness and work to notice my negative thoughts moment to moment, giving myself a greater chance of reaching high performance more consistently.

3. Which of the eight ANTs am I most likely to think? I need to take command over that ANT today!

4. I can share the ANT concept with a friend, family member, or teammate. I'll tell them which ANTs I'm more likely to experience. Together, we can brainstorm a more productive thought to choose instead of the ANT.

My High Performance Power Phrase

I reduce my ANTs so I can reach my fullest potential. I make a commitment to think productive thoughts so that I can do my best.

Chapter 13

Think Like
the World's Best

"If you think you can or think you can't, you're right."
—HENRY FORD

Doctors, scientists, and other experts said for years that the human body was simply not capable of running a mile in under four minutes. Some said it was dangerous. Others said it was impossible. Some thought that a runner's heart would explode! But on May 6, 1954, Roger Bannister did it anyway. In Oxford, England, he became the first person to run a mile in under four minutes. He ran it in 3:59.4, and visualized the accomplishment with certainty and confidence in his mind and body before it happened. He believed it was possible.

Bannister's record-breaking four-minute mile is less about breaking a physical barrier and more about shattering a mental barrier: his run established the possibility that it could be done. Less than two months later, Australia's John Laddy also ran the mile under four minutes. More and more runners quickly followed Bannister's lead. Others had to see it happen before they believed it was possible. But not Bannister. He believed it before he did it. He broke the barrier in the world's mind.

Ample research over many decades shows that the world's best athletes and business people think differently than those who experience less success. They believe in the impossible.

Our thinking is the most important factor in our success, but we are not typically taught how to think like the most successful people around us. Sometimes we are never taught how to think at all—not by our parents, teachers, or mentors. Instead, we figure it out by trial and error. But there is a better way to learn something than by trial and error. That is one of the reasons I am so excited you are reading this book!

The world's best athletes, leaders, and business people will tell you they have learned to master their thinking. They place deliberate energy and focus in mastering the six inches between their ears.

Training your mind takes consistent and daily effort; it is not automatic.

If you don't train your mind, you are letting your thoughts happen by chance. Chance thinking does not lead to success. High performers don't hope their thinking will work for them; they make their thinking work for them. They are intentional and purposeful with their self-talk.

The world's best are intentional with their self-talk.

To experience high performance, your self-talk should be powerful, possibility-oriented, process-focused, and positive. These are called the P4 thoughts. High performers are less likely to experience defeating, restrictive, outcome-focused, and negative thoughts. Remember that your thoughts lead to emotions, and emotions lead to actions. In other words, your thoughts are what can lead you toward or away from your greater potential in this world.

Thinking that Leads to Your Potential	Thinking that Limits Your Potential
Powerful	Defeating
Possibility-oriented	Restrictive
Process-focused	Outcome-focused
Positive	Negative

The best of the best focus on P4 thoughts more often. Their thoughts are:

Powerful. The world's best choose thoughts that make them want to accomplish something and move forward. Their powerful thoughts lead to powerful body language, positive action, and enthusiasm for their day, their team, and their life. High performers realize that weak thoughts lead them to feeling unworthy, defeated, sick, worn-out, and tired. High performers do not let weak thoughts grow and multiply.

Powerful thoughts: I can do anything I put my mind to. I will set a new standard for my team or business. I am pumped and excited to go to work/practice today!

Defeating thoughts: I can't do that. I won't make a difference in the world or on my team. I am not important to my team, family, or business.

Possibility-oriented. The world's best know that when they are focused on possibilities, they stay energized and passionate about their life and work. High performers choose to dream about their future and to visualize what they want to happen in their future. They open their minds to believing in their greater potential and continuously push past the status quo. They don't settle for average; instead, they strive for greatness and consistent high performance.

GET GRITTY

GET PURPOSE

MASTER THOUGHTS

KNOW SELF

DOMINATE CONTROLLABLES

OWN THE MOMENT

CHOOSE EMOTIONS

OWN WHO YOU ARE

LIVE AND LET GO

COURAGE ZONE

Possibility-oriented thoughts: Anything is possible with enough grit! My future is going to be outstanding. The possibilities in my life and performance are endless.

Restrictive thoughts: There is no way he/she could do that. That's impossible. No one could ever do that!

Process-focused: The world's best keep their attention on the process to help them stay in the present moment. They realize that the present moment is the only thing they can control. Focusing on the process allows them to stay in the present. It may seem like the best way to get the result is to focus on the outcome, but outcome-focused thoughts cause pressure, anxiety, heaviness, and a limited belief in our ability—all characteristics of poor performance. As Picabo Street, a U.S. Olympic Skier, said, "I don't think about winning. I think about how I'm going to be fast. If I'm going fast, the winning happens." Focusing on the process allows for creativity, experimentation, and enjoying the moment.

Process-focused thoughts: Focus on the now! I can do anything in the present moment. I am playing fast and powerfully today.

Outcome-focused thoughts: Meeting this deadline is never going to happen. I must win today no matter what. Dang, I can't believe we are losing.

Positive. The world's best know that purposefully not thinking about something will cause them to think about it. For example, if someone asked you to stop thinking about a pink-striped zebra, you probably would find yourself unable to stop thinking about a pink-striped zebra. To avoid thinking about that zebra, you would have to change your focus. If a kicker in football thought, "Don't miss this field goal," he would likely miss it. Or if a golfer thought, "Don't hit it in the water," she would likely hit the ball in the water. Your mind is incredibly powerful! High performers stay focused on what they want to happen instead of what they want to avoid. They use "I will . . ." statements to help them focus on their best.

Positive thoughts: I will kick the ball straight and focus on my routine. I will crush my presentation today! I will be and play the best I can today.

Negative thoughts: Don't crash under the pressure today. Don't miss the next shot. Don't drop the ball. Don't freeze when it matters most today.

The key to experiencing P4 thinking more often is to plan your thinking. Research shows that when we have pre-planned, specific thoughts to address our negative thinking, we do a better job at eliminating the negativity than when we just try not to think negatively.

Consider your next performance: a practice, an athletic competition, a presentation at work, or a meeting you want to go well. What are at least four P4 thoughts that could lead to performing on purpose and at your best?

When you have your thoughts planned out, you have a plan for eliminating the ANTs and negative thoughts that are bound to creep in. When the ANTs appear, choose not to believe what you are thinking and choose P4 thinking instead!

GET GRITTY

GET PURPOSE

MASTER THOUGHTS

KNOW SELF

DOMINATE CONTROLLABLES

OWN THE MOMENT

CHOOSE EMOTIONS

OWN WHO YOU ARE

LIVE AND LET GO

COURAGE ZONE

My High Performance Game Plan
THINK LIKE THE WORLD'S BEST

1. I commit today to choose P4 thinking moment to moment and make it my standard.

2. What was a time I dominated my P4 thinking? What was the result?

3. What was a time I experienced a ton of defeating, restrictive, and outcome-focused thinking? How did the result compare to an experience when I choose P4 thoughts?

4. I will write out at least four P4 thoughts (one for each P) that I can say to myself before my next performance.

My High Performance Power Phrase

I choose powerful, possibility-oriented, process-focused, and positive thoughts to keep me at my best. I make a commitment to not believe everything I think.

Chapter 14

Make "I Will . . . I Can . . . I Am . . ." Your New Standard

"It's the repetition of affirmations that leads to belief. And once that belief becomes a deep conviction, things begin to happen." —MUHAMMAD ALI

CHANCES OF SUCCESS

0%	I WON'T	**60%**	I MIGHT
10%	I CAN'T	**70%**	I WILL
20%	I DON'T KNOW HOW	**80%**	I CAN
30%	I WISH I COULD	**90%**	I AM
40%	I WANT TO		
50%	I THINK I MIGHT		

Let me take you back to 2012. It was my tenth marathon—the Omaha Marathon. I trained more for that marathon than any other that I have ever run. I knew I could run fast. I was ready. I wanted to perform extra well because the most important people in my life were there watching—my parents, my two boys, my husband, and my sister. The race started well, and at mile 13 my husband yelled at me from the side of the road, letting me know I was leading the race as the first woman. *To win a marathon*, I thought, *that would be amazing! I am crushing it!* I had a smile plastered on my face for much of the race. *Today is going to be my day!* kept going through my mind.

But then I hit a wall. As I was running up the biggest hill in the race at mile 22, I felt overwhelmed with defeat and could feel my entire body start to work against me. My arms felt tingly. My legs felt like bricks. My feet ached. It was hard to breathe. *This might be the worst I have ever felt in a marathon,* I thought.

The second-place female suddenly appeared by my side. I could feel her presence on my right. The ANTs got louder and louder in my mind. I thought, *Why did I sign up for this race? She is going to pass me. I feel miserable! I want to drop out! This sucks. All those miles and hours I trained this summer are wasted! I am not going to win today.*

She stayed beside me all the way up and down the hill. My whole body ached. My quads were on fire. It became harder to breathe. I was exhausted, thirsty, and hungry. And then, in a blink of a second, I got a little ahead of her.

As I ran around a U-shaped turn in the course, I got a glimpse of her face. I could see the discomfort in her eyes. *She feels the same way I do,* I thought. This thought jolted me out of my funk and my negativity. I started to think productively again. *She feels the discomfort, too,* I told myself. *This is what marathoning is about. You were born to run marathons!* My mind flooded with P4 thoughts focused on the possibilities for myself in that race.

I planned four Power Phrases because I knew the marathon would get tough, like it always does. For the last four miles of the race, I repeated my Power Phrases over and over: "I am fast. I am fit. I am confident. I am happy. . . . I am fast. I am fit. I am confident. I am happy. . . . I am fast. I am fit. I am confident. I am happy . . ."

As I began to control my thoughts, I felt a powerful shift. I was centered, and my mood improved.

My pace followed my mind. I started running faster and faster. Faster and faster. Soon I was running my fastest pace yet. I sped ahead of my competitor.

I don't remember miles 24 and 25. I was in the flow. Finishing the marathon felt surreal. I finished 4 minutes in front of the second-place female after being inches from her just a few miles before.

As I ran across the finish line, tears rolled down my face—not because I won, but because I had mastered my thinking. I got to the height of my physical ability that day because of my mind. The miles and miles of training paid off because I had decided to think like the world's best!

The quickest way to perform to your wicked awesome potential is to change your thinking.

A powerful way to talk to yourself is to choose Power Phrases. Power Phrases combat destructive phrases such as "I won't . . . ," "I can't . . . ," and "I am not . . ." Power Phrases, or positive affirmations or declarations, begin with "I will . . . ," "I can . . . ," or "I am . . ." These statements focus on a positive change, your wicked awesome potential, and who you are instead of who you are not.

- **"I will . . ." is a statement about a positive change or intention.** When you think "I will . . ." you are talking about what you want and what you intend to make happen. "I will . . ." predicts your future success. For example:

    ° I will start my own company.

    ° I will be more loving with my family.

    ° I will play big this weekend.

- **"I can . . ." is a statement about your potential.** It is a positive statement about your ability to accomplish your goals and dreams. When you think "I can . . ." you focus on your belief in your ability to do something. For example:

GET GRITTY

GET PURPOSE

MASTER THOUGHTS

KNOW SELF

DOMINATE CONTROLLABLES

OWN THE MOMENT

CHOOSE EMOTIONS

OWN WHO YOU ARE

LIVE AND LET GO

COURAGE ZONE

- ° I can stop smoking.

- ° I can build a million dollar company.

- ° I can throw the ball accurately.

- **"I am . . ." is the most powerful power phrase because it is a statement about who you are and your identity.** The phrase "I am . . ." has the ability to shape your reality and your destiny. When you think "I am . . ." you focus on traits that you already have inside you. "I am . . ." statements allow you to take a personal inventory of your strengths, talents, and positive attributes, as well as qualities that you would like to develop (like confident, happy, or relaxed). You can become what you are say you are. For example:

- ° I am resilient and keep going despite obstacles.

- ° I am amazing at connecting with people.

- ° I am strong and powerful.

Powerful Ways to End Your "I Am . . ." Statements

A Leader	Alive	Amazing	Centered	Confident	Creative
Ecstatic	Empowered	Energized	Excited	Extraordinary	Explosive
Fit	Grateful	Gritty	Gorgeous	Happy	Intelligent
Invincible	Juiced	Loving	Passionate	Patient	Present
Raring to Go	Ready	Resilient	Smart	Unstoppable	Worth It

I use Power Phrases daily. I create my "I am . . ." statements by thinking about how I would describe myself when I am fully alive, flourishing, and living with purpose. My "I am . . ." statements are framed by my bed next to my purpose statement, and I say them to myself or sometimes out loud (which is the most powerful) when I first wake up in the morning. They are:

- I am loving.

- I am authentic.

- I am me.

- I am worth it.

I repeat these four Power Phrases when I feel like I need a positive spark, when I am judging others or myself, or when I struggle to fully show up to what I am doing.

Make "I will . . . ," "I can . . . ," and "I am . . ." statements your new standard for how you talk to yourself daily—especially when you feel you aren't at your best. You might not see an impact after saying the Power Phrases just one time, so keep repeating them until they become a habit.

Your mind simply becomes what you tell it the most. What you think about, you create. What you think about yourself, you become. In fact, every thought you think, either conscious or unconscious, is translated to electrical impulses. Those impulses affect every feeling, every action, every habit, and every moment in our lives. The more often you repeat your Power Phrases with passion, certainty, and meaning, the more automatic they become.

GET GRITTY

GET PURPOSE

MASTER THOUGHTS

KNOW SELF

DOMINATE CONTROLLABLES

OWN THE MOMENT

CHOOSE EMOTIONS

OWN WHO YOU ARE

LIVE AND LET GO

COURAGE ZONE

My High Performance Game Plan

MAKE "I WILL . . . I CAN . . . I AM . . ." YOUR NEW STANDARD

1. I commit to improving my self-talk.

2. On a note card, I'll write three or four Power Phrases to bring to work, practice, or my next performance.

3. I'll post my Power Phrases where I'll see them each morning, such as on my Grit Board, and say them out loud or in my mind to powerfully take on my day.

4. Throughout my day, I'll revisit my Power Phrases to improve my self-image and daily performance.

My High Performance Power Phrase

I talk to myself, not listen. I think "I will . . . I can . . . I am . . ." to help me reach my wicked awesome potential.

Chapter 15

Reframe Your Way Back on Your Game

---

*"If you change the way you look at things,
the things you look at change."*
—WAYNE DYER

When I first met Maddie, she was an emerging high school gymnast with big dreams to compete in the state gymnastics meet in the vault. However, in her junior year, she tore the ACL in her knee. Unfortunately, her season ended abruptly. Maddie, understandably, was devastated. When she came to me, we decided that as she was slowly getting back into the sport after surgery, we'd work together to train her mind. Recovering from a season-ending injury can be difficult for any athlete, as their minds can become filled with ANTs like "Why me?" and "I couldn't possibly ever get back to where I was before" and "I can't do this." In a sport like gymnastics, where risk and trust are paramount to performance, addressing ANTs can mean the difference between returning to the sport better than before or becoming fixed in an attitude of defeat.

Maddie and I did what psychologists refer to as cognitive reframing. We created alternative ways to see her life, her gymnastics, and her future. When we reframe, we change our viewpoint. We intentionally choose to see circumstances, challenges, and our desires through a different lens—often a lens that might feel farfetched or uncomfortable. But here's the deal: the world is what we make it, so we can change our lens at any time. Reframing helps us to stay stoked and excited despite hardships, no matter how awful things might feel in the moment. It also helps us overcome obstacles like a loss of a job, a poor performance, or a season-ending injury.

Reframing doesn't require that we ignore the injury, difficulty, or pain. Instead, it allows us to see our circumstance differently. Maddie and I worked to see her injury as an advantage. We talked about how she learned more about her passion for gymnastics during the injury. At one point, Maddie said, "Cindra, I know I can do this. I am ready to get back to gymnastics and reach my goals!" It was clear that grit was urging her to go after her goal of making it to state in the vault. So, together we created the perfect Power Phrase for her that she could repeat in her most vulnerable moments. Her Power Phrase became, "My setback is a comeback."

Maddie could easily have seen her injury as an ending, but through reframing she told herself that injuries happen to even the best athletes; she reminded herself of her guiding goal to make it to the state competition. She also didn't dwell on the negative. When she was tired, she practiced despite her injury. When her knee hurt, she didn't dwell on the discomfort; instead, she reminded herself that the moment would pass. She surrounded herself with family and friends who believed in her comeback and affirmed her dream every day. On her bad days, she repeated her Power Phrase and placed it in a place that she would see throughout the day.

Two years after her injury, Maddie lived the first of many of her dreams and competed in the vault at the state meet. Like Maddie, you can leverage your grit to remain excited, passionate, and on track even when a circumstance, challenge, or tragedy throws you off your path. It's a proven fact that the world's best think like Maddie: they adopt a regular practice of reframing negative events in a positive light.

Here are a few examples of when to reframe:

- A coach or boss provides difficult feedback

- You miss the game-winning shot

- You have a bad race, game, or performance

- You don't get the job that you applied for

- You are experiencing a difficulty in a relationship

- You must perform or drive in rainy or snowy weather

- You don't do well on a test or exam

- You're in a cranky mood

The key is to step back and consider the frame or "lens" of the situation. This doesn't mean you ignore the difficulty or obstacle, but you choose to see a different perspective. How can you challenge the beliefs or assumptions underlying how you see the "negative" event? What is another way of looking at it, an alternative lens? How can you stand in another frame and see a different perspective?

All of the negative events or obstacles are helping you learn more about yourself, your situation, and your desire to reach your goals. The key is to shift your perspective and view each difficulty as an opportunity to grow and learn.

GET
GRITTY

GET
PURPOSE

MASTER
THOUGHTS

KNOW
SELF

DOMINATE
CONTROLLABLES

OWN THE
MOMENT

CHOOSE
EMOTIONS

OWN WHO
YOU ARE

LIVE AND
LET GO

COURAGE
ZONE

My High Performance Game Plan

REFRAME YOUR WAY
BACK TO YOUR GAME

1. I will find ways throughout my day to change my frame or lens.

2. When I feel frustrated and angry, I'll ask myself, "How can I see a weakness as a strength, a setback as a comeback, or a difficulty as an opportunity?"

3. When I reframe, I won't ignore the injury, difficulty, or discomfort, but instead see how the obstacle is helping me.

4. Next time a friend, co-worker, or teammate is complaining about a situation, I'll help them reframe and use a new lens.

My High Performance Power Phrase

I use reframing regularly to keep me passionate and charged for my goals and my life. I see a setback as a comeback.

Chapter 16

Disengage with Overthinking

"Finish each day and be done with it. You have done what you could, some blunders and absurdities have crept in; forget them as soon as you can. Tomorrow is a new day." —Ralph Waldo Emerson

Ashley, an aspiring speaker, coach, and author, called me a few years ago. She wanted to do what I do—speak, coach, and write—and she asked if I could help her get out in the world with her message. I was excited to begin by teaching her tips and tricks to help her speak in a way that came alive, coach in an inspiring way, and write powerfully. But as we began our work together, I quickly realized that she wasn't ready for that yet. She had to work on her mindset first.

If you haven't mastered your mindset, tips and tricks don't help much. Ashley was stuck in the overthinking rut, frequently wondering things like, "Am I horrible at this?" and "Is this really the next step to take?"

Like Ashley, I can easily overthink situations. In fact, we can all experience overthinking; research suggests overthinking is a common problem. In one study published in the *Journal of Cognitive Psychotherapy*, researchers found that 73 percent of young adults and 52 percent of middle-aged adults can be classified as overthinkers. The research of University of Michigan psychology professor Susan Nolen-Hoeksema suggested that roughly 57 percent of women and 43 percent of men can be classified the same way. My experience as a high performance coach confirms these findings.

In other words, we all can needlessly, passively, endlessly, and excessively ponder the meanings, causes, or consequences of things. We can overthink anything: our athletic performance, our success, our failure, our families, our appearance, our career, or our health. When we overthink, we can ask ourselves questions like:

- Why did I make that mistake?

- Why was I so terrible in practice today?

- What do others think of me?

- What did he mean by that comment?

- Why I am so unhappy?

Overthinking is a serious problem because we cannot perform at our highest level when we engage in it. Overthinking interferes with our problem-solving ability, zaps our motivation, impairs our ability to think like the world's best, fosters ANTs, and prevents us from pursuing our goals. Overthinking can drive our family, friends, teammates, and coworkers away because of the negative thoughts and emotions that are generated. Overthinking gives us a distorted, pessimistic view of our life. It can feel like quicksand!

It is great when we have family, friends, or coaches who can help us through these moments, but we can catch ourselves, as well. To do so, the first step is to recognize that overthinking is not your friend. Overthinking does not help you! When we feel down, we might think that focusing inward and evaluating our situation is good and meaningful, but when we ruminate while we are upset, what we think can be toxic. We can feel powerless, self-critical, and pessimistic.

To help reduce overthinking, I've outlined a three-step process. I call this process the CAR Shift. CAR helps you shift gears in your mind instead of in your car. Using the CAR Shift can help you make your thinking more productive.

"C" is for Catch it

You can't do your best if you don't notice when something is throwing you off. The key is to "catch it" or notice the thought. Self-awareness moment-to-moment will help you identify when negative thoughts impact your mood and body. When you are angry, sad, mad, or irritated, your brain releases chemicals that make your body feel miserable. Notice your thoughts at these moments and then don't follow the unhealthy ones. Remember: A thought is just a thought. That's all. A thought is not a fact!

"A" is for Address it

Don't let negativity grow. Instead, decide to address it and confront it head on. You have two choices in addressing the ANTs. One option is looking for evidence on why your thought is not accurate or true. Poke holes in the negativity and find the ways your thought is not accurate. When you have a bad race, game, or performance, remind yourself of the times you have had a great performance. If you didn't get the job that you wanted, tell yourself that it is an opportunity to grow and develop your skills. A second option is to take a mindful approach in addressing negativity, which is discussed in depth in Chapter 28. Imagine the negative thought moving out of your mind like a cloud passing by. You could say a phrase like "Let it go" or "Focus on the now" if that helps. Decide how you will release the negativity and then follow through with your decision.

"R" is for Refocus it

To get out of your head, refocus on the next step to reach your goals. What is the next thing you need to do to move forward? What is the next step in your process? If you are an athlete, commit to the next step on the field, court, or track. If you are a leader, coach, or business manager, consider the next step you need to lead your team effectively. Move your focus to a task or your next step so you don't keep ruminating or overthinking.

GET GRITTY

GET PURPOSE

MASTER THOUGHTS

KNOW SELF

DOMINATE CONTROLLABLES

OWN THE MOMENT

CHOOSE EMOTIONS

OWN WHO YOU ARE

LIVE AND LET GO

COURAGE ZONE

Here is an example of how Ashley used the CAR Shift when she was overthinking.

- **Catch it:** She noticed this thought: *"Will I ever be great at this speaking, writing, and coaching thing?"*

- **Address it:** She reframed her thought and replaced it with this: *"Each day I am growing, learning, and getting better! I will trust myself and the process."*

- **Refocus it:** She committed all her focus to the next task she needed to do to be successful, which was to write her first blog post.

Where in your day-to-day can you use the CAR Shift? What do you tend to overthink about and how could this be useful? You can use the CAR Shift in any part of your life—in your business, family life, or as you are leading your team or group. Remember, the world is what you make of it. You have the power to change your focus at any time.

Becoming happier and being your best self means learning how to disengage from overthinking. Every day, in all parts of our life, we can experience minor setbacks and hassles. Learning to stop overthinking about them will help you reach your highest level of performance and think like the world's best.

My High Performance Game Plan
DISENGAGE WITH OVERTHINKING

1. What was a time in the past when I engaged in overthinking? What did I overthink about and what were the consequences?

2. How does overthinking impact my life and why should I disengage from it? For example, does it personally zap my motivation, destroy my creativity, or take away my passion for what I do?

3. I will write down one or two things I tend to overthink. Then, I'll write out how I could use the CAR Shift to address these things.

4. The next time I want to be at my best—at an upcoming job interview, a big game, a try-out, or a presentation—how can I use CAR in that situation or while preparing for it?

My High Performance Power Phrase

I notice when I excessively and endlessly think too much. I remind myself why I should be confident in my plan and myself.

CONCLUDING THOUGHTS

Wow! You are continuing to make progress toward thinking like the world's best!

Here are the things you learned from Master Your Thoughts.

* You can practice thinking like an optimist and choose to use the OPP Strategy.

* We all experience Automatic Negative Thoughts, but you can use the CAR shift to address your ANTs.

* You can think like the world's best by choosing P4 Thoughts and using Power Phrases that start with "I will . . . I can . . . I am . . . "

* And a key to staying fulfilled is to reframe each obstacle as an opportunity.

Now, take a moment to record the following on your Grit Board:

* Four P4 Thoughts you want to say to yourself regularly.

* Your 4 Power Phrases to use daily.

* An example of your new reframe.

4

Know Yourself to Master Yourself

The world's best understand themselves and their tendencies, and are in tune with their thoughts, emotions, and actions. They know they need to master themselves to be successful.

Chapter 17

The ABCs of Self-Awareness

"I think self-awareness is probably the most important thing towards being a champion." —BILLIE JEAN KING

Jonathan is President and CEO of Greater Mankato Growth, the town I live in. He is also the most positive person I know. In fact, his positive energy is contagious. You can feel it when he walks in the room—people want to be around him. His interview is one of the most powerful so far on the *High Performance Mindset Podcast*.

Jonathan is on a journey that may seem unimaginable. Three years ago, he was diagnosed with prostate cancer. Six days after his diagnosis, he developed an infection which led to his diagnosis of kidney cancer. Through the treatments, while he often felt tired, he continued to embrace challenges that came his way. His mindset helped him thrive for the past three years, even though he was given only a 3-10 percent chance of living that long.

As Jonathan explains it, he first tried to "tame" cancer, but soon realized that he had to "take what the defense gives him." He meant that he had to listen to and understand his body. Thanks to his determination and grit, he wouldn't stop living just because he had cancer. "If I am going to get out of bed, why not give it my best?" he said.

Jonathan now sees his cancer as a "tremendous blessing" and says that the last three years have been his "most blessed period in his life." He said that cancer has helped him become a better version of himself. He has more compassion for others. He can connect more with people. He has a clearer understanding of how things beyond work impact lives. He has become more intentional and has a heightened sense of the now.

He sees that his mission is to change the way we see cancer. "People can live with cancer," he says. He encourages us to be open to the blessings that come from our difficulties. To stay positive, he encourages people to focus on what can come from a difficulty.

Self-awareness means to be able to understand your tendencies and be in tune with your thoughts, emotions, and actions in the moment. Jonathan gets that, or he wouldn't be thriving with cancer. He listens to his mind and body while living intentionally.

Self-awareness is important in everything we do and is the foundation of our ability to deal with challenges and adversity. If you have a high degree of self-awareness, you are in tune with how your body is dealing with a challenge or adversity.

When we are self-aware, we know ourselves—what we do well, how we can improve, what jazzes us, and what people or situations push our buttons. Athletes, leaders, and business people who are self-aware can accurately perceive their emotions in a nonjudgmental way.

Travis Bradberry and Jean Greaves, in their book *Emotional Intelligence 2.0*, argue that 83 percent of high performers in sports, business, and life are highly self-aware. They suggest that if two people with similar talent and skill apply for a job, the one with higher self-awareness is more likely to get it. According to their research, high self-awareness is also related to life satisfaction and the ability to reach goals.

Self-awareness is key in your journey to reach the next level and think like the world's best. When you are self-

GET GRITTY

GET PURPOSE

MASTER THOUGHTS

KNOW SELF

DOMINATE CONTROLLABLES

OWN THE MOMENT

CHOOSE EMOTIONS

OWN WHO YOU ARE

LIVE AND LET GO

COURAGE ZONE

aware, you understand yourself, pursue your passion (instead of someone else's), and don't let emotions like fear and anxiety hold you back. Developing an honest and nonjudgmental understanding of yourself will help you stay gritty and move forward each day towards your vision.

People or situations don't make us feel a certain way—we choose how to feel and what we do.

Self-awareness can improve your performance in many situations, including:

- A job interview

- A final play in the game when you are up to bat, run, throw, kick, or block

- A championship game, meet, or situation

- A keynote presentation

- A meeting to propose or finalize a contract with a client

- A surgery

- A negotiation

- A game in front of a scout or when someone is evaluating your performance

- A time where your child is throwing a tantrum

You can use the ABC's to increase your self-awareness:

A – **Awareness** of your thoughts, emotions, and actions. Notice what you are thinking, feeling, and doing.

B – **Breath,** taken deeply, as you notice your thoughts, emotions, and actions.

C – See yourself and the situation with **compassion** and nonjudgment. Make adjustments to your thoughts, emotions, and actions to do so.

Without self-awareness, you can lose yourself. Your thoughts, emotions, and actions can go on autopilot, which may not be helpful. You can be overwhelmed with anxiety, doubt, and frustration. Instead, take a huge step forward in your awesome, gritty future by moving forward with increased self-awareness.

GET GRITTY

GET PURPOSE

MASTER THOUGHTS

KNOW SELF

DOMINATE CONTROLLABLES

OWN THE MOMENT

CHOOSE EMOTIONS

OWN WHO YOU ARE

LIVE AND LET GO

COURAGE ZONE

My High Performance Game Plan
THE ABCS OF SELF-AWARENESS

1. I'll use the ABC method to increase my self-awareness and change my thoughts, emotions, and actions when needed.

2. What people or situations push my buttons? What can I do to stay in control in those situations?

3. When I feel pressure or stress, I'll pay attention to what led me to feel that way.

4. During my best moments, I'll pay attention to what led me to feel that way.

My High Performance Power Phrase

**I work to understand myself and my tendencies.
I master myself to reach a new level.**

Chapter 18

Respond, Not React

*"Between stimulus and response there is a space. In that space,
is our freedom and power to choose our response.
In our response lies our growth and freedom."*
—VICTOR FRANKL, *Man's Search for Meaning*

In his bestselling book *Man's Search for Meaning*, Victor Frankl, a neurologist and psychiatrist, described his experiences as a concentration camp inmate during the Holocaust. In his highly influential book, Frankl described the importance of finding meaning in all forms, even in the most brutal conditions. He argued that the meaning of life is found in every moment, even in suffering and death. Our life is about how we interpret moments of difficulty and respond to them.

The quote at the beginning of this chapter emphasizes that we can control our reactions to life. But in practice, we often react with heightened anxiety, fear, guilt, or doubt, believing that things make us feel this way. We react without thinking. We too easily accept our reflexive reactions. We don't always see that we choose our response. When we react without thinking, we stay stuck where we are without growing.

When we are self-aware, we notice what Frankl calls the "space" between the stimulus and response. Frankl said that we can grow, change, and be in control when we increase and make use of this space. We can find inner happiness and be in control of our response.

When we choose how to respond, we can act with purpose and intention.

By increasing our self-awareness, we are less likely to have our buttons pressed. When we are aware of our thoughts, feelings, and actions in the moment, we give ourselves control of our reactions and our response. We have greater choice and freedom when we are aware. We can respond instead of react.

To consider the importance of responding, not reacting:

- Notice the outcome of your reactions. Observe what happens when you put space between the stimulus and response and when you do not. How does that change the situation and how you feel in the moment?

- Think about a reaction you would like to change in yourself. Perhaps you would like to have less of a temper or show more love for your family. Consider how you see the world's best respond to adversity and challenge and how you would like to respond to be more of an ideal version of yourself.

- Think back on a few moments when you lost control of your emotions and when increasing the space between the stimulus and response could have helped you. In your sport, perhaps the stimulus was a bad call by an official or a rude comment by a coach. In your home life, perhaps the stimulus was your child throwing a tantrum or a family member who didn't show up for a gathering. In business, maybe the stimulus was a client who refused to pay their bill or a complaint that came in over the phone. Consider how increasing the space between the stimulus and your response could have helped you stay in control and calm to increase your performance.

When we react, we let our emotions take a central role. Our face heats up and we become defensive and emotional; we can lose our grit and focus.

Responding, however, is thoughtful and guided by logic. It is active and intentional. When you respond, you stay gritty, in control, and focused to be a higher performer. When you respond, you think and act like the world's best. Choose to respond today!

GET
GRITTY

GET
PURPOSE

MASTER
THOUGHTS

KNOW
SELF

DOMINATE
CONTROLLABLES

OWN THE
MOMENT

CHOOSE
EMOTIONS

OWN WHO
YOU ARE

LIVE AND
LET GO

COURAGE
ZONE

My High Performance Game Plan
RESPOND, NOT REACT

1. I commit to increasing the space between the stimulus and response today.

2. Who is a person I consider to be successful in sports, business, or life? How do they respond in frustrating or anxiety-provoking situations?

3. What are a few times in the past few weeks where increasing the space between the stimulus and response could have benefited my performance or happiness?

4. What is the impact I have on the outcome of situations and other people when I respond, not react?

My High Performance Power Phrase

**I choose to respond with purpose and intention.
I put space between the stimulus and response
to stay calm, collected, and in control.
I respond, not react.**

Chapter 19

Discover Your MVP Level

"What I tell people is be the best version of yourself in anything that you do. You don't have to live anybody else's story."
—STEPH CURRY, 3-TIME NBA MOST VALUABLE PLAYER

Steph Curry, the Golden State Warriors point guard, was named a unanimous choice for MVP in the 2015-16 season—a first in the NBA. Basketball greats like Charles Barkley, Kevin Durant, and Steve Nash have described his skill set as "scintillating" and "amazing," and others have simply called Curry "the best shooter in the NBA."

Curry provides an extraordinary example of someone who works consistently and deliberately to reach his MVP level. At 6'3" and 190 pounds, he is smaller than the average NBA player—four inches shorter and thirty pounds lighter. In fact, during the 2009 NBA Draft, scouts said that Curry was not a true point guard, was out of control at times, had a frail frame, relied too heavily on his outside shot, and had only average athleticism, size, and wingspan. Some scouts expected him to struggle at the professional level.

Of course, that is not how the story turned out. Analysts have described Curry's success to date as largely a product of his exceptional work ethic. Others have called his preparation "spectacular." His pregame routine has gone viral, watched by over 2 million people on YouTube.

He works diligently on refining his ball-handling skills. He dribbles two basketballs, one with each hand, in quick repetition, and then follows with a variety of shots from various angles and positions all over the court. Fans love Curry because he has a strong character, is confident but not boastful, and has fun. "There's nothing left to say except that he's the MVP," Steve Kerr, the head coach of the Golden State Warriors, said after Curry's 45-point performance in the 2016 post season.

Curry is a great example of someone who is consistently gritty. You, just like Curry, cannot perform at your MVP level—your personal best—if you are not using your mind in a productive way. Every decision goes through your mind; the key is to keep your mind working for you, not against you. To do this, it's important to understand when you perform at your best and what leads to your MVP level.

When researchers asked athletes, entrepreneurs, and business leaders what their best performance feels and looks like, they identified the following characteristics:

- High self-confidence

- Feeling in control (energized yet relaxed)

- Positive self-talk

- Ability to bounce back from mistakes

- Optimistic, positive attitude

- Clearly defined goals

- Automatic (not forcing performance)

- Adaptively perfectionistic (high standards, yet flexible)

- Viewing difficult situations as exciting challenges

- Motivated, determined, and committed

- Seeing arousal as helpful to performance

- Ability to cope well with distractions and stress

- Present-moment focused

- An energy giver (not an energy drainer)

In sports, developing these characteristics can mean the difference between medaling at the Olympics or not, winning the Super Bowl or not, or becoming a professional in your sport or not. In business, it can mean the difference between starting your own business or not even taking the first step, closing the big deal or letting someone else finish for you, or getting the job of your dreams or freezing at the interview. And you can develop these psychological characteristics if you choose to do so.

It is personally rewarding to play at your MVP level. When you are at your best, you have no regrets because you are giving your life your all. There is nothing that you would change because you gave all that you could. Your MVP level is meaningful, fulfilling, and fun.

What does it mean for you to be an MVP?

- First, think about a time when you were at your MVP level. What thoughts, feelings, and actions led you to be at your best? What did your body feel and look like? List your answers.

- Next, think about a time you were not at your best or when you performed poorly. What thoughts, feelings, and actions led to this performance? What did your body feel and look like? Were there any distractions present? List these answers, as well.

- Finally, compare and contrast your lists. What led to you being at your best? What did not? What are the biggest differences between the lists?

GET GRITTY

GET PURPOSE

MASTER THOUGHTS

KNOW SELF

DOMINATE CONTROLLABLES

OWN THE MOMENT

CHOOSE EMOTIONS

OWN WHO YOU ARE

LIVE AND LET GO

COURAGE ZONE

In graduate school, I studied the Individualized Zone of Optimal Functioning (IZOF) created by Yuri Hanin. This model helps us understand that there are individual differences in our best performances and helps us to name the emotions that help us be at our best. It can help you go deeper into what gets you to your MVP level.

To explore your MVP level, try a simple exercise. Draw an upside down U on a blank piece of paper. To the left of the U, draw a vertical line that says "performance." Under the U, draw a horizontal line that says "emotions." Your MVP level happens at the peak of the inverted U. That's where a combination of emotions (not just one emotion) leads to your best. We all have individual differences and have different emotional makeups. That is why it is important for you to understand your own emotional profile to help you get to your MVP level purposefully and intentionally.

What do you need to know about the IZOF model?

Some emotions help us and some do not. Even some so-called negative emotions can help us perform at our best. For example, you might play well when you are aggressive or are dissatisfied with your previous performance.

Helpful emotions can be very different for different activities. For example, a baseball pitcher's MVP emotional profile might be confident, calm, and loose, whereas a running back's might be charged, quick, and determined. In business, a customer service center manager might feel calm, alert, and charismatic at their best, whereas a motivational speaker might feel energetic, inspired, and pumped at their best.

We are more likely to thrive, experience achievement and success, and advance to the next level when we perform with emotions that support our MVP level.

Exercise: Find Your MVP Profile

You can find your MVP emotional profile by using the following exercise.

Circle five emotions from the list below that lead to your MVP level. Remember that even emotions that we might consider negative might help you be at your best.

Then, put a box around five emotions from the list below that hinder your performance.

Absorbed	Accepting	Aching	Agitated	Aggressive	Alert
Amazed	Angry	Animated	Annoyed	Balanced	Brisk
Calm	Charged	Confident	Connected	Courageous	Dissatisfied
Eager	Engaged	Fearless	Flexible	Focused	Free
Friendly	Gentle	Grateful	Happy	Hopeful	Humble
Irritated	Kind	Loose	Motivated	Nice	Optimistic
Overjoyed	Pleased	Quiet	Reliable	Resourceful	Wired

GET GRITTY

GET PURPOSE

MASTER THOUGHTS

KNOW SELF

DOMINATE CONTROLLABLES

OWN THE MOMENT

CHOOSE EMOTIONS

OWN WHO YOU ARE

LIVE AND LET GO

COURAGE ZONE

My High Performance Game Plan
DISCOVER YOUR MVP LEVEL

1. When I've experienced my MVP level in the past, what thoughts, feelings, and actions led to it?

2. What has stopped me from reaching my MVP level consistently? What thoughts, feelings, and actions led to it?

3. I will complete the exercise to find and understand my MVP level.

4. I'll consider one strategy I can use to reach my MVP level consistently.

My High Performance Power Phrase

I work to reach my MVP level consistently and understand what leads to me being at my best. I think, feel, and act like an MVP.

Chapter 20

Find Your Flow

*"It's important to push yourself further than you think you can go
each and every day—as that is what separates
the good from the great."* —KERRI STRUG

I remember watching the 1996 Olympics from my childhood living room. The U.S. women's gymnastics team had never won an Olympic team gold medal. This year would be different, they said. On the final day of competition, the U.S. was in a commanding lead over Russia, but that lead evaporated after the first four Americans took an extra step on their landings in the vault and Dominique Moceanu fell twice.

The gold medal was now in the hands of Kerri Strug, a quiet gymnast who had been overshadowed by her teammates Moceanu, Dominique Dawes, and Shannon Miller. As she approached the vault, Kerri used self-talk to reduce her doubts and fears. She said, "This is it, Kerri. You've done this vault a thousand times, so just go out and do it." She took a deep breath and sprinted down the runaway. As she landed her vault, she heard a snap in her left ankle. Two ligaments in her ankle tore. Her score was not enough to beat the Russians.

Kerri's ankle was throbbing. Pain was shooting up her leg. Still, she had one more vault. Watching the event on television, I wondered if she would complete it. Bela Karolyi, her coach, walked over to her and said, "We need you one more time. We need you one more time for the gold."

Kerri put her pain of her injury, doubt, and fear aside. She rose to the occasion despite numerous distractions. Again, she talked to herself and said, "I know I can do it one more time, injured ankle or not . . . I've done this more than a thousand times."

So she began. She sprinted down the runaway, did a back handspring onto the vault in a near perfect fashion, and descended to the ground. As she landed hard without stumbling, she heard another crack in her same ankle. Kerri gingerly picked up her ankle and gently moved it behind her other leg to keep her balance. She stood tall in her traditional finishing salute as if her ankle was just fine.

The 32,048 people in the Georgia Dome let out a roar. A 9.712 flashed on the giant scoreboard: with this score, the U.S. won the gold medal. Her coach Karolyi later described the powerful moment: "In my 35 years of coaching I have never seen such a moment . . . people think these girls are fragile dolls. They're not. They're courageous."

Kerri made the impossible possible that day. She blocked out the pain, dealt with the pressure, and stayed in the moment. She flowed.

Psychologist Mihaly Csikszentmihalyi, the author of bestselling book *Flow: The Psychology of Optimal Experience*, is considered to be the grandfather of flow and the first to coin the term. You can experience flow in any activity you enjoy: flow is the ultimate optimal experience. When you experience flow, you are using your skills to their fullest and are so absorbed in the task that nothing else matters. You feel effortless. You are performing at your best.

Flow is possible when the challenge of what you are doing and the demand of the situation match. What you are doing needs to be hard enough to stretch you but not so hard that you snap like a rubber band. Steven Kotler, in his book *The Rise of the Superman: Decoding the Science of Ultimate Human Performance*, argued that to experience flow, what you are doing should be 4 percent greater than your skill level in order to keep your attention and to release neurochemicals like dopamine. If you stretch yourself more than 4 percent, you move beyond the flow state and feel over-challenged. Kotler suggested that if you want to increase your performance over the long haul, push yourself 4 percent harder, day after day, month after month. The impossible becomes possible and your progress skyrockets. In return, you create more flow and optimal experiences.

Csikszentmihalyi suggested that there are ten core components to flow including:
- A balance between skill and challenge
- Immediate feedback
- Clear goals
- Action and awareness merging
- High concentration on the task at hand
- A sense of control
- A loss of self-consciousness
- A transformation of time
- The activity is intrinsically motivating or "autotelic"
- Absorption in the task

When you experience a few of these components, it's microflow. When all of the ten components happen at once, it's macroflow.

Let's think about you:

Think about a time that you were in the flow. What did your flow zone feel like? What led to that feeling? What were your expectations and goals before the performance?

Contrast this to a time you were not able to focus and you struggled. What were the differences between these times for you?

Sometimes when I am working with athletes, coaches, and business leaders, they want a magic ticket to get in their flow zone. Unfortunately, flow isn't like a light switch that you can turn on and off. Finding your flow zone starts with your mind and channeling your focus to the present moment. Your mind is a muscle; it takes daily practice to master it. If you try to force flow, you get further away from it. But there are things you can do that increase your chances of finding your flow zone. Many of them appear in this book!

Train your mind with the strategies and tools presented in the chapters you've already read and the chapters to come. If you use these tools, flow will more likely occur.

GET
GRITTY

GET
PURPOSE

MASTER
THOUGHTS

KNOW
SELF

DOMINATE
CONTROLLABLES

OWN THE
MOMENT

CHOOSE
EMOTIONS

OWN WHO
YOU ARE

LIVE AND
LET GO

COURAGE
ZONE

My High Performance Game Plan
FIND YOUR FLOW

1. I'll spend some time this week thinking about times that I have experienced flow. What was I doing and how was I feeling?

2. During times I was not in the flow and struggled, what got in my way of experiencing flow?

3. How can I push myself by 4 percent each day so challenge is just outside my current skill level? I'll reflect back on the process goals I set earlier for ideas about what this could look like.

4. I commit to using the mental tools and strategies in this book to increase my chances of experiencing the ultimate experience.

My High Performance Power Phrase

My mind is like a muscle. I train my mind using mental tools to increase my chances of finding flow.

Chapter 21

Master Your Green Light

---

*"Checking in on yourself gives you awareness.
Awareness is like feedback on what, if any, adjustments are
necessary to improve your performance. The best excel at
coaching themselves." —*KEN RAVIZZA AND TOM HANSON

I remember the first time I drove a car. I was 15 years old and in driver's education class. I was nervous. I overthought every turn, where my hands were on the steering wheel, and what the instructor thought of me. I even slowed down for the green light, thinking it might change as I drove through. My performance that day was not automatic. I was in my own head, unsure of my ability, and way too nervous.

Your performance every day can be understood using a traffic light model. I first read about this concept in Ken Ravizza and Tom Hanson's book *Heads-Up Baseball: Playing the Game One Pitch at a Time* and have used it with a number of my clients, both individuals and teams.

In this model, think of your body as a traffic light. Green means "go," yellow means "caution," and red means "stop." Unless you are just learning to drive a car, you don't even see the traffic light when it is green. You keep driving. The same is true when you are at your best throughout your day. The green light represents your flow zone. It represents you at your best. You feel confident, in control, and focused on the task at hand. You don't need to make adjustments to yourself, your reaction, or your actions. All is phenomenal. You are thinking, acting, and responding like the world's best.

The yellow light is when you are starting to lose your high-performance mentality. You are just going through the motions, are a little too anxious or tense, or feel rushed. Perhaps you have made one mistake in the game, at your job, or during your presentation, and that mistake starts to impact your confidence. You are in the early stages of losing control or performing unconfidently.

Think back to the last time you came to a yellow light while driving: Did you speed up or slow down? The majority of people I know speed through the yellow light. But if you speed through the yellow lights throughout your day or when you are performing, things will get worse for you. You will become more nervous, unconfident, or feel less in control. In the traffic light model, the key is this—when you feel in the yellow light, you must make adjustments to get back to your green light.

When you experience the red light in your body and performance, you have completely lost the high-performance mentality. You are struggling. Your mind is racing. You feel tense. Your performance and play are on the decline. You may have lost control of your emotions and your mindset. Maybe you missed a field goal or catch, yelled at your child in a public place, or flipped someone off in traffic. If you don't intervene with yourself, your performance will bottom out and you will probably regret it. You will continue to be in an ugly, unproductive state until you do something to change it up.

To reach high performance and be at your best consistently, day after day, month after month, year after year, self-awareness is key. The traffic light model helps you master your green light by:

- Learning about yourself and how you typically experience and respond to stressors.

- Helping you develop a plan to deal with situations the at lead to your yellow or red lights.

- Providing a language for you to use with your company, team, or family.

Ideally, it would be great to live in your green light: to stay confident, in control, and focused all the time. But even the world's best—professional athletes, CEOs, and presidents of million dollar companies—experience situations that lead to their yellow and red lights. The key is to regain control of your mind and body as soon as possible; it's easier to regain control after a yellow light than a red one. Choose to pay attention to yourself and make adjustments as necessary.

Let's consider your green, yellow, and red lights to help you reach high performance more often. Here are a few examples to get you started:

In Your Green Light:	In Your Yellow Light:	In Your Red Light:
I am saying to myself: *I am strong. I am fast. I am mentally prepared. I stay in control. I am amazing at what I do.*	I am saying to myself: *Crap, I made that mistake again. How long until I screw up again? I feel like crap.*	I am saying to myself: *I am such an idiot. I am a loser. I never do anything right. They might as well just cut me or fire me. I want to quit.*
I am feeling: *Confident, calm, in control, energized, excited, passionate, unstoppable, and ready to be at my MVP level.*	I am feeling: *Tightness, frustration, too much anxiety, tension in my shoulders or body, like I have a million things running through my mind.*	I am feeling: *Depressed, uncertain, sluggish, crushed, resentful, hostile, incapable, fearful, and doubting my ability or the ability of my team.*

GET GRITTY

GET PURPOSE

MASTER THOUGHTS

KNOW SELF

DOMINATE CONTROLLABLES

OWN THE MOMENT

CHOOSE EMOTIONS

OWN WHO YOU ARE

LIVE AND LET GO

COURAGE ZONE

I am focused on:	I am focused on:	I am focused on:
Being at my MVP level in the present moment. Just playing, not thinking. What is going well. Letting mistakes go quickly.	*The weather, such as the heat, cold, or wind. A mistake I made or a teammate made. A call by a ref or ump in a game.*	*Other people, several mistakes I have made or others have made, what frustrates me, and how miserable or fearful I feel.*

Exercise: Complete a Stop Light Grid

Now, complete a Stop Light Grid of your own to reflect on your green, yellow, and red lights:

In Your Green Light:	In Your Yellow Light:	In Your Red Light:
I am saying to myself:	I am saying to myself:	I am saying to myself:
I am feeling:	I am feeling:	I am feeling:
I am focused on:	I am focused on:	I am focused on:

To master your green light or move to your green light from your yellow or red light, one mental strategy is key. I call it the Power Pause Strategy.

The Power Pause Strategy

Power Breath + Power Phrase

1. When you are in your yellow or red light, take at least one Power Breath. A Power Breath takes only fifteen seconds. Focus on your breathing; breathe in slowly through your nose for six seconds, hold for two seconds, and breathe out slowly through your mouth for seven seconds. Take multiple Power Breaths as needed until you feel calm and collected.

2. Then, say a Power Phrase in your head; an "I will . . . I can . . . I am . . . " statement to stay calm and in control such as, "I am in control of myself and my reactions. I stay calm despite things around me." (Review Chapter 14 to dig back in to these statements.)

High performers use pictures, signs or stickers to remind them to stay focused on the present moment. Several of the teams and athletes I have worked with place a stoplight sticker on their water bottle or on the sideline bench. Other teams have taken it one step further and placed green laces in their cleats, or have used a marker to make a green dot on their wrist.

One professional baseball player, Jason Hoppe, placed a stoplight sticker inside the bill of his baseball cap. When he needs to refocus, he steps off the mound, takes several power breaths, and looks at his sticker to stay in his green. (You can listen to his story on the *High Performance Mindset Podcast*.)

GET GRITTY

GET PURPOSE

MASTER THOUGHTS

KNOW SELF

DOMINATE CONTROLLABLES

OWN THE MOMENT

CHOOSE EMOTIONS

OWN WHO YOU ARE

LIVE AND LET GO

COURAGE ZONE

My High Performance Game Plan

MASTER YOUR
GREEN LIGHT

1. I will spend some time this week completing the Stop Light Grid to better understand my green, yellow, and red lights.

2. I commit to spending more time in my green light, the place where I'm at my ultimate best.

3. I will practice using the Power Pause Strategy this week to stay in my green light.

4. I'll place a stoplight sticker or another reminder of this exercise in my locker, by my bed, on my mirror, or in another spot where I'll see it regularly.

My High Performance Power Phrase

I master my green light. I check in with myself to stay confident, in control, and focused. I coach myself.

Chapter 22

Fly Your Butterflies in Formation

"Nerves and butterflies are fine—they're a physical sign that you're mentally ready and eager. You have to get the butterflies to fly in formation, that's the trick." —STEVE BULL

An NFL coach once approached me with a problem: one of his team's most talented athletes was struggling to perform. "He should be leading the NFL. That's how much talent he has!" the coach said. As I began to work with the athlete, I could see and hear how anxiety had overtaken him. When I asked, "What is getting in the way of you reaching your MVP level in this league?" he didn't hesitate. He knew. Just like you know deep down what is getting in the way of you reaching your MVP level consistently.

His problems? He was replaying mistakes in his mind. He was questioning if his contract would be renewed. He was wrapped up in many things he couldn't control, like negative fans, coaches' comments, and the weather. He hadn't thought about the 10,000+ hours he had put in to develop his craft in a long time, or the hard work he had been putting in daily. As a result, he felt anxious and tense when he performed. He missed several important opportunities. He started to listen to the haters more and more. His confidence was at an all-time low.

Sometimes we forget that people at the highest levels of their careers are human too!

I began teaching him week after week many of the tools in this book to build his High Performance Toolbox. As a result, he began to act, think, and feel like a mentally strong NFL athlete and soon led the NFL in his category by the end of the season. He had the tools to make it happen, and he did. His talent shone.

Anxiety is a silent killer of too many people's dreams. When you have too much anxiety, it is debilitating. You can't think straight. You feel tense and tight. You are focused on what you are not instead of what you are. You don't perform at your highest level consistently.

Some arousal or energy actually helps you to perform at your highest level. Gary Mack, the author of *Mind Gym: An Athlete's Guide to Inner Excellence*, compared your performance to guitar strings. If your strings are too loose, you feel and perform flat. But if they are too tight, you feel and perform too wound up. You snap. Your body needs to be in the right tension for you, based on your internal makeup and the activity you are performing.

Notice the words I used to describe high performance. We all need arousal or energy to reach high performance and to perform at our best, but anxiety doesn't help us perform at our best. In performance psychology, we describe anxiety as a negative interpretation of your energy. In other words, how we see the energy matters.

Anxiety can influence performance in pressure-provoking situations like these:

- Before or during an important performance such as the Super Bowl, a championship game, or the Olympic Trials

- Before or during a job interview, speech, or presentation to your dream client or organization

- Before or during judging-based performances such as a speech competition, a gymnastics meet, or a presentation

- In a moment when your coach or boss tells you "We need you right now" or "The team needs you to score"

- As you return from an injury or illness

In these situations and many others, it is easy to focus on the future—on the result, outcome, or consequences of not performing at our best. You might fear that you don't have what you need to do what you need to do. This fear creates tension in your body.

The best way to take control of your anxiety is to understand it. Let's look at the two types of anxiety, cognitive and somatic, to better understand how anxiety shows up in your body.

- **Cognitive anxiety** happens when you worry about your ability to perform. You question if you have what it takes to reach high performance and experience success. Your anxiety is in your mind and is reflected in your thoughts.

- **Somatic anxiety** is when you feel tense and jittery. You feel the butterflies in your stomach. Your heart rate, breathing, and sweating increase. Your anxiety is in your body and it creates tension. For an athlete, muscle tension can be problematic because you can't perform at your best if you are too tight. You can't throw, kick, or hit the ball accurately with lots of tightness in your shoulders, arms, or legs.

Which type of anxiety (cognitive or somatic) do you experience most often?

When you live up to your high performance potential, you move with little worry or tension in your body. To reach high performance consistently and to think like the world's best, you have to know the early warning signs of anxiety and then intervene before it takes over. Signs could be tightness in your body, shortness of breath, a racing heart, throwing up, worry, or self-doubt.

GET GRITTY

GET PURPOSE

MASTER THOUGHTS

KNOW SELF

DOMINATE CONTROLLABLES

OWN THE MOMENT

CHOOSE EMOTIONS

OWN WHO YOU ARE

LIVE AND LET GO

COURAGE ZONE

But there are ways to get your butterflies to fly in formation! When you feel the early warning signs of anxiety, you can:

- **Get your mind back to the present.** It's likely that your thoughts are focused on the future. Notice the thoughts that are causing your anxiety and gently bring your mind back to the present moment.

- **Remind yourself of your preparation.** List or imagine the concrete evidence that you have to show you are ready. Think back to the hours you have put into your craft, or the hours you put in for the performance.

- **Remember your past successes.** Like a film's highlight reel, imagine in detail at least three to five times you have been successful. Picture these successes two or three times a day.

- **Use your Power Phrases.** A few examples that could be helpful during anxiety-provoking situations are: *"I can handle anything that comes my way. I am confident. I am relaxed. I will be at my best today."*

- **Reframe your anxiety as excitement.** A recent study published in the *Journal of Experimental Psychology* suggested that viewing your anxiety as something positive and exciting can make all the difference. Focus less on the potential for things to go wrong and more on how excited you are to be on center stage. Show your strengths and be a member of your team.

- **Remind yourself to take Power Breaths.** Many people ignore the power of deep, intentional breathing. They think it is silly or become self-conscious doing it, but it works! Count when you breathe so that you stay focused on the numbers and not what is creating your anxiety. (See Chapter 21 for a refresher).

FLY YOUR BUTTERFLIES IN FORMATION

1. Which type of anxiety do I experience most often, cognitive or somatic? I'll choose two or three strategies to use the next time I feel anxious.

2. When in the past did I feel anxious? What can I do next time I experience a similar situation?

3. I can reframe my anxiety as excitement so that I am prepared the next time I feel stressed.

4. When in the future do I want to perform at my highest level? I'll make a list of two or three ways I can be sure that I'll be fully confident in that situation.

My High Performance Power Phrase

I gently bring my mind back to the present. I see my butterflies flying in formation as I perform.

CONCLUDING THOUGHTS

Bravo! Your focus and hard work continues! You are on your way to mastering your thoughts, emotions and actions! Here are the things you learned from Know Yourself to Master Yourself:

- You can use the ABC's to level up your self-awareness and increase the space between the stimulus and response.

- You can find your MVP level—or your personal best—consistently.

- What leads to flow and how you can experience it more often.

- And how you can use the stop light analogy and the Power Pause to stay in your green light.

Now, take a moment to record the following on your Grit Board . . .

- 5 words that describe your MVP Level.

- A few key phrases from this section, such as "Respond Not React," "Increase the Space," or "Find My Flow."

- A picture of a stoplight to remind yourself to stay in your green.

5

Dominate the Controllables

The world's best

dominate what they have control over—their attitude,

preparation, and effort—instead

of what they cannot.

Chapter 23

Dominate Your APE

---

*"I fear not the man who has practiced 10,000 kicks once,
but I fear the man who has practiced one kick 10,000 times."*
—BRUCE LEE

In the 2004 American League Championship Series, Pedro Martinez pitched for the Boston Red Sox at the New York Yankees Stadium. Pedro didn't have a stellar night; as a result, the Yankees won the game. After the game, the reporters asked him about his performance. He said, "They [the Yankees] beat me. They're that good right now. I just tip my hat and call the Yankees my daddy." By calling the Yankees his "daddy" he was paying respect to the other team.

Five years later in the 2009 World Series, Pedro pitched in Game 2 of what turned out to be a six-game series against the Yankees. This time he was a starting pitcher for the Philadelphia Phillies. The fans didn't forget his famous phrase, and started chanting, "Who's Your Daddy . . . Who's Your Daddy . . . Who's Your Daddy . . ." Can you imagine over 100,000 people in Yankees Stadium chanting *against* you and doing their best to distract you? A pitcher who didn't take command over his reactions would crumble under that kind of pressure!

Despite the distractions, Pedro remained calm, cool, and collected on the mound. He dominated the controllables. If you watched closely that day, Pedro had a smirk on his face. He stayed in control even as he walked off the mound and the Yankees came up victorious. The chant by the 100,000+ fans then turned to, "Still Your Daddy! Still Your Daddy! Still Your Daddy!"

After the game, reporters asked Pedro how he performed so well despite the constant and distracting chanting. Pedro replied, "Several years ago I was sitting under a mango tree and didn't have a cent to my name. Today, I was one of the most important people in one of the biggest cities in the world."

Pedro controlled the controllables that day! He could have cracked under pressure, taken the chanting personally, blamed himself for the previous comment he made in 2004, and become frustrated and annoyed by the fans. But he didn't! He reframed the difficulty into an opportunity and was grateful to be the center of attention. He chose to dominate the controllables!

Dominating the controllables is an essential part of reaching high performance, thinking like the world's best, and growing your grit. Life, athletics, and business can be simply divided into two areas: 1) things that you can control, and 2) things you cannot control.

So what do I mean by the "uncontrollable?" In sports, you cannot control your teammates; coaches; referees or umpires and the calls they make; fans; field conditions; the weather; the administration; your uniforms; your competitors; or winning. (You might be wondering about why winning is on this list! It's because you can't control the other team or those you compete against.)

In business, you cannot control your competitors; changing technology; your boss; your clients; the economy; or other people's thoughts, actions, or perceptions that impact your business. In life, you cannot control your family, your friends, your neighbors, or any other person you interact with throughout your day.

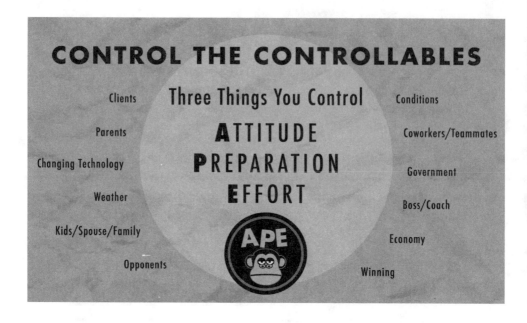

When we focus on things we have no control over, we tend to experience frustration, anxiety, and fear. We are not thinking or acting like the world's best. Uncontrollables, or the things outside the circle in the image here, can take us off our game and further away from reaching our high-performance potential consistently. For every minute we are focused on things we cannot control, we are taking away energy and passion for our goals. We are draining our mindset and passion instead of fueling them.

When we focus on what we can control, we are more likely to experience high performance. We are more likely to reach our goals and dreams because we are not wasting energy focusing on things we have no control over.

What we can control boils down to three things: our attitude, preparation, and effort, or our APE for short. When we dominate our APE, we are showing up in the world, on our team, and with our family as the best version of ourselves. When we are dominating our APE, we don't let our attention go to things we cannot control even for one minute. We are working hard toward our goals, staying gritty, and choosing to engage in thinking that contributes to our success.

- **A**ttitude – We have complete control of our attitude every minute of every day. We control the positive or negative attitude we choose when we interact with our family, coworkers, or teammates. We control how we approach everything in our lives, and can see either the good or the bad in every situation. Both the good and bad perspectives always exist. High performers and the world's best choose to focus on the good, to see the silver lining in every difficulty. They choose to see the good despite a bad game, an argument with a coworker, or the loss of a big client. What kind of attitude are you using every minute of every day? Is your attitude moving you closer to your goals or further away?

- **P**reparation—We are in complete control our preparation. High performers relentlessly pursue excellence and mastery. They master themselves so they can master their craft. They stay gritty and keep their focus on their long-term goals and dreams. They attend extra training, hire coaches, ask for feedback, and are the first to arrive at practice and the last to leave. They work daily to develop their knowledge and skills. High performers master their schedule. They know we all have the same amount of time in each day: 86,400 seconds to be exact. High performers utilize those 86,400 seconds in the best way to reach their goals. Is what you are doing with your 86,400 seconds moving you closer or further away from your long-term goals?

GET GRITTY

GET PURPOSE

MASTER THOUGHTS

KNOW SELF

DOMINATE CONTROLLABLES

OWN THE MOMENT

CHOOSE EMOTIONS

OWN WHO YOU ARE

LIVE AND LET GO

COURAGE ZONE

- **E**ffort—We completely control our effort. High performers give their absolute best day after day. They go hard toward their goals and dreams. High performers know how to control the amount of focus and intensity they use to pursue mastery. When you do your best daily, your best just becomes better. Now, you can choose to just go through the motions, or engage like a high performer and deliberately pursue mastering your craft with energy, passion, and full engagement. High performers and the world's best stay gritty and develop the skills they need to achieve their goals. High performers stay with the boring things to pursue their goals. They keep going despite losing, a mistake, or heartbreak. Are you showing up in this world, at practice, at work, and with your family in a way that demonstrates that you are all in? Or are you just going through the motions? Are you putting in the effort level needed to achieve your biggest goals and dreams? If not, decide today to dominate your APE!

Now that you have decided to dominate your APE, let's talk about how you can do so. When you are focused on things you cannot control, use these three steps:

1. First, catch yourself in a nonjudgmental way. No need to beat yourself up. Just notice when you are focusing on things you can't control.

2. Next, say a phrase that reminds you to stay focused on what you can control. You might say, "Dominate my APE!" "APE Up," "C & C," or "Control the Controllables."

3. Finally, redirect your attention to what you can control. Focus on dominating your attitude. Smile and choose to see the positive in the situation. You might even want to point out the positive to others (in a nonjudgmental way). Decide to give full effort and choose to be 100 percent prepared so you can reach high performance.

Next time you get worked up or bothered by what someone else did or said, or frustrated by a bad "call" in the game or a mistake someone else made, control the controllables. Decide to focus on your attitude, preparation, and effort. You have everything it takes to dominate your reaction to events or people around you! Now, go make it happen!

GET GRITTY

GET PURPOSE

MASTER THOUGHTS

KNOW SELF

DOMINATE CONTROLLABLES

OWN THE MOMENT

CHOOSE EMOTIONS

OWN WHO YOU ARE

LIVE AND LET GO

COURAGE ZONE

My High Performance Game Plan
DOMINATE YOUR APE

1. When in the past did I dominate my APE? What was the outcome when I was fully committed to my best attitude, preparation, and effort?

2. What things do I focus on that are outside of my control?

3. I commit to fully using the 86,400 seconds in my day. I'll make the necessary changes to my mindset and schedule to stay gritty.

4. I commit to using an APE phrase such as those presented in the chapter to help me focus on the controllables.

My High Performance Power Phrase

I dominate my APE. I use the 86,400 seconds in my day to develop my knowledge and skills. I give my best attitude, preparation, and effort day in and day out.

Chapter 24

Register for Responsibility 101

"Life is 10 percent of what happens to me and 90 percent of how I react to it." —JOHN MAXWELL

In his book *The Obstacle is the Way*, Ryan Holiday shares the story of when George Clooney first arrived in Hollywood. Clooney was rejected at most of his auditions. He blamed the system and the decision makers for not seeing what he was and who he could become. But then Clooney changed his perspective. He reframed the difficulty as an opportunity. He realized that casting was a problem and obstacle for the producers. He stood in the producers' shoes and saw auditions as a chance to solve their problems. He chose to no longer take a victim perspective but shift to a creator. This shift changed things for him. He went from blaming to taking responsibility. Clooney began to study and understand what the casting directors and producers were looking for. He saw himself as the person with something special to offer. He began to project that he was the man for the job and that he could solve their problems. That change made all the difference.

Most of us are conditioned to blame someone else for our suffering. We might have heard our family members or talk radio or even our friends blame the economy, their own parents, or the president for problems. We blame the weather. We blame our spouse. We blame our boss. We blame our teammates. We blame our genetics. We blame our education. We blame ownership. We blame our kids.

When we blame others, we weaken our power and our ability to be high performers. Every time we blame someone or something, we dwindle our chance of success and reaching our goals. We don't think or act like the world's best. The more we blame others, the less gritty we become.

Blame is the most dangerous and poisonous ANT because we don't face the problem. We become a passive victim to our circumstances. We don't change our situation or work to solve our problems. We ruin relationships. We live in a negative state with a limiting perspective. We say things like "Why me?" and "That wouldn't have happened if . . ." and "It's all their fault."

The world's best know that they are the only person responsible for their quality of life. They look inside and create the life and performance they desire. Instead of asking "Why me?" high performers ask, "Why not me?" They see problems as puzzles to be solved. They learn from the difficulty and rise to the challenge.

High performers take responsibility for their past and future. They realize that their choices and decisions led them to where they are today. They accept responsibility for their past but don't dwell in it. They choose to think clearly about themselves and grab ahold of their future.

While working on my Ph.D., I taught several personal development classes for students on academic probation. In these courses, we used Skip Downing's book *On Course* and discussed strategies for success. The majority of the students on academic probation had the intelligence to succeed in college, but they blamed others—their professors, their parents, their high school teachers, their friends— for their circumstances. Because of that, I had to quickly clarify the difference between victims and creators and the language they use in those classes.

Victims	Creators
Victims create excuses and blame others. They complain and feel like they "have" to do things. They pretend their problems belong to others. They repeat actions that are ineffective. They seldom reach their goals.	Creators solve problems, take action, and accept responsibility. They *choose* to follow through and own their problems. They commit and take control of their lives. They achieve their goals because they work hard and are gritty.
Victim Language: • "I am overweight because my parents are overweight." • "I was cut from the team because the coach was unfair." • "That's such a stupid requirement." • "He is such a lousy boss." • "It's not my fault that I am late to practice." • "I wish I could run faster."	*Creator Language:* • "I will reclaim my energy by losing weight." • "I will put more effort into developing my skills and ability to make the team." • "I am going to complete this requirement with full effort." • "My boss has a lot of great qualities." • "I was late because I didn't look at my watch." • "I will improve my speed by running twice a week."

Take a minute to write down victim statements that are not helping you take responsibly for you and your future. Then cross them out and restate them in the language of a creator to generate energy for your future.

To change your future, you have to take responsibility for your life right now. To achieve high performance in sports, business, and life, recognize you are in the driver's seat in your life. You have the steering wheel. Take control and drive!

GET GRITTY

GET PURPOSE

MASTER THOUGHTS

KNOW SELF

DOMINATE CONTROLLABLES

OWN THE MOMENT

CHOOSE EMOTIONS

OWN WHO YOU ARE

LIVE AND LET GO

COURAGE ZONE

My High Performance Game Plan

REGISTER FOR RESPONSIBILITY 101

1. When I notice myself engaging in the blame game, I'm going to stop, take responsibility for my perspective, and decide to think and act like a creator.

2. When faced with a problem this week, I'll own it, taking control of my perspective and solving the problem like a creator, not a victim.

3. When I notice a friend, coworker, or teammate engaging in the blame game, I'll nonjudgmentally help them see the creator perspective.

4. I will write out my victim statements to become aware of my limited language, then rewrite them so I am free to act and think like a creator.

My High Performance Power Phrase

From this moment forward, I accept 100 percent responsibility for my future and my past. I give up excuses and victim language. I own my power.

Chapter 25

Believe in the Best-Case Scenario

"Don't spend a lot of time imaging the worst-case scenario. It rarely goes down as you imagine it will, and if by some fluke it does, you will have lived it twice." —Michael J. Fox

---

Kristi Schuck, founder and co-owner of WYSIWYG (What You See Is What You Get) Juice Company, recently shared her story of resilience on the *High Performance Mindset Podcast.* It was through her husband's diagnosis with Stage 4 Colon Cancer that they both discovered the power of juicing. Her husband, Wes, was given only four short months to live. It was shocking news, but they believed they had a choice in how they dealt with his diagnosis. "Attitude is everything," she said. They made a decision to feel empowered every day despite the diagnosis. They made a choice to see cancer as an opportunity to learn and grow.

Wes, Kristi, and their family could have focused on the worst-case scenario after his diagnosis. Taking the worst-case scenario perspective might have seemed like the natural or easy way to look at things. Instead, their family continued to believe he would live for many years, and that he could thrive even with this diagnosis. As a result, they found ways to help him thrive by juicing and establishing a caring and loving environment in their home.

In a powerful interview on the one-year anniversary of Wes's death,

Kristi talked about how she turned the difficulty of losing her husband to colon cancer into a journey of establishing her juice company in Wes's honor. Her company, WYSIWYG Juice, was founded to help others thrive.

Kristi and Wes's story is a powerful example of how believing in the best-case scenario can mean the difference between thriving or surviving, between loving or fearing.

What you see is what you get.

The science supports this statement. Neuropsychologists found that when your brain expects something to happen, it works to achieve it at a subconscious level. Your expectation creates it. Your brain takes over the job of accomplishing what you see. If you expect the worst, you will get the worst. If you expect the best, you are more likely to get the best.

As John Nabor, a five-time Olympic medalist in swimming and former world-record holder, said, "Life is a collection of self-fulfilling prophecies." Expectation impacts your behavior, which can cause what we expect to actually happen. We can develop self-fulfilling prophecies unknowingly, and they are incredibly powerful. For example, if you believe an athlete on your team doesn't have the skills to be successful, you will treat them that way. You might ignore them or not give them the feedback to develop their skills. Then the athlete will likely conform to your expectations. If you believe your employee or spouse is disloyal, you might treat them in a way that results in the response you expect. If you believe you can't make the team, you might not stay gritty and develop your ability and skills to succeed as part of it.

Negative self-fulfilling prophecies lead to a vicious cycle. Your negative self-fulfilling prophecies create expectations that lead to events happening in your life, business, and sport. Those negative expectations then result in a lack of motivation or mistakes, and these can lower your self-esteem and self-confidence. Then, your lack of self-confidence creates future mistakes or a lack of motivation. If you expect to have a bad practice, you will. If you expect to make only seven out of ten good reps in practice, you will. If you expect your business or marriage to fail, it will. You create your future in your mind. Only you make it happen!

The better option? Believe in the best-case scenario.

The key is to focus on what you want to happen, not on what you don't want to happen. Think, "The sky is the limit for me," or "I am a champion in the making," or "My success will continue," instead of "Oh, crap. Here I go again," and "I will never amount to anything," and "Something bad is about to happen." Focus on thinking like the world's best, and high performance will happen. The first step is believing high performance can happen for you. Only after you believe can you put a plan in place to make it a reality.

The next time you think of the worst-case scenario, focus on what you want to happen instead. Choose a gritty perspective and shift your thoughts away from the worst-case scenario, instead considering the best-case scenario and what I call the "my-scenario." Your my-scenario is what you plan and can create. It focuses on the process, not the outcome, and on what you can control.

I use this exercise often. For example, recently I was entering the taper period of my training for a marathon. (The taper is a period where you decrease mileage each week to be fresh for race day.) Because I was not running as much as I had been, my mind could lose its focus, so I used the best-case and my-scenarios in my head to stay gritty.

- The Worst-Case Scenario: *I will crash and burn at this marathon. I will hit the wall!*

- The Best-Case Scenario: *I will run a personal best time. I know I can do this because I am the most prepared I have ever been.*

GET GRITTY

GET PURPOSE

MASTER THOUGHTS

KNOW SELF

DOMINATE CONTROLLABLES

OWN THE MOMENT

CHOOSE EMOTIONS

OWN WHO YOU ARE

LIVE AND LET GO

COURAGE ZONE

- My-Scenario: *I will run my heart out. I will run fast and strong.*

After completing this exercise, I had more energy and excitement for the race. I was reminded that I can control my effort in the race, which was the most important thing and is reflected in the my-scenario response. I also reinforced that I was the best prepared I have ever been for a marathon.

You can try this for yourself—consider an upcoming event in your life. Write out the best-case scenario and the my-scenario. Then, put a plan in place to go after your dream.

My friends, what you see is what you get! To create the life, performance, and business that you desire and deserve, you have to see it first. You have to have a positive expectation about yourself, other people, and the circumstances in your life.

Continually believe in the best-case scenario and make it happen with your my-scenario. This will change your future and bring your grit to a whole new level.

My High Performance Game Plan

BELIEVE IN THE BEST-CASE SCENARIO

1. I will keep my self-fulfilling prophecies in check and continue to believe the sky is the limit.

2. I will focus on what I want to happen, not on what I don't want to happen.

3. When my mind goes to the worst-case scenario, I'll write out the best-case scenario and the my-scenario. I'll choose to believe that the positive expectation will help me to stay gritty.

4. When I notice a friend, coworker, or teammate talking about the worst-case scenario, I'll share how the my-scenario exercise can help them stay gritty and believe.

My High Performance Power Phrase

I focus on what I want to happen. I think like a high performer and believe the sky is the limit for me.

Chapter 26

Design a Contingency Plan

"Expect the best. Prepare for the worst. Capitalize on what comes." —Zig Ziglar

---

Several years ago, I was in Boston to run the Boston Marathon for the second time. Forecasters predicted that it would be near 90 degrees at race time. It was going to be hot! The heat is problematic for marathoners given the possibilities of heat stroke. Marathoners typically run best at temperatures between 60-70 degrees. The 26.2 miles in 90 degrees was going to be tough.

The day before the race, I received five emails from the race director, who wanted to make sure all runners would take extra precautions in the heat. I appreciated it, though five emails seemed obsessive to me. Everywhere I went, people complained about the weather. They couldn't stop talking about how hot it was going to be! With each email and comment, I grew more and more frustrated and anxious. By that evening, I was livid. I was angry with Mother Nature.

That night, as I walked into my hotel room after dinner, I caught myself. I remember the exact moment when I finally said, "Woah, woah, woah, Cindra! Dominate your APE!"

I caught myself. I was reacting to the weather and the emails from the race director. I wasn't responding. I was focused on things I could not control. I needed to intervene with myself. If I didn't, I was going to be angry, frustrated, and anxious on race day, and that is *not* how I race my best.

All of the research I've done on the High Performance Mindset ran through my mind. Study after study. I searched through them in my mind, asking myself, "What would the world's best do right now?"

Then I remembered the work of one of my mentors, Dr. Dan Gould. Dan and his graduate students have conducted numerous studies examining Olympic teams and athletes, comparing and contrasting those who thrived with those that did not. They found those who succeeded at the Olympics had a plan to deal with distractions and were detailed in their competition plans. They had a contingency plan. They had a plan for the things that might get in their way of being their best. By planning, they were ready for anything and could stay confident, calm, focused, and on their game.

A contingency plan is a plan to deal with the unexpected.

I quickly grabbed a sheet of paper when we arrived at our hotel room and wrote this:

Imperfection #1: _____

My planned reaction or strategy:

Imperfection #2: _____

My planned reaction or strategy:

Imperfection #3: _____

My planned reaction or strategy:

GET GRITTY

GET PURPOSE

MASTER THOUGHTS

KNOW SELF

DOMINATE CONTROLLABLES

OWN THE MOMENT

CHOOSE EMOTIONS

OWN WHO YOU ARE

LIVE AND LET GO

COURAGE ZONE

I called the problems "imperfections" to emphasize that they are just blemishes or undesirable features. They are not problems, just imperfect things happening to me or around me. I felt more liberated and less frustrated by calling them imperfections than problems. After "Imperfection #1," I wrote "THE HEAT" in big capital letters. After "My planned reaction or strategy," I wrote: "Drink one Gatorade every mile at the water stations. Pour two glasses of water over my head. Pay close attention to your hands. If they are swollen, drink more!" I included a few other imperfections in my list, including negativity or self-doubt and an overly fast start in the race.

The next day, as I ran, I thrived. I was very wet at the end of the 26.2 miles, but I ran a personal best time in 90-degree heat! I was grateful for Dan Gould and his research. If I had not written a contingency plan that night, I would not have had a strategy. I would have just grown more and more frustrated, angry, and anxious. Perhaps I would have just gone through the motions in the race and not given my best effort. I would not have had grit that day or been able to capitalize on the race.

Life, sports, and business are not perfect; therefore, it is best to plan for things that might happen so you are ready for anything and can capitalize on what comes. When you plan for imperfections, you have a back-up plan ready and can stay calm and confident.

In my work with NFL athletes and elite teams as well as entrepreneurs and business leaders, we plan for imperfections like:

- Self-doubt

- Weather conditions (i.e., cold, windy, hot, snowing, raining, etc.)

- Field conditions (i.e., wet, dry, hard, soft, etc.)

- Forgetting something

- Making a mistake

- Being behind in the score

- The loss of a valuable employee or client

- Anxiety or pressure increases during the performance

We don't dwell on or expect these things, but by planning for the unexpected, we are prepared.

Reflect on an important event you have coming up and consider at least one imperfection that could occur. What could get in your way of an ideal performance? Then, plan your reaction or strategy. For example, failed technology, anxiety, or pressure could get in your way of dominating your athletic performance, presentation, or sales pitch. How would you deal with that imperfection?

As a result of your planning, you can remain confident, focused, and calm. You have programmed into your subconscious what you plan to do when imperfections arise. Then, in the moment, you won't have to think twice about what you will do because you already know. You can respond with purpose and intention and stay in control of your attitude and effort. You can dominate like the world's best!

GET GRITTY

GET PURPOSE

MASTER THOUGHTS

KNOW SELF

DOMINATE CONTROLLABLES

OWN THE MOMENT

CHOOSE EMOTIONS

OWN WHO YOU ARE

LIVE AND LET GO

COURAGE ZONE

DESIGN A CONTINGENCY PLAN

1. I commit to expecting the best while preparing for anything that comes my way.

2. I'll remember to see things that get in my way merely as imperfections. They are blemishes and I can handle them.

3. What are three or four imperfections that get in my way?

4. I will think like a high performer and design a contingency plan that addresses those imperfections.

My High Performance Power Phrase

**I expect the best but prepare for anything.
I respond with purpose and intention. I know
I can handle anything that comes my way.**

Chapter 27

Don't Take Things Personally

"Quit worrying about what other people think and follow your heart." —JACK CANFIELD

I love Jimmy Kimmel's regular segment called *Mean Tweets*. During the segment, stars, leaders, and politicians read mean tweets about themselves that others have posted on Twitter. Some of my favorite segments include:

- Steph Curry, the Golden State Warrior point guard and 2015 & 2016 NBA MVP, reading, "Imagine the damage Steph Curry would be doing in the NBA if he didn't have such a girly name. #ChangeItToSteve"

- Rascal Flatts, the country music band with thirteen #1 hits, reading, "Please do us all a favor and stop making music. You are so awful. #sobad #spareus #soundsofdeath."

- Barack Obama, former President of the United States, reading: "How do you make Obama's eyes light up? Shine a flashlight in his ears."

- Erin Andrews, ESPN Football Commentator and host of the ABC hit show *Dancing with the Stars*, reading, "Hopefully a ball to your temple will knock the stupid out of you."

If any of these stars or leaders had taken these tweets (or any of the other things that people have said about them) personally, they would not be where they are today. They wouldn't be following their goals and dreams, and wouldn't be leading in their country, industry, or craft.

Many of the young athletes I work with take their teammates' comments or coach's feedback to heart. Even the elite athletes I work with get stuck, from time to time, in listening to the haters and doubters. Especially in today's social media culture, the haters seem to be everywhere for NFL, NBA, and MLB stars and other public personalities. And I know the haters don't stop there. There have likely been times in your own life when you've experienced hate or doubt. How did you respond?

To be real, this is one of the concepts in this book I personally struggle with the most. It is not a habit for me yet, but it will be with time. My strategy is to notice whenever I take other people's actions or words too personally. I remind myself that I am giving the other person power over my destiny. I am letting the other person dictate my goals and dreams. I want to be in the driver's seat! I know you do too.

In his book *The Four Agreements*, Don Miguel Ruiz wrote, "Nothing people do is because of you. What others say and do is a projection of their own reality, their own dreams." Yes, what people say and do is a projection of their beliefs and thoughts. It is a projection of their world, not yours. People do things because of themselves.

When you take things personally, you act and think selfishly. You think it's all about you. You let criticism and negativity eat at you. You overreact, get offended, and hold grudges. You create conflicts that can impact your relationships long-term.

When you take things personally, you allow the words of others to poison you. You start to believe their opinions. You allow your confidence bank to dwindle. You get further away from your goals and dreams. You cannot be a high performer or reach your full potential when you take things personally.

When you decide to protect yourself and not to take things personally, you avoid needless suffering. You cannot be hurt by others. Your anger, irritation, jealousy, frustration, and conflicts with others lessen. You are happier and at your best more often. Now, does that sound good?

Here are a few things you can do when you notice yourself taking what others say or do personally:

- Remember that it is more important what you think about yourself than what others think about you. Keep your belief in yourself high and maintain confident thoughts and body language.

- Consider what is going on in the other person's life. Put yourself in their shoes. Maybe they had a bad day or someone in their family is sick. You might have no idea what the other person is dealing with.

- When you get feedback from a coach, supervisor, or boss, listen or read it like a text message. Take it in objectively for what it says, not what you think it means.

- Ask yourself, "Will I care about this in one year or six months from now?" If yes, then address it. If not, let it go.

- Think like a 60-year-old. When you take things personally, remember these wise words from Dr. Daniel Amen: when you're 18, you worry about what everybody is thinking of you; when you're 40, you don't give a darn what anybody thinks of you; when you're 60, you realize nobody's been thinking about you at all.

My High Performance Game Plan
DON'T TAKE THINGS PERSONALLY

1. When do I take what people do or say personally?

2. Whenever I catch myself taking other people's thoughts and actions personally, I'll remind myself that I'm giving the other person power over my destiny.

3. I will think and act like the world's best by maintaining my confidence and belief in myself.

4. I will think like a 60-year-old and keep in mind that others probably aren't thinking about me at all!

My High Performance Power Phrase

I don't take what other people do or say personally. I decide to protect my grit and confidence. I keep my belief in myself high.

Practice 5
CONCLUDING THOUGHTS

You are over halfway through this book! From Dominate the Controllables, you learned about the following:

- You can dominate the controllables—or your APE— to be in control or your destiny.

- You can think and act like a creator to take the driver's seat of your life.

- You can write out the best-case or my-case scenarios to change your perspective and stay gritty.

- And you can choose to not take what others do or say personally.

Now, take a moment to record the following on your Grit Board:

- Your APE phrase to say focused on what you can control.

- A few key phrases from this section, such as "I am a Creator!" "Believe in My-Scenario" or "Think Like a 60-year-old!"

6

Own the Moment

The world's best
        stay present-moment focused.
They recognize that they can't control the
past or the future, but they are empowered
to reach their highest potential when they
are engaged in the present moment.

Chapter 28

Be Mindful

"Most people don't realize that the mind constantly chatters. And yet, that chatter winds up being the force that drives us much of the day in terms of what we do, what we react to, and how we feel." —JON KABAT-ZINN

What do Phil Jackson, Joe Namath, Arthur Ashe, Misty May-Trainor, Kerri Walsh, Kobe Bryant, Shaquille O'Neal, Michael Jordan, and Russell Wilson have in common? They are all top-level athletes in their sport, and they all practice mindfulness training. Phil Jackson, who has won eleven NBA titles as a coach, has been nicknamed the "Zen Master." While coaching the Chicago Bulls, he hired meditation teacher George Mumford to work extensively with the players, including the team's star player, Michael Jordan.

In his book *The Mindful Athlete: Secrets to Pure Performance*, Mumford described Michael Jordan's and Phil Jackson's last game with the Bulls. The Bulls were playing for their sixth championship and the second three-peat. Mumford could tell Jordan was in his flow zone. He recounts Jordan's own recollection of when the game came together for him. "When I got the rebound, my thoughts were very positive. The crowd got quiet, and the moment started to become the moment for me. That's what we've been trying to do . . . once you get into the moment, you know when you are there," Jordan explained. "Things start to move slowly, you start to see the court very well. You start reading what the defense is trying to do. I saw that moment. When I saw that moment and the opportunity to take advantage of it . . . I never doubted myself. I never doubted the whole game."

Similarly, Russell Wilson, the Seattle Seahawks quarterback, described in an *ESPN the Magazine* article how he uses mindfulness practices to gain control and increase awareness. During a recent NBA season, I saw cameras focused on LeBron James with his eyes closed, focused inward, and engaged in deep breathing. Even in the Silicon Valley, corporations like Google, Twitter, and Facebook encourage their staff to practice mindfulness not just to have more inner peace, but also to get ahead. Classes on meditation and mindfulness are helpful to unlock productivity and boost creativity.

Last fall, I took a mindfulness mediation class so I could offer a similar experience to the high performers I work with. After each class, I felt calmer, happier, less stressed, and increasingly self-aware. I now practice mindfulness daily.

You might be wondering what I mean by mindfulness. I believe mindfulness is the practice of connecting with your emotional, mental, and physical self in the present moment in a nonjudgmental way. It is intentionally focused awareness. As Jon Kabat-Zinn stated in his bestselling book *Full Catastrophe Living*: "Mindfulness means paying attention in a particular way, on purpose, in the present moment, nonjudgmentally."

Mindfulness is choosing to be awake in the moment and know what you are thinking, feeling, and doing. The nonjudgmental component promotes the acceptance of what is and is not working to change what is happening around you. You don't work to fight or judge your situation. Instead, you notice it and become aware.

Mindfulness will inevitably improve your self-awareness, enhance your performance at work and at home, increase happiness, reduce stress, help you think like the world's best, and help you free yourself of the habits that you don't like—the stuff that prevents you from getting to your next level. When you train yourself to pay attention to your thoughts, feelings, and actions, you'll notice right away what

GET GRITTY

GET PURPOSE

MASTER THOUGHTS

KNOW SELF

DOMINATE CONTROLLABLES

OWN THE MOMENT

CHOOSE EMOTIONS

OWN WHO YOU ARE

LIVE AND LET GO

COURAGE ZONE

your needs are, whether that means more rest, distance from a toxic person or situation, time to work on something creative, or a yoga class to calm and center yourself. When we work to bring our attention back to the moment over and over again, we bring ourselves relief from becoming lost in the minutiae of our lives and the weight of our demands.

For the record, mindfulness is a lot easier said than done. In fact, the Buddha referred to our mind as a "monkey mind," meaning that our mind is like a monkey in search of fruit in a forest, moving from one tree to another. I get it. I feel like I have a monkey mind far too often. Like you, my mind can be restless, easily distracted, hard to control, and easily agitated. I can easily and quickly go from thought to thought.

Exercise: Mindful, Not Monkey Mind

Try this mindful exercise to increase your self-awareness and reduce your monkey mind:

Sit in an erect position. Take a moment to notice what is going on for you, right here, right now. Breathe in and breathe out. Ask yourself: "What am I thinking right now? What am I feeling right now? What is going on with my body?" Take a moment to name these thoughts, feelings, and sensations and put them into words. For example, you might think, "I am feeling frustrated right now and my body is boiling," or "I am being self-critical and not kind to myself. I feel sad and lonely." Notice what is without judgment even if it doesn't feel good.

There are several ways you can practice mindfulness to bring your attention back to the moment and increase your self-awareness. Here are a few:

- Take 5-15 minutes in the morning to quiet your mind and notice your thoughts, feelings, and body. Engage in a mediation practice or take a slow, mindful walk to hear what your body and mind might be trying to tell you. Couple that with your Grit Focus Activities discussed in Practice I to thrive.

- While driving, notice how you feel. Where is there tension in your body? Are your shoulders raised? Is your stomach tight? Can you stretch or move your body in a way that dissolves the tension you feel?

- While walking into practice or work, notice your breath, your pulse, and your emotions.

- Try mindful eating. Shift from autopilot eating to intentional eating. Take mindful bites and bring all your senses into it. Breathe in the smell of the food, notice the texture, and truly taste each bite.

- Take a break at work every hour. Take 1-2 minutes to become aware of your thoughts, feelings, and body. Breathe and allow yourself to connect with your feelings and your body in the present moment.

- Notice negative thoughts like "I can't believe I did that" and "I'm so stupid for saying that." Remember that you don't need to let your thoughts sway your emotions.

- Take a mindfulness meditation class in your area or online to learn deeply about how to incorporate mindfulness into your daily life.

GET GRITTY

GET PURPOSE

MASTER THOUGHTS

KNOW SELF

DOMINATE CONTROLLABLES

OWN THE MOMENT

CHOOSE EMOTIONS

OWN WHO YOU ARE

LIVE AND LET GO

COURAGE ZONE

My High Performance Game Plan
BE MINDFUL

1. Who do I know that practices mindfulness? I can ask them about the benefits they experience by nonjudgmentally being in the present moment.

2. I will work to be nonjudgmental in the moment by accepting what is. I won't try to change or judge it; instead, I'll just notice and become aware.

3. This week, I'll notice a time when my monkey mind moves from thought to thought. Then I'll take a deep breath and let the thoughts pass.

4. I commit to a mindfulness exercise in my life, incorporating it into my week at the same time or place.

My High Performance Power Phrase

I work to notice my thoughts, emotions, and body in the present moment. I quiet my monkey mind by staying in the present moment.

Chapter 29

Attack the Process

---

*"You win a national championship by focusing on what it
takes to get there, and not on getting there."*
—NICK SABAN, ALABAMA HEAD FOOTBALL COACH

The story of Olympian Brenda Martinez provides a prime
example of what happens when you focus on the process
over the outcome. In July of 2016, she was positioned to win the
800-meters at the Olympic Trials in Eugene, Oregon. With less than
100 meters to go, Alysia Montano made a move behind Martinez
and tripped. As a result, she clipped the back of Martinez's shoes.
Martinez stumbled but regained her speed. Meanwhile, a handful of
runners who maintained their speed throughout the final 100 meters
finished in the top three earning Olympic spots. After the race, she
stayed in control of her emotions, responded not reacted, and said,
"The track doesn't care about your feelings. You've just got to move
forward."

Less than one week later, she raced the 1500 meters and dove across
the finish line to secure her spot at the Olympic Games by three one-
hundredths of a second. When she was asked what her key to success
was, she said, "I just quickly let go of what happened in the 800
meters and got back to my routine, to focusing on all the little things
I could do that would give me the best chance of running well later
in the week."

She didn't get caught up in the outcome of her previous race and what it could mean. She didn't get caught up in the uncontrollable factors such as Alysia Montano clipping her shoe. Instead, she dominated her attitude, preparation, and effort for the next race. And that focus on the process landed her a spot on the Olympic team. She will forever be known as an Olympian.

"The process" includes all the small things you need to do to become a champion or the best at your craft. The process is what you do day in and day out to be successful—to think and act like the world's best. To focus on the process, you must break down your goal and focus on what it takes to get there. For Martinez, that meant maintaining a positive attitude, reducing stress from outside sources, and ensuring her body was recovered before her next race.

Perhaps the coach that best understands "the process" is Nick Saban, Alabama Football's Head Coach. Saban is a master of the mental game and preaches the importance of focusing on the process daily. He keeps his team's attention on the present moment—on dominating the opponent for 60 minutes—instead of on the outcome. "Don't look at the scoreboard is one of our philosophies," Saban wrote in his book *How Good Do You Want to Be? A Champion's Tips on How to Lead and Succeed.* His team and staff never talk about championships, and they don't get caught up in the hype around the program, even though they have won four National Championships. He said, "We simply focused on the process of becoming champions." For the Crimson Tide, focusing on the process had led to big results.

The process requires daily discipline and a focus on executing the fundamentals. Let's take a football team as an example. A quarterback must focus on reading the defense, not on scoring a touchdown. The kicker must focus on staying relaxed and executing the fundamentals instead of on scoring three points. The punter must focus on kicking high and straight instead of on the number of yards he wants the ball to go. A receiver must trust he will catch the ball instead of trying to catch the ball.

One of the biggest issues that I see professional athletes struggle with is over-trying. Instead of trusting the process, they simply try too hard. They press, trying to force things to happen instead of letting them happen. When we over-try, we tense up. We worry about the score, the competition, or our last failure.

Over-trying comes when we focus on the outcome.

A common misconception is that trying harder will lead to success. Truth is, it won't. Instead, trust yourself and the process. Care more about executing the process than the score or your competition. Focus on the journey, not the destination. Notice the joy you feel from doing the task.

The habit of focusing on the process over the outcome can be applied to any goal—receiving a promotion at work, improving your marriage, or showing more love to your kids. But how?

First, set your goal and write it down. You have to know what you desire and want. Look back at the earlier chapters of this book or your notes from them if you need to review what you are after.

Next, outline the steps that are in your control to get there. What is the process needed to get where you want to go? What are the daily steps you need to take that will lead to extraordinary results? Your daily focus should be on these steps.

Keep Your Eyes on the Prize, but Focus on the Process Daily

When you stay focused daily on the process, you are more likely to persist, and persistence and grit are needed to accomplish your goals. You will be more likely to stay passionate about your work and have a higher sense of satisfaction and accomplishment. Focusing on the process will ensure your self-worth isn't directly tied to the results.

GET GRITTY

GET PURPOSE

MASTER THOUGHTS

KNOW SELF

DOMINATE CONTROLLABLES

OWN THE MOMENT

CHOOSE EMOTIONS

OWN WHO YOU ARE

LIVE AND LET GO

COURAGE ZONE

You'll think less about failure and what other people think. You will be more likely to try new things. You'll be thinking like the world's best. When you focus on the process, you will put forth your best effort and thus you will experience high performance more often.

My High Performance Game Plan
ATTACK THE PROCESS

1. This week, I will write down a goal and outline the steps, or the daily process, that I need to follow to get there. I'll attack that process each day.

2. Next time I focus on winning or the outcome while in a game or other situation, I'll bring my attention back to the present moment and the process.

3. I commit to not getting too high or too low, staying focused on the daily steps.

4. I will post the phrase, "Keep My Eyes on the Prize, but Focus on the Process Daily" in my home, planner, locker, or car to remind myself to focus on the process daily.

My High Performance Power Phrase

I attack the process it takes for me to reach my highest potential. I keep my eyes on the prize, but my focus on the process daily.

Chapter 30

Take One Play at a Time

"Live in the moment. Take one day at a time. One play at a time."
—ADAM THIELEN, WIDE RECEIVER FOR THE MINNESOTA VIKINGS

Adam Thielen grew up playing football in the small town of Detroit Lakes, Minnesota. He loved the game and dreamed of playing at a higher level. He didn't get recruited, however. "I didn't have the size or speed," he said on an interview on the *High Performance Mindset Podcast.* Just a few weeks before camp, the football coaches at Minnesota State University decided to give him a shot and offered him a small scholarship to play.

Fast-forward four years, to after his senior year in which he led the Mavericks to a third undefeated regular season: Thielen knew he could play at the next level, this time in the NFL, but the draft came and went.

Then the Minnesota Vikings provided him an opportunity after the draft to attend the rookie tryout and evaluation session. He took full advantage of the opportunity. Thielen said, "If I would have known then what I know now, I probably wouldn't have made it. I was oblivious to how everything worked and the chances of making it in the league, especially coming from a Division II school. I just took it one drill at a time. I was just living in the moment. Giving it all I got. And now I am here." Thielen made the practice squad, and the next year, the team.

In his third year in the league, he was named Special Teams Player of the Year for the Minnesota Vikings after providing a 75-yard punt return against Kansas City Chiefs en route to a NFC North title for the Vikings. In his fourth year, he led the Vikings in receiving yards. As a result, he was rewarded by the Vikings with a three-year contract extension.

As you read in the preface of this book, I had the opportunity to work with Adam while he was a senior at Minnesota State University when I was providing mental training for the football team. Years later, when I interviewed Adam for the *High Performance Mindset Podcast*, he said these mental training principles were keys to his quest: taking it one play at a time, letting go of mistakes, getting in flow, using imagery to put himself in situations to ensure he was ready, and not dwelling on the past. He said: "Mindset is huge! Your mind can do a lot for you, or it can really hurt your performance. At this level, you realize it more than ever."

Like Adam, you perform your best in the present moment by taking one play at a time. That play could be the assignment you are working on, the client you are serving, or the conversation you are having. No matter the situation, the present moment is the only place your best performance can take place. The present moment is the only place you can experience flow. Your best performance cannot happen if your mind is focused on the past or the future.

Your mind can be one of three places—the past, the present, or the future.

Past	Present	Future
Anger	You can do and	Fear
Frustration	be anything in the	Anxiety
Regret	present moment	Doubt
Depression		Pressure
		Results/Outcome

GET GRITTY

GET PURPOSE

MASTER THOUGHTS

KNOW SELF

DOMINATE CONTROLLABLES

OWN THE MOMENT

CHOOSE EMOTIONS

OWN WHO YOU ARE

LIVE AND LET GO

COURAGE ZONE

When you are focused on the **past**, you are more likely to experience negative emotions such as anger, frustration, regret, and depression. When you are focused on the **future**, you are more likely to experience negative emotions such as fear, anxiety, self-doubt, and pressure. You are more likely to have an outcome-focus over a process-focus when you are focused on the future.

In the **present** moment, however, you can do anything you want to. In the present moment, pressure does not exist. In the present moment, you can be focused on the process. The great thing is that you can train your present moment focus. Getting back to the present moment is about two practices: awareness and choice.

"Life is available only in the present moment."
—THICH NHAT HANH

1. Awareness. You must be aware of your focus. You can tell where your mind is by noticing what you are focusing on. That's why you need a moment-to-moment observation of your thoughts to reach high performance frequently. You have to be able to notice when your mind is not in the present. To gain awareness, ask yourself

° Where are my thoughts right now?

° Are your thoughts in the present?

2. Choice. If not, know that you can make the choice to bring your focus back to the present any time you want to. Remember, awareness first, choice second.

Present moment focus is all about awareness first, choice second.

Once you make the choice to bring your focus back to the present moment, you can use refocusing strategies like these to get you to the present moment:

- Gently bring your mind back to the present moment. You could use a key word like "focus" or "next play" to get your attention back. In sports, when there is a break, the most important play is always the next one. Say "next play" to direct your attention to where you want it to be, on the present.

- When distracted, take a deep Power Breath and refocus your attention. Remember, everyone gets distracted; it's not a big deal. Just ask yourself, "What's Important Now?" (or say its abbreviation, "WIN") and then direct your attention to what's important at the present moment.

- Use mindfulness practices to non-judgmentally focus your attention on the present moment. There are mindfulness practices in Chapter 28. These practices can help reduce your anxiety and stress and allow you to think more clearly under pressure.

Your success is determined by your ability to stay in the present moment. To stay focused on the here and now, commit to staying aware of your focus, moment by moment. It's all about awareness first, choice second.

GET GRITTY

GET PURPOSE

MASTER THOUGHTS

KNOW SELF

DOMINATE CONTROLLABLES

OWN THE MOMENT

CHOOSE EMOTIONS

OWN WHO YOU ARE

LIVE AND LET GO

COURAGE ZONE

My High Performance Game Plan

TAKE ONE PLAY
AT A TIME

1. What are one or two practices or tools I can use regularly to bring my focus back to the present moment?

2. Next time I'm focused on the past or future in a negative way, I will remember that these are the places where negative emotions live.

3. When I want to maintain a present moment focus, I will remind myself, "Awareness first, choice second."

4. I can learn more about mindfulness practices. I'll review Chapter 29 and search for apps or websites that will help me to practice mindfulness regularly.

My High Performance Power Phrase

**I live in the moment. I take one play at a time.
I can do anything and be anything
right here, right now.**

Chapter 31

See Pressure as a Privilege

"Pressure is a privilege—it only comes to those who earn it."
—BILLIE JEAN KING

Billie Jean King understood pressure. She learned to rise to the occasion when it mattered most. As a result, she won 39 Grand Slam titles, including six Wimbledon and four U.S. Open titles. She's considered one of the greats, an icon in tennis.

In 1973, she took on something larger than herself. She wanted to show the world that women belonged in sports. In what came to be dubbed "the Battle of the Sexes," she took on a previous top male player, Bobby Riggs. Riggs believed that the women's game was inferior to the men's game. He believed that even a 55-year old man could beat the top female player. Their game attracted an audience of over 50 million people from 37 countries. King said, "I thought it would set us back 50 years if I didn't win that match. It would ruin the women's [tennis] tour and all women's self-esteem." While those words seem filled with pressure to me, Billie Jean called it "thrilling." She beat Riggs in three straight sets, 6-4, 6-3, 6-3.

We often see pressure as something we don't want to experience. We avoid it. If we see it as something we want to avoid, we crumble under it, and thereby limit our opportunities and ourselves. We don't take risks. We don't go after big dreams or goals. We play small.

The world's best see pressure differently. They see pressure as a privilege. They see it as a challenge. They don't avoid pressure; they use it. They reframe it as a good thing. They know that if they had not accomplished something meaningful or experienced success in the past, they wouldn't be in the situation. They know it's normal to feel something in their body when they perform, that it's their body's way of saying, "This is important!"

For example, LeBron James, 4-time NBA MVP, was asked how he planned to handle the pressure during Game 6 of the 2013 NBA playoffs. He said, "There's no pressure. It is going to be fun, a great game, and I look forward to meeting the challenge." He played well and his team won.

In their book *Performing Under Pressure: The Science of Doing Your Best When it Matters Most,* Hendrie Weisinger and J. P. Pawliw-Fry examine how the Top 10 percent handle pressure. Weisinger and Pawliw-Fry found that these high-achievers use natural tools within themselves to preform to their best during moments of high pressure. They use these tools to counteract pressure's negative effect. They reframe their thoughts, focus on their breathing, and stay focused on the process. These are some of the very tools identified in this book!

Weisinger and J. P. Pawliw-Fry also provide three factors that explain why we underperform under pressure:

° The outcome is important to us.

° The outcome is uncertain.

° We feel that we are responsible for and are being judged on the outcome.

Think about the last time you felt pressure. You were likely doing something you wanted to do well at. The outcome likely was unknown. And you were likely responsible for or being judged on the outcome. At work, it might have been a presentation or meeting. In sport, it might have been before or during a big play, or during playoffs. If we don't learn to change our perception of pressure and manage ourselves during it, then we risk falling behind those who can and do just that.

> *We all must learn to perform under pressure*
> *to be successful and effective.*

Awareness is the first step in seeing pressure as a privilege. You can't live a life without pressure. The key is to manage your reactions to it. Notice your thoughts and emotions. Your thoughts and emotions determine the pressure you experience. You might be focused on failure or the worst-case scenario, or on thinking about things you cannot control like other people's perceptions. Use these three steps in the Pressure Shrinker to see pressure as a privilege. Remember POP the pressure to make the strategy stick.

1. Power Breaths: Take several deep Power Breaths and gently bring your attention back to the present moment where peak performance happens.

2. Opportunity: Reframe the pressure as a great opportunity.

3. Process: Focus on the process and the steps you need to execute.

Use the Pressure Shrinker every time you feel pressure, not just in the moments that matter the most, so that you can get used to dealing with pressure in a positive way. If you do, you will be training your mind to not see pressure as a threat that will undermine your performance but as an opportunity to thrive. Acknowledge the skills, experience, and qualities you have. List them. Use a highlight reel and flash back to your previous successes. Remind yourself to embrace pressure and to

GET GRITTY

GET PURPOSE

MASTER THOUGHTS

KNOW SELF

DOMINATE CONTROLLABLES

OWN THE MOMENT

CHOOSE EMOTIONS

OWN WHO YOU ARE

LIVE AND LET GO

COURAGE ZONE

see it as great opportunity, not as something that happens when things go wrong. Remember the Pressure Principle:

Pressure is a privilege. Pressure allows me to get better.
Pressure is an honor. Pressure leads me to greatness.
I have earned the right to feel pressure.

My High Performance Game Plan
SEE PRESSURE
AS A PRIVILEGE

1. I will make a list of high-pressure situations I'm experiencing and reflect on them. How could my thoughts impact my performance?

2. I will envision a successful high-pressure situation in my future. I'll sit back in a comfortable chair, breathe deeply, and visualize the moment in detail, with color, sound, and location. I'll see myself executing my plan.

3. I can post the Pressure Principle somewhere I can see it regularly in order to remind myself to see pressure as a privilege.

4. Next time I feel pressure, I'll use the four steps in the Pressure Shrinker to stay in the present moment.

My High Performance Power Phrase
**I see pressure as a privilege.
I have earned the right to feel pressure.
Pressure leads me to greatness.**

Practice 6
CONCLUDING THOUGHTS

You are crushing it! You are well on your way to developing a High Performance Mindset! In Own the Moment, you learned:

- You can practice mindfulness daily like the world's best to reduce your stress and improve your performance.

- You can keep your eye on the prize, but your daily focus should be on the process to reach your highest potential.

- You can decide to stay in the present by being aware first and making a choice second.

- To use the Pressure Shrinker next time you feel the pressure to stay in the present moment.

Now, take a moment to record the following on your Grit Board:

- 2-3 process goals you want to focus on to stay gritty.

- The pressure principle.

- A few key phrases from this section such as "Awareness First, Choice Second," "One Play at a Time," or "Pressure is a Privilege!"

Choose Empowering Emotions

3:1

The world's best
thrive because they regularly experience
positive emotions. They know that when people
experience three positive emotions for every one
negative emotion, they flourish.

Chapter 32

Choose Positivity

---

*"Being positive won't guarantee you'll succeed.
But being negative will guarantee you won't."* —JON GORDON

Unchecked negativity leads to health-harming emotions like guilt, depression, bitterness, shame, hate, distrust, and stress. It impacts your whole body. Your blood pressure rises, your muscles feel weak and tight, your head pounds, and you can't think clearly. You blame and find fault in everything—your teammates, your coaches, your kids, your spouse, your boss, and yourself. You can't see solutions or opportunities. You feel stuck.

Negativity has real implications to your performance, your family, and your life. It impacts the culture of your family and team. It impacts your health and your wellness. It impacts every part of your life.

Barbara Fredrickson's groundbreaking book *Positivity: Top-Notch Research Reveals the 3-to-1 Ratio That Will Change Your Life* explains that we need a positivity percentage of at least 75 percent to flourish. That means we need a ratio of 3 positive emotions to 1 negative emotion to thrive and feel alive. When you flourish, you are remarkably resilient. You believe in and are excited about your future. You perform at a high level, physically, socially, and psychologically. You celebrate the greatness in others. You are gritty and go after your goals and dreams.

Fredrickson's work suggested heartfelt positive and uplifting emotions such as joy, gratitude, pride, fascination, inspiration, hope, wonder, confidence, amusement, or love need to be felt 75 percent of the time. Negative emotions like embarrassment, dissatisfaction, anger, or stress should only be felt 25 percent of the time. The ratio of 3:1 can go all the way up to 11 positive emotions for every 1 negative emotion (a positivity percentage of 92 percent), which represents what she calls our "upper bound of flourishing." This means there is appropriate negativity, and more positivity is not always better. For example, if your ratio was 100 to 1, you might likely feel you are just forcing a smile on your face. Your positivity isn't genuine. You are faking it. You might be suppressing negative emotions that are not helpful to ignore. You aren't yourself. You drive others away. You are not consciously practicing high-performer habits of authenticity.

Negative emotions can be helpful in small doses. For example, if you lose your job, a family member passes away, or you miss the game-winning shot of the state championship, it is okay to feel upset, angry, or frustrated. Those feelings deserve to be felt and are important for us to process what is happening in our lives. Some appropriate negativity is important and helpful.

But too much negativity has real consequences. In fact, Fredrickson's research suggests that the opposite ratio of 3 negative emotions for every 1 positive emotion (or 25 percent positivity percentage) predicts depression. When we experience a 1-to-1 ratio (or 50 percent positivity percentage), we stagnate. We don't grow or change. We don't improve.

Most of us could use improvement in our positivity percentage. In fact, Fredrickson estimates that only 20 percent of people are above the 75 percent positivity percentage that predicts a flourishing life.

Her research is confirmed in many other studies. Marcial Losada's impressive research on sixty management teams found that high-performing teams have a positivity percentage of 85 percent, medium performance teams had a positivity percentage of 66 percent, and low-performing teams had a percentage of 29 percent. High-

GET GRITTY

GET PURPOSE

MASTER THOUGHTS

KNOW SELF

DOMINATE CONTROLLABLES

OWN THE MOMENT

CHOOSE EMOTIONS

OWN WHO YOU ARE

LIVE AND LET GO

COURAGE ZONE

performing teams were also more connected and asked more questions of others, whereas the lower performing teams had little connectivity and asked almost no questions.

John Gottman's research on marriages, highlighted in Malcolm Gladwell's *Blink*, argues that flourishing marriages have a positivity percentage of 83 percent, whereas marriages that end in divorce have a 42 percent positivity percentage. In fact, just by paying attention to their positivity percentage, Gottman could predict with 90 percent accuracy if newlyweds would still be married or would be divorced in four to six years.

Positivity drives our performance, happiness, and effectiveness in many areas of our lives! Here are the positivity percentages that have been found in the following areas:

- 85 percent = High Performing Teams

- 83 percent = Flourishing Marriages

- 75 percent = Flourishing Individuals

- 66 percent = Medium Performing Teams

- 50 percent = Stagnant Individuals

- 41 percent = Divorce of Marriages

- 29 percent = Low Performing Teams

- 25 percent = Depressed Individuals

Why do we need more positivity than negativity to flourish? As humans, negativity has a much stronger impact on us than positivity. For example, let's say a friend compliments you on your performance while another friend suggests you were horrible. The compliment might make you feel better for a couple of minutes, but you might think about that insult for several hours or even days. Negativity can have a strong impact on our performance and happiness.

In case the positivity percentage evidence isn't enough for you, there are a host of other benefits to choosing positivity. Additional research by Barbara Fredrickson, Martin Seligman, Shawn Achor, Tal Ben-Shahar, and Sonja Lyubomirsky finds that positivity:

- Allows you to be more creative and receptive to others

- Broadens your view of yourself and your capabilities

- Allows you to experience deeper relationships

- Enhances your performance

- Can help you live up to 10 years longer

- Allows you to build new skills and new knowledge

- Is related to higher salary and better health

Many people think that positivity needs to come from an event; they think, "I need to play well, do well, receive a compliment, or treated well to be positive." But the world's best know this isn't true. Positivity is a choice. Positivity does not need to come from an event. Nothing needs to happen for you to be positive. Positivity is a state of mind. It starts with a choice!

And that choice starts with making a decision to increase your positivity percentage. It starts with setting a daily intention to notice your negativity and change your thoughts and emotions. No one else can change your thoughts, emotions, or mindset. It is only up to you.

Exercise: Choose Empowering Emotions

One of the first steps in choosing empowering emotions daily is to consider the empowering emotions that you want to feel and the disempowering emotions you don't want to feel. You might feel the disempowering emotions from time to time, but you don't want to get stuck in them. Intentionally making

GET GRITTY

GET PURPOSE

MASTER THOUGHTS

KNOW SELF

DOMINATE CONTROLLABLES

OWN THE MOMENT

CHOOSE EMOTIONS

OWN WHO YOU ARE

LIVE AND LET GO

COURAGE ZONE

a decision on how you want to feel helps you choose your emotions. There are over 4,000 words to express emotion in the English language, but most people only experience fewer than a dozen in a given week. In the exercise below, I've provided a few examples of emotions to jump-start your thinking. I encourage you to consider new emotions that you don't typically use to name how you feel and expand your emotional range.

1. Write down three empowering or positive emotions you consistently want to feel. Empowering emotions might include authentic, blessed, confident, compassionate, courageous, creative, energized, excited, fascination, gratitude, hopeful, happy, loved, inspired, joyful, motivated, optimistic, passionate, proud, smart, or wonder.

2. Write down three disempowering or negative emotions you don't consistently want to feel. Disempowering emotions might include anxious, angry, annoyed, ashamed, confused, depressed, dejected, discouraged, dissatisfied, embarrassed, frustrated, guilt, judged, tired, stressed, weak, worried, or worthless.

3. Identify at least two things you commit to doing every day to choose to feel more empowered emotions and fewer disempowered emotions. Select strategies from your High Performance Toolbox like addressing your ANTs (Chapter 12), reframing your negativity (Chapters 15), or engaging in a daily mindfulness practice (Chapter 29).

Your mind is a powerful thing. When you fill it with positivity and choose to feel empowered, your life and performance will change. Today, make the choice to choose positivity! Feel empowering emotions like the world's best!

My High Performance Game Plan
CHOOSE POSITIVITY

1. I commit to striving for at least a 75 percent positivity percentage in my mind and my interactions with others.

2. I commit to bringing more positivity to my family, business, or team to help me and others thrive and flourish.

3. I will complete the Empowering Emotions Exercise and commit to two strategies to increase my positivity percentage and performance.

4. I will think like the world's best and keep negativity in check. I'll set a daily intention to notice negativity and change those negative thoughts and emotions when they arrive.

My High Performance Power Phrase

I choose positivity. I choose to bring positive energy each day and in each situation.

I choose empowering emotions.

Chapter 33

Choose Confidence

"You have to believe you're good enough to excel at the highest level if you ever expect to get there." —PAT SUMMIT

The 2016 NBA Finals were epic. The Golden State Warriors dominated every phase of the game in the first two games in the series. As a result, the Cleveland Cavaliers lost the first two games by 48 points. It looked like the Golden State Warriors, the 2015 NBA Champions, were well on their way to win another championship. LeBron James, the hometown star of the Cleveland Cavaliers and arguably one of the best to ever play the game, was searching for what to do. If he didn't find the answer, he wouldn't be able to bring a championship to his home state. He was searching for the answer that would help his team be the first team ever to rally from a 3-1 series deficit.

LeBron stepped up his mental preparation. He studied the film of the first two games carefully. He painstakingly picked apart his performance, watching closely how he played in the arena that held 19,596 Golden State fans, and analyzed how he could improve. He also spent the weekend watching old Muhammad Ali fights, in awe of Ali's grit and perseverance. He watched how Ali carried himself and maintained his confidence in his long 12- or 15-round fights. Then, LeBron gathered all of his teammates in the locker room to watch Steve Jobs' 2005 commencement speech at Stanford University (see Chapter 6).

The commencement speech made all the difference for the Cavs team.

One of the Cavs players and a fifteen-year veteran in the NBA, Richard Jefferson, said he was inspired by Jobs' words to reflect on how past events lead him to the Cavs this season. These words from Jobs stood out to him: "You can't connect the dots looking forward; you can only connect them looking backward. So you have to trust that the dots will somehow connect in your future." Kevin Love, the Cavs center and three-time All-Star, said that one phrase from Jobs' speech hit him in the heart: "Stay hungry, stay foolish." He wrote the phrase on his shoes to remind him to play loose: to focus on the process with high energy and effort instead of judging himself on statistics.

LeBron and the Cavs went on to do it, completing the biggest comeback in NBA Finals history and delivering a championship to Cleveland for the first time in 52 years. LeBron and the Cavs could not have done it without confidence and without mental preparation. LeBron would have never stepped up his preparation without the belief that he and his team could succeed. He provided an opportunity for his teammates to hear messages of confidence, and it paid off.

Confidence is belief and trust in your ability. It is your certainty that you will be successful. Having skills and talent is not enough; we have to believe in our skills in order to use them to the best of our ability. To cultivate your grit and think like the world's best, you need the confidence to do so. Confidence is a key to high performance.

Confident leaders, athletes, and entrepreneurs trust they have what it takes to succeed and prepare to perform at their best daily. They don't let mistakes, bad games, or less-than-stellar performances impact their confidence. They know they are not perfect and that mistakes are the best way to learn. They use both positive and negative feedback to help inform their game. If they do experience poor performances back-to-back, they don't believe they are in a slump. They believe

GET GRITTY

GET PURPOSE

MASTER THOUGHTS

KNOW SELF

DOMINATE CONTROLLABLES

OWN THE MOMENT

CHOOSE EMOTIONS

OWN WHO YOU ARE

LIVE AND LET GO

COURAGE ZONE

they can turn it around at any time. They do not accept negative labels about themselves.

But let me get one thing super clear: confidence is not about acting cocky or arrogant. When I work with athletes, entrepreneurs, and leaders at all levels, I am clear that being mentally strong is about having inner arrogance, not outer arrogance.

Confident people don't brag. They don't feel the need to shout their greatness from the rooftops. Instead, they show their confidence with their performance and by showing up when it counts.

In other words, high performers are confidently humble. As Norman Vincent Peale wrote, "People with humility don't think less of themselves. They just think about themselves less." High performers who are confidently humble realize they can always grow and learn. They care about others including their family, teammates, and coworkers. They help others reach their full potential. They don't believe they are more important than others.

Confidence is one of the strongest predictors of your daily performance and is essential for your development. Confidence modifies how you perceive and respond to everything that happens to you in life, business, and sport.

Research within performance psychology shows that confident people work harder, set more challenging goals, and persist longer. They are grittier and stay the course to go after their goals and dreams over the long-term. Research by Dan Gould and others shows that confident athletes perform better than less-confident athletes. Olympic coaches named confidence as one of the strongest indicators of success at the Olympic Games. Confidence is key to you reaching high performance.

Your confidence is shaped by what you focus on, how you think, your beliefs, and your actions.

Here is what I mean. Confident people think "I will . . . I can . . . I am," not "I won't . . . I can't . . . I am not." These P4 thoughts create a focus and meanings that lead to confidence. Confident people's thoughts and focus create unstoppable action.

The Confidence Equation

Thoughts + Focus + Actions = Confidence

What you think about, you focus on.
What you focus on, you act upon.

Confidence requires constant nurturing. Even if you are at the top of your field, sport, or company, nurturing your confidence is key if you want to remain at the top. As Joe Montana, the quarterback for the San Francisco 49ers and four-time Superbowl Champion, said, "Confidence is a fragile thing." You can make the decision to let mistakes, failure, and negative people to impact your confidence, or you can choose confidence on a daily basis. As Mia Hamm, the all-time leading goal scorer in women's soccer said, "The thing about confidence I don't think people understand is it's a day-to-day issue. It takes constant nurturing."

How do you develop your confidence? Here are ten essential decisions you can make to increase your confidence.

Decision 1: Make a Choice to Be Confident. High performers make a daily choice to think, be, and act with confidence. They think like a winner and act in a way that maintains confidence. They make a daily decision to nurture their confidence and they stack one good day on top of another.

Decision 2: Remind Yourself of Your Accomplishments. The most powerful sources of confidence are past performances or achievements. When you have accomplished good things in the past, you are more likely to believe you can do so in the future. Your past accomplishments are tangible evidence that you can do it, because you've already done it! Remind yourself daily of how you have

GET GRITTY

GET PURPOSE

MASTER THOUGHTS

KNOW SELF

DOMINATE CONTROLLABLES

OWN THE MOMENT

CHOOSE EMOTIONS

OWN WHO YOU ARE

LIVE AND LET GO

COURAGE ZONE

improved your skills over time.

Decision 3: Make a Decision to be Fully Prepared. Preparation is the second most powerful source of confidence and is fully under your control. You have to deliberately and daily put in the work. Then, when it is time, review your training and your preparation to feel confident. Remind yourself of the miles you put in, the hours that you practiced, and the extra work you dedicated yourself to.

Decision 4: Be Your Own Best Friend. Your self-talk has a direct impact on your confidence and daily performance. If you are not confident, you are likely telling yourself all the reasons you can't do something instead of all the reasons you can. The words "I won't . . . I can't . . . I am not . . ." disempower you and make you physically weak. Notice the voice inside your head, and if you need to, change it. Change "can'ts" into "cans." Like your best friend would, give yourself evidence why you can experience success.

Decision 5: Change Your Body Language. When we are not confident, we tend to slouch. Our body language is small, closed up, and inward instead of big, open, and outward. As Amy Cuddy's book *Presence: Bringing Your Boldest Self to Your Biggest Challenges* argues, standing for two minutes in a power pose can make all of the difference. Some power poses include standing with your hands on your hips, your chest slightly out, and your shoulders slightly back; or stretching out while sitting down with your hands behind your head and your feet on a table; or leaning back in your chair with your hands behind your head and your ankle on the other knee. Cuddy demonstrated actual chemical changes after a 2-minute power pose, including a 20 percent rise in testosterone (the "dominance" hormone), and a drop in cortisol, the stress hormone. Simply put, by engaging in a power pose, we can change our own body chemistry and the way others perceive us.

Decision 6: Put on Your Confidence Armor. Confidence Armor is a mindset steeped in unshakeable focus, not taking things personally, and a belief that you are the best at what you do. When you're wearing your Confidence Armor, you understand that you're the only you there is and you like what you see in the mirror. With your armor on, you're able to process instructions and feedback like a text message, applying the technical aspects of how to improve without zeroing in on how the instructions are communicated. The world's best don't allow coaches, teachers, or friends' comments to sear their confidence, grit, or intrinsic motivation.

Decision 7: Let Go of Mistakes and the Past. Your past has led you to where you are today. Everything has been perfect so far at leading you here. Instead of looking back and feeling regret, depression, or anger, see the difficulties you have experienced as opportunities that have made you stronger and more confident. And when you make mistakes—and you will—use the tool "Learn, Burn, Return" described in Chapter 47 to help you stay confident and in the present moment. As LeBron James, the three-time NBA Champion and four-time NBA's Most Valuable Player, said, "I think the reason why I'm the person who I am today is because I went through those tough times when I was younger."

Decision 8: Use Imagery Daily. Confident people imagine their past successes and future successes. They create the future in their mind, and then they live it. To improve your confidence, develop your own personal highlight reel, whether in your mind or actually on video if you have past performances available (See Chapter 36). Then visualize future performances in which you are at your best and rise to the occasion when it matters the most.

Decision 9: Surround Yourself with Success. As Jim Rohn, author and motivational speaker, said, "You are the average of the five people you spend the most time with." Choose carefully and surround yourself with confident people who are interested in developing their high performance potential. Choose to surround yourself with gritty people who want to think like the world's best and can help you get where you want to go. Watch for successful role models who are already doing what you want to do. Then, follow their lead. Remind yourself, if they can do it, you can do it, too!

Decision 10: Finish Your Day with Confidence. Keep a confidence-building journal in which you write down three things that went well each day followed by one thing you learned. Use the 3-to-1 ratio to focus positively on the day and see the one thing you learned as an opportunity to grow. Remember to view the thing you learned as happening for you and in your best interest as you master your craft. If you are a coach or leader, have your team state their 3-and-1 at the end of practice or at the end of the day.

Confidence is a choice you make daily. Your belief and trust in your ability is your choice. Intentionally decide today to take control of your confidence. Believe and trust that you can!

My High Performance Game Plan
CHOOSE CONFIDENCE

1. I commit to nurturing my confidence daily. I'll use the ten daily decisions to improve or keep my confidence high and to reach high performance.

2. I'll remember the Confidence Equation and develop my confidence by changing my focus and what I think, feel, or react.

3. When I feel the need to brag, I'll remind myself that confident people are humble.

4. When I make a mistake this week, I'll remind myself that a mistake is an opportunity to grow and learn, and does not need to negatively impact my confidence.

My High Performance Power Phrase

I choose confidence. I choose to believe and trust in my ability. I constantly nurture my confidence to be at my best for myself and my team.

Chapter 34

Choose Happiness

"The greatest discovery of any generation is that a human can alter his life by altering his attitude."
—WILLIAM JAMES, PSYCHOLOGIST

I heard Tony Hsieh, the CEO of Zappos.com, speak a few years ago in Las Vegas. Zappos, the online retailer that's doing over $1 billion a year in gross merchandise sales selling shoes, clothing, and accessories, didn't become successful without growing pains. In early 2002, Zappos used a company called ELogistics to fulfill their inventory and delivery needs, yet customers were not getting what they had ordered on time. Customers were not happy and the company was struggling. It was then that Tony realized that they were outsourcing their key core competence, ignoring what could make Zappos unique: customer service.

In his *New York Times* bestselling book, *Delivering Happiness*, Hsieh described the ah-ha moment he had when he decided to make happiness his business model. As a result of this moment, Zappos opened their own warehouse to meet customer needs quickly and started policies that customers loved. They offered free shipping, free returns, and a 365-day return policy. He applied research on the science of happiness to running his company, incorporating three types of happiness—pleasure, passion, and higher purpose—into Zappos. He saw how companies with a higher sense of purpose outperformed those without. He believed that by focusing on increasing the happiness of those around him, he and everyone at Zappos could also drastically increase their own happiness, too. And it worked. After becoming the highest-ranked newcomer to Fortune Magazine's annual "Best Companies to Work For" list in 2009, Zappos was acquired by Amazon and valued at over $1.2 billion on the day of closing.

Tony was on to something. He knew that happiness was a powerful model for achieving success. Happiness is not the result of what you do or accomplish. Instead, happiness comes from your perspective: by recognizing and appreciating what you have. Happiness is a choice each of us can make daily, regardless of our circumstances or surroundings. And making a choice to be happy can make us more productive.

Sonya Lyubomirsky, in her book, *The How of Happiness: A New Approach to Getting the Life You Want*, suggested that up to 40 percent of our happiness is within our power and can change simply through how we think and act. Her research suggests that a small amount (only about 10 percent) of our happiness comes from our life circumstances or situations, like if we are rich or poor, healthy or unhealthy, married or divorced. The remaining 50 percent is what she calls the "set-point" and is determined by our genetics. What this all means is that a large percentage of our happiness is up to us. We each have the potential to change up to 40 percent of our happiness by engaging in daily, intentional activities that impact how we act and think. Will you choose happiness?

The research in positive psychology suggests that happy people share some key traits. Imagine the incredible impact it could have on your life if you chose to be happier!

- Happier people are more energetic, sociable, and have richer networks of social support.

- Happier people make better teammates because they are more cooperative and want to help others.

- Happier people perform at a higher level and are more productive, creative, and engaged.

GET GRITTY

GET PURPOSE

MASTER THOUGHTS

KNOW SELF

DOMINATE CONTROLLABLES

OWN THE MOMENT

CHOOSE EMOTIONS

OWN WHO YOU ARE

LIVE AND LET GO

COURAGE ZONE

- Happier people are gritty and deeply committed to their goals and dreams.

- Happier people are more likely to marry and stay married.

- Happier people make physical exercise a habit and have stronger immune systems.

- Happier people live longer.

- Happier people devote time to their family and friends and enjoy those relationships.

- Happier people are comfortable expressing gratitude for what they have.

- Happier people are more resilient in the face of adversity. They show poise, grit, and strength despite the challenges.

Decide to work on being happier and learn how to do so today. Just by deciding to be happier, you will see an impact. For example, two experimental studies published in the *Journal of Positive Psychology* found that simply *trying* to be happier can actually elevate your mood and well-being.

When you choose happiness, you start committing to better mental habits, choose environments that support your decision, and are more committed to reprograming beliefs that hold you back.

My High Performance Game Plan
CHOOSE HAPPINESS

1. I will choose happiness this week. Decide to be happier!

2. How much can I improve my happiness percentage? Could I improve it by 5 percent this week, or perhaps 20 percent in the next year? I'll record my goal as a personal commitment.

3. Who is someone I know who is consistently happy? I can ask them how they choose happiness to identify two or three strategies they use to do so.

4. What is one happiness-improving question that I can use each day this week to focus on what is great in my life? For example, will I ask "What is great about my situation?" or "What am I happy about right now?"

My High Performance Power Phrase

I choose happiness. I focus on what is great about my situation. I savor the small positive moments.

Chapter 35

Choose Gratitude

"When you are grateful, fear disappears and abundance appears."
—Tony Robbins

Gabriele Grunewald, known by many as Gabe, is an Olympic hopeful who won the USA Track & Field Indoor Championship in the 3,000 meters and has experienced setback after setback. As a track and field athlete at the University of Minnesota, she noticed a lump below her left ear where her jawline ended. The lump was more of a nuisance than anything, but when she finally decided to get it checked out, the doctors told her she had Adenoid Cystic Carcinoma, a rare form of cancer in her salivary gland. She underwent surgery and face radiation that ended her season.

Gabe was determined to come back, even though a comeback would require an additional year of college. In fact, she said, "I had unfinished business and I was more determined than ever. With all that I'd experienced with the cancer and then surgery, I was just grateful and happy to be running again. I visualized myself running faster than I ever had." And Gabe accomplished what she'd always set out to do, but this time as a cancer survivor. The next year she finished second in the 1,500 meters at the NCAA championship.

While training, she pressed forward with a new attitude. The NCAA championship race had put her on the map and doors started opening. No limiting beliefs would hold her back. She signed a contract and reached her dream of becoming a professional runner.

Four months after the National Championship, however, doctors diagnosed Gabe with cancer for the second time. This time she had an aggressive thyroid gland cancer, completely unrelated to her first diagnosis. Can you imagine how defeated she could have felt? Who would have blamed her if she had simply thrown in the towel, believing that her professional running career just wasn't in the cards?

The thing is, she didn't do that because she has unbelievable grit. She continued to believe and imagine her full recovery. She shared with me on the *High Performance Mindset Podcast*, "I had overcome cancer before, so I knew I could do it again. I knew I would do it again!" She embraced her struggle and what it meant to be a two-time cancer survivor.

She imagined improving her times and becoming one of the best runners in the United States. She gives that exercise the credit for getting her through her second bout of cancer. She explained, "I never feel more alive than when I am racing and doing my best. I thought, if I can get stronger as a person through the cancer, I can be a stronger runner, too." Gabe's setback was only a setup for a comeback.

And come back, again, she did! She thrived, finishing fourth place at the 2012 Olympic Trials in the 1500, just one spot away from representing the United States at the Olympics. The experience only made her more interested in the Olympic Team.

Her next chance was in 2016. But just before that, again, a setback appeared. During the fall and winter of 2015, Gabe was diagnosed with a sacral stress fracture. She could not run for four weeks, and then had to slowly ease back into running at all. Taking time off is not an order that an elite athlete wants to hear mere months before Olympic Trials.

During a period where most Olympic hopefuls are training hard, Gabe cross-trained and focused on her mind. She visualized herself doing all the remarkable things she wanted to do and accomplishing every one of her gritty goals. She imagined her fitness coming together

GET GRITTY

GET PURPOSE

MASTER THOUGHTS

KNOW SELF

DOMINATE CONTROLLABLES

OWN THE MOMENT

CHOOSE EMOTIONS

OWN WHO YOU ARE

LIVE AND LET GO

COURAGE ZONE

in time for the Olympic Trials. She envisioned herself fresh and ready to go. "I could turn this into my advantage," she told me.

You wouldn't believe it, but that's just what happened. She competed in both the 5,000 and 1,500 meters at the 2016 Olympic Trials and made the finals in the 1,500. Though she raced her heart out, the time off from training took its toll and she didn't finish where she wanted to. A few weeks after the trials, she discovered cancer again for a third time—this time in her liver. Again, Gabe vowed to beat cancer and said she would be ready to "hit the track harder than ever in 2017."

She recently sent a tweet to her followers from her hospital bed as she prepared to go into surgery. She said, "My pre-op mantra is, 'Anything painful or uncomfortable happening during this hospital stay is not being done to me, it is being done for me and for my benefit.' The only way out is through." Remarkable, right?

Despite her setbacks, Gabe stays positive and grateful. When I asked her recently about her "why" and her decision to compete on the pro running circuit while battling cancer, she said, "I want to show others that even in the face of adversity and uncertainty, living a fulfilling life is still possible. I want to make the time I have mean something." Instead of being bummed about cancer and dwelling on the negative, she opts to find things to be grateful for. Gratitude is more than saying "thank you"—it is about seeing difficulties as opportunities and problems as gifts. It's about not taking the small things for granted.

We aren't automatically thankful. Gratitude is an intentional practice that heightens our performance and grit. When was the last time you were grateful for an injury, an argument, a poor job performance review, or a loss of a game or race? Maybe it's been a while! But that should change. Gratitude is the perfect antidote to negative emotions because it's impossible to feel gratitude and fear, anxiety, worry, envy, or anger at the same time.

Gratitude reminds us to appreciate things that can't be scored or counted, things like teamwork, friendship, and improvement. By being grateful, we tap into what makes us tick, and this helps drive us to do better. It allows us to fall in love with our game or work again, and when we do that, we are more likely to experience our flow zone and high performance. A series of studies on gratitude in sports, including one published in the *Journal of Applied Sport Psychology*, found that gratitude decreased athlete burnout, increased athlete self-esteem, and helped athletes perceive more support from coaches and teammates while also appreciating the accomplishments of others.

Here are five scientifically proven tools to help you feel more gratitude:

1. **Tool 1: Take a gratitude visit.** Write a note, send an email, or go visit someone to let him or her know you appreciate him or her or what he or she did for you.

2. **Tool 2: Start a gratitude journal.** Set aside time to write down one, two, or three things you are grateful for at the start or end of your day

3. **Tool 3: Write a birthday gratitude list.** Choose a person you are grateful for or someone you want to be more grateful for (such as a family member, teacher, coach, or friend). Every day, write one thing you appreciate about that person in a notebook or journal. Give them the list on their next birthday.

4. **Tool 4: Use gratitude language.** Grateful people use words like *blessed, blessings, fortunate, lucky, abundance, privileged, gifts,* or *givers* instead of *unfortunate, unlucky, regret, disastrous, doomed, hopeless, lack,* or *scarcity.*

5. **Tool 5: Take a gratitude walk.** Take a 5- or 10-minute walk to start your day or over your lunch hour. During the walk, make a mental list of all the things that you are grateful for.

GET GRITTY

GET PURPOSE

MASTER THOUGHTS

KNOW SELF

DOMINATE CONTROLLABLES

OWN THE MOMENT

CHOOSE EMOTIONS

OWN WHO YOU ARE

LIVE AND LET GO

COURAGE ZONE

Gratitude is one of the greatest human virtues because it lays the foundation for a fulfilling and worthy life. Take a few simple moments each day to channel your inner Gabe and be thankful for the experiences, people, and moments that increase your happiness, performance, and grit. When you do, you will feel like the world's best!

My High Performance Game Plan
CHOOSE GRATITUDE

1. I commit to intentionally practicing gratitude daily.

2. Next time I experience a difficulty, I'll remember to use gratitude-rich words such as blessed, fortunate, privileged, or lucky.

3. I will start a gratitude journal in which I record a few things that I'm grateful for at the start or end of my day to build my long-term happiness.

4. I can post a gratitude reminder on my refrigerator, planner, or mirror to remind myself to intentionally practice gratitude today.

My High Performance Power Phrase

I choose to intentionally practice gratitude daily. I focus on what I am grateful for to stay fueled and excited for my life, sport, and business.

Chapter 36

Choose to Imagine Greatness

"If you can imagine it, you can achieve it. If you can dream it, you can become it." —WILLIAM ARTHUR WARD

A lbert Einstein used imagery to conceptualize his theory of relativity. He visualized how the world would look while it was traveling inside a beam of light. Adrian Grenier, actor and star on *Entourage*, uses imagery to prepare for each event or meeting. He asks himself, "What kind of performance do I want to give here? Who do I want to be? What is the outcome? And then I go through the mental process of creating that outcome in my mind."

Mikaela Shiffrin, the 18-year-old American skier who won the slalom at her first Olympic Games, used imagery many times to mentally rehearse. As a result, she didn't feel like a rookie or like it was her first time at the Olympics. Jack Nicklaus, the legendary golfer, said, "I never hit a shot, not even in practice, without having a very sharp, in-focus picture of it in my mind. It's like color movie." Tiger Woods used imagery as a second-grader when he played in his first international tournament. When his dad asked him what he was thinking about on the first tee, he said, "Where I wanted the ball to go, Daddy."

Imagery involves systematically using your senses to create a past or future event in your mind. Imagery is not just causal daydreaming, but a systematic process of visualizing to improve your performance. It is focused preparation.

You can use imagery to learn a new skill or strategy as well as visualize future success. Imagery is a powerful mental skill and is reportedly used by 99 percent of the world's best. It's so powerful because your mind doesn't know the difference between a vividly imagined event and a real one; your brain uses the same systems for both real and imagined events.

One study showed that visualization can be nearly as effective in improving performance as actual practice, and another found that when practice is combined with imagery, performance can skyrocket. According to some studies, every minute of imagery is worth seven minutes of physical practice. Bottom line, imagery increases the probability that you will experience success.

Imagery works by sharpening your mental blueprint and strengthening muscle memory. The more you use imagery, the better you will become at it.

You can use imagery for more than just sports. You can use imagery to improve your ability and confidence for a public speech, a job interview, or an important audition.

Use the VICE acronym to use this powerful mental tool properly:

V: Vivid. Create a crystal-clear and detailed image in your mind. Use colors and all five senses. Where are you? What are you wearing? What are you hearing? What does it smell like? Who is with you? See yourself performing on the field or behind the podium from your point of reference. Picture the details. See the image from inside your body the way your eyes would normally see it. The more vivid the image, the more it will come alive.

I: Intensity. Feel the image with same intensity as you would when performing. Feel the physical sensations in your body. Feel the breath coming into your body, the weight of the book in your hand, or the texture of ball. Don't worry about the outcome; just imagine the details of performing at your best. Imagine the process of getting the hit, nailing the presentation, or being at your best for the job interview.

GET GRITTY

GET PURPOSE

MASTER THOUGHTS

KNOW SELF

DOMINATE CONTROLLABLES

OWN THE MOMENT

CHOOSE EMOTIONS

OWN WHO YOU ARE

LIVE AND LET GO

COURAGE ZONE

C: Controllability. Controlling the image is key to imagery's success. Imagine exactly what you want to happen and manipulate the images in your mind. Imagine the beginning through the end. You can image yourself making mistakes and overcoming them; just always end on a positive note. Imagine yourself rebounding from adversity, in control of your mind, body, and response. If you imagine something that you don't want to keep repeating the image in your mind until you imagine it the way you'd like to. As you practice imagery, you will improve your control of the process.

E: Emotions. Feel the emotions and energy of the performance to make it real in your body. Feel the excitement, happiness, satisfaction, and sense of accomplishment present in your body when you stay gritty and reach your goals. Feel and imagine your friends, coaches, parents, or teachers' reactions. What would it feel like to score that game-winning goal or to rock that presentation in front of potential clients? How excited or stoked will you be? The more passion and energy you can imagine with, the more powerful the result will be.

When I work with elite athletes, championship teams, leaders, and entrepreneurs, I usually recommend that they systematically practice imagery every other day for ten or fifteen minutes. I recommend the same for you. You could use imagery before you go to bed or at the beginning of the day. Turn off your phone and eliminate any distractions that might be around you. Start with four or five Power Breaths so that you relax and eliminate any fear, anxiety, or self-doubt.

If you are not using imagery consistently, you are missing out on a powerful way to improve your performance. Include imagery as part of your daily routine. It will help you think like the world's best and accomplish even more than you thought was possible!

My High Performance Game Plan
CHOOSE TO
IMAGINE GREATNESS

1. When I feel disappointed in my situation or circumstances, I will imagine myself coming back stronger.

2. I commit to practicing imagery regularly.

3. I will remember to use VICE (Vividness, Intensity, Controllability, and Emotions) to use imagery in the most powerful way.

4. The next time I want to increase my confidence, motivation, focus, or sense of calm and control, I'll use imagery to do so.

My High Performance Power Phrase

I imagine success. I create success in my mind first and then I live it. I use the most powerful performance weapon I have: my mind.

Chapter 37

Choose to Create Your Own Energy

"You get some momentum going, get the adrenaline flowing, and anything can happen."—FRANK PERMUY

It's a game that I will never forget. In front of a home crowd, the Minnesota State Mavericks football team was taking on a conference rival. The Mavericks had started the season undefeated, which was a testament to the mental training the team engaged in that year. It was the first year they tried it, and the impact was profound. The athletes looked more confident, motivated, and focused, and their performance improved.

The Mavericks were down 10 to 24 with 7 minutes and 33 seconds remaining in the fourth quarter. They got the ball on the 35-yard line, and despite the score, the team played like they could win. They started to intentionally build momentum, the focus of our workshop just a few days before. You could see the momentum in the athletes' faces, energy, and body language. They were jumping up and down, locked into the game, and pumping up their teammates. Looking at them, you wouldn't have guessed they were down by two touchdowns.

As I stood on the sidelines, one athlete came rushing over to me. "Dr. Kamphoff, don't worry. We are going to pull this off. Watch me!" he said as he ran off the field. On the next play, the Mavericks scored.

Then they scored again. They were unstoppable. The game went into overtime, and in overtime, the Mavericks won.

In my experience, most football coaches believe that a team needs a "big play" to turn the tide in a game like this: an interception, a score, or big stop. I disagree. By building positive energy, any team—not only a football team—can create a psychological edge. You can create momentum by waking up your actions, voice, and energy and creating a shift. Energy can help win games and championships.

I call this the "Law of Mojo." Mojo, or momentum, is positive or negative changes in motivation; when positive, it involves feeling optimism, energy, and control over the situation. In sports, business, and life, momentum impacts whether things seem to be going right or going wrong.

To understand the Law of Mojo, think of a power plant. It doesn't have energy; it generates energy. You, your family, and your team are the same way. You decide to either generate positive or negative energy in a situation, the game, or your family. You can either build Mojo or lose it, and that decision impacts the outcome you receive.

Researchers in sport psychology have found that positive momentum leads to an increase in performance, whereas negative momentum leads to a decrease in performance. Most football coaches agree that momentum makes a difference. In fact, 92 percent of football coaches believe team performance is "crucially determined by momentum."

Psychological momentum does not just apply to sports. Albert Einstein taught us that the universe is made of energy. Everything we see is made up of the same energy as our bodies. Energy is everywhere. Your thoughts are loaded with energy. Your energy grows from your thoughts when you focus on gratitude, happiness, and your vision for the future. Behaviors like complaining, blaming, and thinking like a victim decrease your energy.

Other people can also increase or decrease your energy. The culture

GET GRITTY

GET PURPOSE

MASTER THOUGHTS

KNOW SELF

DOMINATE CONTROLLABLES

OWN THE MOMENT

CHOOSE EMOTIONS

OWN WHO YOU ARE

LIVE AND LET GO

COURAGE ZONE

of your family and your team at work or in sports can increase or decrease your energy. Each person contributes to a culture's collective energy. That means that, no matter your role, you can impact the energy of your group.

People who generate momentum around them know their role, understand how important their work is, and decide to bring liveliness to their work. They have unfailing enthusiasm and a clear purpose in their life. Their sense of purpose propels them forward.

How do you generate positive energy and momentum in your life and on your team? Here are the four ways that I teach the people and teams I work with to do so.

1. **Wake up.** To create more energy, wake up your actions and voice. Create energy with high-fives, smiles, and physical touches like a pat on the back. Changing your voice means only allowing positive statements in your mind such as "Way to go!" and "Nice play!" and "Keep up the great effort!" Negativity drains energy. The positive energy you create is contagious and can be spread through strong and confident body language and an unfailing enthusiasm in your work, life, and sport.

2. **Decide to be a momentum giver, not taker.** Consider what you bring to your team, your work, and your family. Do you bring positive energy, or take it away from the situation? Are you noticing what is great with your team or spouse? Are you focusing on what is right, not wrong, in the situation? Take an honest and compassionate look at your focus, and if needed, decide to change it.

3. **Make your positive energy greater than other people's negativity.** This step is actually one of my favorite quotes from Jon Gordon's book, *Energy Bus*. Use Jon's wise words as a guideline and decide to bring more positive energy than other people's negativity. Negativity will always be there, but decide to feel good no matter what is going on around you.

4. **Celebrate the victories of others.** Make a decision to celebrate what other people accomplish. Make sure your team knows about other people's wins and recognizes them no matter how small they are. How can you recognize others more? Praise them for doing things right. People need to know that they are appreciated. They work hard at their jobs and on their teams. Energy givers reinforce the worth of people's work.

How can you use these tools to develop your mojo on your team and in your life? Momentum is key to staying gritty and to consistently experiencing high performance, and it starts with one positive thought or action in the moment. When you keep your positive energy high, negativity can't leak in.

GET GRITTY

GET PURPOSE

MASTER THOUGHTS

KNOW SELF

DOMINATE CONTROLLABLES

OWN THE MOMENT

CHOOSE EMOTIONS

OWN WHO YOU ARE

LIVE AND LET GO

COURAGE ZONE

My High Performance Game Plan

CHOOSE TO CREATE YOUR OWN ENERGY

1. I commit to bringing positive momentum to my life, team, and family.

2. I will be aware of the energy I bring to conversations and situations this week. I'll notice if I bring positive momentum or take it away and make adjustments as necessary.

3. I will put myself in charge of bringing positive energy to every situation and leading with drive, vitality, and empowering emotions.

4. I will celebrate the accomplishment of two other people today by congratulating them or sending them a note, email, or text message.

My High Performance Power Phrase

I generate energy and positive momentum. I bring energy in each situation. I am full of enthusiasm, energy, purpose, and happiness.

Chapter 38

Choose Your Friends Wisely

"You are the average of five people you spend the most time with." —JIM ROHN, AUTHOR AND MOTIVATIONAL SPEAKER

In his book *Rich Dad, Poor Dad*, Robert (Guy) Kiyosaki described his experience having two dads. His biological, government-employed dad was stuck in a middle-class mindset with limiting viewpoints about money. This was his "poor dad." His poor dad had the habit of saying, "I can't afford it." His "rich dad" forbade those words and instead insisted on saying, "How can I afford it?" Guy's "rich dad" was his best friend's entrepreneurial dad, one of the wealthiest men in Hawaii. Robert chose to spend time with his rich dad so he could learn from him. And sure enough, his rich dad taught him the importance of a mindset that leads to wealth while teaching him the importance of hard work.

Robert observed, "The poor and the middle class work for money. The rich have money work for them." He continued, "Going into our fear and confronting our greed, our weaknesses, our neediness is the way out. And the way out is through the mind, by choosing our thoughts." Spending time with his rich dad eventually led to Robert's success as an investor and businessman. His eighteen books have sold over 26 million copies. Because Robert chose to spend time with this rich dad at thirteen years old, he impacted his future and the future of millions of people who read his books.

I love Jim Rohn's quote that starts this chapter: "You are the average of five people you spend the most time with." These words force you to think about whom you spend your time with, and to reflect on how your friends, family members, and teammates impact you. This idea is supported by research; many studies show that the people you choose to spend time with can either limit your future or expand it.

We tend to underestimate the importance of the company we keep. When I discuss this topic with clients, including professional athletes and successful entrepreneurs, many are surprised to learn how much the people you spend time with influence the person you will become. You conform to others around you, and the values of others influence your own. The people around you can either elevate your game or bring it down.

Observe high performers and you'll notice that they surround themselves with people that help them be great. They hang around optimistic and confident people who design their futures.

Friends of high performers talk about the exciting opportunities and projects they are jazzed about. They also talk about their future as if it has already happened. High performers and their friends share the same values because attitudes and energy are contiguous. The world's best don't let friends regularly complain, blame, or hold a victim mindset.

You can use the **Five People Exercise** to help you identify and gather your own gritty group.

1   Consider the five people you spend the most time with. Write down three qualities that stand out to you about each person. Do these qualities help you get to where you want to go? Reflect on if you need to decide to spend more or less time with each person. Ask if each of these people provides positive or negative momentum. Then, put a positive or negative sign by each name to indicate if you need to spend more or less time with each

person on your list.

2. Write down five attributes that you need to embody to reach your goals and dreams. These could be attributes that you already have but need to develop more fully, or attributes you do not currently have. Then, identify the friends, colleagues, or teammates that have those qualities from the list above. Circle their names from your list above.

3. Finally, write down five people who are not on your current list but who could support you in getting to where you want to go. List some of the attributes that each person has and record how each person could help push or support you in staying gritty and reaching your vision. Write down how you plan to reach out to these people. Will you email, call, send a message on social media, or approach them face-to-face?

Remember: you can't be exceptional on your own. You need support and a crew of like-minded superstars who believe in your vision and push you to be the very best version of yourself. You can't choose your family members, so you should love them regardless of their energy. But you can choose your friends, and perhaps this exercise helps you see the friends you should spend less time with.

The world's best know that their friends can either elevate their game, or not. Choose your friends wisely!

GET GRITTY

GET PURPOSE

MASTER THOUGHTS

KNOW SELF

DOMINATE CONTROLLABLES

OWN THE MOMENT

CHOOSE EMOTIONS

OWN WHO YOU ARE

LIVE AND LET GO

COURAGE ZONE

My High Performance Game Plan
CHOOSE YOUR FRIENDS WISELY

1. This week, I'll notice how the energy of others positively or negatively impacts my energy and momentum.

2. I will make smart decisions about who I spend time with and choose optimistic, confident people who are designing their future.

3. I will spend less time with toxic people who decrease my energy.

4. I can complete the Five People Exercise to reflect on who I want to spend the most time with in the days ahead.

My High Performance Power Phrase

**I surround myself with optimistic, confident people who are jazzed about their future.
I choose people who bring me energy.**

Practice 7
CONCLUDING THOUGHTS

Your High Performance Toolbox is getting very full! In Choose Empowering Emotions, you learned:

- You can experience at least a 75 percent positivity percentage by choosing to feel empowering emotions.

- You can use the 10 decisions to feel more confident by choosing what you think about, focus on, and act upon.

- You can feel more happiness by recognizing and appreciating what you have.

- You can choose to feel gratitude instead of fear, anxiety, or worry.

- And you can use the VICE acronym to powerfully practice imagery daily.

Now, take a moment to record the following on your Grit Board:

- 3 empowering emotions that you consistently want to feel.

- 1 happiness-improving question you could use daily such as "What's great about my life right now?"

- A key phrase from this section such as "Channel My Inner Gabe," "Imagine Greatness," or "Bring Mojo!"

8

Own Who You Are

The world's best make the conscious choice to show up as themselves every day and in every interaction. They know who they are and own who they are.

Chapter 39

Do You

"Often people attempt to live their lives backwards;
they try to have more things, or more money, in order
to do more of what they want so that they will be happier.
The way it actually works is the reverse. You must first be
who you really are, then do what you really need to do,
in order to have what you want." —MARGARET YOUNG

Simone Biles dominated the gymnastics competition in the 2016 Rio Olympics, becoming the most-decorated American gymnast ever with 19 Olympic and World Championship medals to her name. Her elevation and execution were unmatched. In her floor routine, she performed "the Biles," a signature move that includes a double layout with a half twist. The crowd was awestruck by her performance.

Her story also struck a chord with viewers. Every four years during the Olympics, we hear about the dedication, grit, and hard work of champions. But Simone's story stands out. By the age of three, it was clear that her biological mother could not care for her and her sister, Adria, because of drug and alcohol addiction. Biles could have bounced from one foster care family to another, but instead her grandparents, Ron and Nellie Biles, adopted her. They cared for her and became her mom and dad. They provided unwavering support for her as a person and gymnast.

Growing up, Simone was fearless. Before enrolling in a gymnastics class, she taught herself to do backflips off her family's mailbox. As a six-year-old, she visited the gym on a fieldtrip. There she saw older girls flipping and twisting, and immediately sought to copy them. The gym owner could tell Simone was unique. In a bold move, he sent a letter to her family encouraging Simone to join the gymnastics program, and her family did just that.

After years of hard work and pushing her limits, Biles entered a league all her own at the Rio Olympics. In route to the all-around gold medal, she achieved a 2.1 point margin of victory, larger than any gymnast from 1980 to 2012. After her all-around win, she wanted to set the record straight. There was no reason to compare her to any top male athlete or former gymnastics gold-medalists. Instead, she embraced her uniqueness, her story, and her gifts. She said, "I'm not the next Usain Bolt or Michael Phelps. I'm the first Simone Biles." She truly blazed her own trail.

I'm a big fan of Brene' Brown's work on authenticity. In her book *The Gifts of Imperfection,* she says that authenticity is a practice: it's not something we have or don't have, but a conscious choice of how we want to live. We can practice authenticity: we can choose to make a decision to be us and be real instead of trying to be someone we are not. Simone Biles showed up as herself, with her own moves, as her own person, without comparing herself to someone else.

Brown's research suggests that there are some people who consciously practice authenticity daily. The rest of us are authentic some days and not other days. When we mindfully and purposefully practice authenticity, we invite happiness, gratitude, and joy into our lives, and this impacts our performance. As Brown said, we let go of who we think we should be, and embrace who we really are—even though we are not perfect. When we mindfully practice authenticity, we are less likely to experience anxiety, blame, resentment, and depression, emotions that undermine our performance.

Authenticity is a foundation of performance. To be successful in sports, business, and life, you must be

GET GRITTY

GET PURPOSE

MASTER THOUGHTS

KNOW SELF

DOMINATE CONTROLLABLES

OWN THE MOMENT

CHOOSE EMOTIONS

OWN WHO YOU ARE

LIVE AND LET GO

COURAGE ZONE

yourself. When you are real, people connect with you. People can tell when you are a phony. In sports and business, you have to be comfortable with who you are to use your strengths and be confident. Plus, you can't actually be someone else. It is impossible!

I've learned this lesson personally. When I first started working in performance psychology, I tried to be like one of my mentors, Dan Gould. I tried to talk like him, conduct workshops like him, and consult like him. I wasn't really connecting with my audience like I knew I could. I was happy with my work, but I wasn't bringing my heart and soul. Something was missing because I wasn't showing up as the real Cindra Kamphoff. Once I started reading more of Brown's work, I began applying her teaching and showing up like myself: full of energy, passion, and heart, as the person my coach calls "Dynamo Cindra." I try to do this when I'm on the football sidelines, speaking in front of a group of business executives, and writing this message to you. When I do, I feel so much more alive.

I learned that most of us are drawn to people that are real and down to earth. These people know who they are, and their ego isn't out of control trying to prove something about themselves to others. We celebrate people like Simone Biles who own their uniqueness, because we all want to do the same.

Sometimes it can be tough to show up as ourselves. We may judge ourselves or fear being judged by others even though we celebrate authenticity. As E. E. Cummings wrote, "To be nobody-but-yourself in a world which is doing its best, night and day, to make you everybody but yourself—means to fight the hardest battle which any human being can fight—and never stop fighting."

"Doing you" can be the bravest battle you fight. But when you "do you," you show your true gifts to the world. You make the choice to let your true self be seen. You are able to reach a whole new level of performance when you are not worried what others think about you. You are not evaluating your worthiness from critics in the stands. Instead, you are being yourself, doing what gives you energy without worrying what will people think. You can take risks like the world's best. You accept who you are and let go of believing you are not enough. You speak up about your uniqueness.

How do you show up 100 percent authentically, guaranteed? Notice when you are not yourself. Remember that being yourself is how you connect with others. When you are yourself without judgment, you are free to perform to your potential. By showing up as yourself, you remove the barrier that can exist when we interact with others.

We all have unique gifts and strengths. When we aren't ourselves, we hide those strengths. We live and perform in a shadow. The world needs you and your gifts. Don't hold back!

GET
GRITTY

GET
PURPOSE

MASTER
THOUGHTS

KNOW
SELF

DOMINATE
CONTROLLABLES

OWN THE
MOMENT

CHOOSE
EMOTIONS

OWN WHO
YOU ARE

LIVE AND
LET GO

COURAGE
ZONE

My High Performance Game Plan
DO YOU

1. When am I not myself? I need to remember that being authentic is how I can best connect with others and let my gifts be seen.

2. What are a few times that I wasn't "doing me?" What were the consequences?

3. I can learn more about the power of authenticity by reading Brene' Brown's *The Gifts of Imperfection*.

4. When I lose focus on being me, I can remember that to get what I really want, I need to be who I really am.

My High Performance Power Phrase

The world needs me and my gifts. I will show up as myself and let my true self be seen. I will "do me."

Chapter 40

Let Go of Comparison

"Comparison is the thief of joy." —THEODORE ROOSEVELT

People who focus on the thoughts of others struggle to reach their greatness and greater potential. An image that made this clear to the world was the picture of South African swimmer Chad Le Clos looking at American Michael Phelps during the 200-meter butterfly at the Rio Olympics. In it, Phelps focused forward, whereas Le Clos has his head turned to watch Phelps as they raced. Even though Le Clos had beaten Phelps just four years earlier in the same race, Le Clos swam poorly. Phelps won the Olympic gold, beating Le Clos by over a second, with Le Clos finishing in fourth place.

Reporters and commentators were floored Le Clos did so poorly. They couldn't explain it. "For some reason, Le Clos didn't medal," they said. Of course, the reason was that Le Clos was focused on Phelps instead of on being his best. He wasted time and energy on another competitor instead of staying focused on getting in his flow zone.

Even from the ready room, it was clear that Le Clos' sole focus was on Phelps. He was standing a few feet in front of the folding chair in front of Phelps, peacocking, jabbing, and shaking his muscles, hoping that Phelps was watching. He was attempting to intimidate Phelps. It didn't work. Phelps was watching in his seat with his hood up. As he listened to the music on his headphones, he grimaced. When they both stepped onto their blocks to start the race, Le Clos was still focused on Phelps. He looked at Phelps one more time before the start of the race, whereas Phelps turned his back to Le Clos and focused on getting in his flow zone.

It's easy to get caught up in the competition, take your eyes off the lane in front of you. It's easy to compare yourself or your performance to others instead of staying focused on your own improvement. It's easy because we live in a culture obsessed with comparison. Sometimes even the world's best forget to stay focused on themselves, as Le Clos showed us.

Go deep for a minute: How have you shifted your eyes toward your competitors or others' achievements or things? How has this impacted your performance or happiness? Would you like to change your focus?

We compare our appearances, our businesses, our number of friends, our athletic abilities, our families, our Facebook or Twitter followers, and our belongings to other people's. In sports, we might compare the goals we score or the times we run. We all do this to evaluate ourselves and to get a sense of our place in the world. But the problem is that we usually don't do it in a fair way. We compare the highlight reel of others to our behind-the-scenes footage. We compare our beginning to somebody else's middle or end.

Comparison makes us feel like we are never enough: not good enough, smart enough, powerful enough, thin enough, athletic enough, successful enough, strong enough, certain enough, extraordinary enough, fast enough. The list goes on and on.

Comparison is a trap. Comparison can spin us into a tail-chasing frenzy of self-doubt. Researchers have found that comparing breeds feelings of low self-confidence and judgment. It leads to anxiety, depression, separation, and loneliness. Comparison negatively impacts our motivation at work and in sports and decreases our passion and zest to go after our goals. Comparison interferes with our ability to be and stay gritty.

Comparison also has a dramatically negative impact on team performance. It fosters competition more than teamwork, superiority and inadequacy more than collaboration. For my master's thesis on jealousy and sports, I found that jealousy negatively related to both team cohesion and satisfaction, both of which are essential for high performance.

When we compare ourselves to others, we have a hard time being happy for other people and their successes. We are less likely to celebrate our team members and their accomplishments. The happiest and most successful people take pleasure in other people's successes. They show concern when other people fail instead of celebrating their failure. As T. Harv Eker said in his book, *The Secrets of the Millionaire Mind*, "Bless that which you want. If you see a person with a beautiful home, bless that person and bless that home. If you see a person with a beautiful car, bless that person and bless that car. If you see a person with a loving family, bless that person and bless that family. If you see a person with a beautiful body, bless that person and bless their body."

People who find themselves paying too close attention to others and comparing themselves to others often find themselves chronically insecure, threatened, and anxious. Comparison is about being "better" than others, not about getting better yourself. The less attention you pay to others around you, the happier and better you will become.

You likely compare yourself to others more often than you think. So, what should you do instead? The first step is to notice when you are comparing yourself to others. To gain awareness of when you compare yourself to others, fill in the blank:

I believe I am not _____ enough when I

compare myself to _____.

Next, you have two choices. The first choice you can make is to celebrate your progress instead of comparing

GET GRITTY
GET PURPOSE
MASTER THOUGHTS
KNOW SELF
DOMINATE CONTROLLABLES
OWN THE MOMENT
CHOOSE EMOTIONS
OWN WHO YOU ARE
LIVE AND LET GO
COURAGE ZONE

yourself to that other person. Focus your energy on being your best you. Think back to where you have come from and the progress you have made toward your goals and dreams since yesterday, last week, last month, or last year. Go back even further: compare where you are now to 1, 3, or 5 years ago.

Or you can ask yourself, "What can I learn from this person?" Acknowledge the other person and be excited for his or her success and talent. Part of what makes life amazing and interesting at the same time is that we can learn from the talents of others. How can you embrace the person as a role model? Learning from someone you admire is the best way to make massive gains in your performance.

Next time you catch yourself using someone else as a benchmark for your own worth, stop and remind yourself how ineffective this strategy is. Comparison is about being better than others; instead, you want to redirect your energy and attention to your own goals and what is required to achieve them. Amazing things happen when you focus on being your best, one stroke, step, pass, or client at a time. My friends, stay gritty and work to be the best version of yourself along the way.

My High Performance Game Plan
LET GO OF COMPARISON

1. I will notice when I compare myself to others, remembering the negative consequences of comparison on performance, confidence, and mental state.

2. Fill in the blank: I believe I am not _____

    _____ enough when I compare myself to

    _____.

3. I will stay focused on my lane. I'll stay focused on my own progress and on comparing myself to where I was yesterday, last week, last month, or last year.

4. When I compare myself to others, I will choose to instead celebrate their successes by complimenting them out loud or writing them a note sharing something that I've learned from them.

My High Performance Power Phrase

I pursue my standard of excellence. I stay focused on my lane and my progress. I stay gritty and work to be my best one step at a time.

Chapter 41

Own Your Story

"When writing the story of your life,
don't let someone else hold the pen." —ANONYMOUS

In 2011, Sheryl Sandberg, chief operating officer at Facebook, was
named to *Forbes* annual World's 100 Most Powerful Women list. At
first, she was horrified that she was ranked as the fifth most powerful
women in the world (right after the Secretary of State Hillary Clinton
and before First Lady Michelle Obama). She felt embarrassed and
exposed on the list, and when colleagues at Facebook stopped her in
the hallway to say congratulations, she would call the list "ridiculous."

After a few days of calling the list ridiculous, her long-time assistant,
Camille Hart, asked her to come into the conference room. Hart told
Sandberg that she was handing the *Forbes* thing poorly. She offered
advice: stop showing people that you are uncomfortable and simply
say, "Thank you."

Sandberg, the year before, gave an electrifying TED Talk describing
how women hold themselves back in their careers. The talk, watched
by over two million people, encouraged women to "sit at the table,"
seek challenges, take risks, and follow their goals with grit. In it,
Sandberg instructed, "We must all chart our own unique course and
define which goals fit our lives, values, and dreams."

Five years after her TED Talk Sandberg told her story again in a
commencement address at University of California—Berkeley.

She had just lost her husband, Dave Goldberg, in a terrible and unexpected accident. In the commencement address, Sandberg told graduates that it is the hard days, not the easy ones, that determine who you are. She said, "You are not born with a fixed amount of resilience. Like your muscle, you can build it up, draw on it when you need it. In that process, you will figure out who you really are, and you just might become the best version of yourself." She shared how her friend, Adam Grant, a psychologist and author of *Give and Take: A Revolutionary Approach to Success*, suggested she think about how much worse things could be after her husband passed away. "What!?" she thought. "That's counterintuitive." But then Adam said, "Dave could have had that same cardiac arrhythmia while he was driving your children." Seeing what could be worse made her more grateful for her health and for her children.

Sandberg owned her story. In both her books, *Lean In: Women, Work, and the Will to Lead* and *Option B: Facing Adversity, Building Resilience, and Finding Joy*, she shared her story, her struggles, and her triumphs as one of the most powerful female leaders in the country. She fueled a national conversation about women in the workplace, and then resiliency in the face of adversity several years later. She allowed others to see the value of living life full-out and shared how modifying the story of her husband's death made all the difference.

What do I mean by "story"? I don't mean to offer tips on how to tell good stories so you get more listeners. Instead, I mean the story we tell ourselves about ourselves to ourselves. Your story creates your reality about life, and your destiny follows the story you create. As performance psychologist Jim Loehr said in his book *The Power of Story*, "Your life is your story. Your story is your life." You are telling your story right now whether you know it or not.

When you own your story, you begin to connect with it in a deeper way. You are proud of what you have overcome and who you are now. You understand the times in your life when you have experienced difficulty, darkness, or struggle. When you connect to those times, you get energy because you are no

GET GRITTY

GET PURPOSE

MASTER THOUGHTS

KNOW SELF

DOMINATE CONTROLLABLES

OWN THE MOMENT

CHOOSE EMOTIONS

OWN WHO YOU ARE

LIVE AND LET GO

COURAGE ZONE

longer ashamed of the difficulties, struggles, or transition. When you own your story, you inspire others because you connect with them. We have all experienced struggles. You seem real and relatable when you tell your story. You motivate others to share their true self, too. When you own your story, you let people see you and they trust you.

As Brene' Brown said in the book *Daring Greatly*, "When we deny the story, it defines us. When we own the story, we can write a brave new ending." When we own our story, we take control of our perspective, how we see ourselves, and how we view the world. We might feel ashamed or guilty about our story, which leaving us feeling powerless. When we own our story, we release the guilt and negativity. We experience empowerment.

We can design a new ending to our story. Jim Loehr, author and performance psychologist, suggests we tell our story in five major subjects: work, family, health, happiness, and friendships. Your overall story of your life has many components, smaller stories within the larger story of your life.

Exercise: Consider Your Story

I challenge you to think about your story. Here are a few questions to consider:

- How did I get to where I am right now, both mentally and physically?

- What drove my passion to enter my chosen sport or career?

- What's my story about family? How important is family to me?

- What value do I place on my health? What led me to where I am with my health?

- How have I come to understand happiness and what leads me

to be happy?

- What's my story about friendship?

- How has my story about these areas defined how I see the world?

I also challenge you to write a brave new ending to your story. Here are a few questions to consider:

- What stories in my life are working and not working?

- Which story could use a fresh perspective?

- Which parts of my story are lies and not the complete truth?

- Which story will not allow me to get to where I want to in my life?

- What's the brave new ending that I want to write to my story?

Now, go write your brave new ending. I mean physically write it. Because when you change your story, you change your life. When you change your story, it will inspire you to move forward with what may be holding you back so you can stay gritty.

GET GRITTY

GET PURPOSE

MASTER THOUGHTS

KNOW SELF

DOMINATE CONTROLLABLES

OWN THE MOMENT

CHOOSE EMOTIONS

OWN WHO YOU ARE

LIVE AND LET GO

COURAGE ZONE

My High Performance Game Plan
OWN MY STORY

1. Next time I am faced with a difficulty, I'll ask, "How could this be worse?"

2. I'll begin to own my story by writing reflections on the questions in this chapter and considering the brave new ending I am creating.

3. Fill in the blank: I know I need to revise this story about

   _____

   in my life so I can create more happiness and reach my potential.

4. I can help others own their story by helping them understand how they got to where they are now, both physically and mentally.

My High Performance Power Phrase

I own my story! I am in control of my perspective and how I see myself and the world. This story creates my reality.

Chapter 42

Defeat Your Limiting Beliefs

"Many people are passionate, but because of their limiting beliefs about who they are and what they can do, they never take actions that could make their dream a reality." —TONY ROBBINS

Rebecca Williams didn't see herself as a runner. In fact, she had never even run a mile! But one day, while out for a walk, she had a moment of inspiration. She thought, *I can run a 5K . . . no, bigger . . . I can run half a marathon . . . no, bigger . . . I can run a marathon!* After that walk, running a marathon was something she just knew she had to do.

The training was not easy. "Preparing and training for a marathon is an all-consuming endeavor," she said. She started spending more time running and less time with her family. She had few people to run with; the only running groups she knew of were for elite runners, and she felt like she didn't belong with them. She didn't see herself as an athlete, and training for a marathon was so out of her comfort zone. Many of her training runs ended in tears. Still, she kept going. "If I don't do this, I won't ever do anything!" was the phrase that got her through.

Rebecca made it to race day. The first half of the marathon went well, but as the miles increased, the race got tough. By mile 20, Rebecca was struggling. She thought, "The wall is real. Everything hurts. I am going to collapse. Will I make it?" As other runners passed her, she knew that she would be the last person to finish the marathon that day. She kept going, putting one foot in front of the other. "What is harder? Quitting or explaining to people why I quit?" ran through her head.

I met Rebecca during the final mile of her marathon where I was volunteering as a member of the Sport Psych Team. She told me and a fellow member her story as we headed to the finish line. It had been a long 26.2 miles for her as she walked across the finish line. In fact, organizers were taking down the finish line as she crossed it. She finished just over seven hours—but she finished! She inspired loads of runners and spectators that day—including me—and was featured in *Runner's World Magazine* because of her courage, grit, and determination on that course.

Rebecca overcame her limiting beliefs about herself that day. She explained, "A lot of people would consider finishing dead last a shameful failure. But there was a boldness and confidence in me that was unleashed that day. I no longer struggle with self-doubt. I no longer shrink back from conflict. I stand and face any challenge life throws at me now. When faced with a challenge, I think to myself, 'I finished a marathon. Yes, it will be hard. But I can do anything!'" Rebecca faced her limiting beliefs head on. While doing so, she finished a marathon, something less than 1 percent of the population has done!

Limiting beliefs are beliefs that constrain us in some way. They can be about others, the world, and ourselves. They are typically broad statements that exist only in our head. We have a lot of limiting beliefs that we may not even be aware of, and these limiting beliefs reflect self-doubt and feelings of unworthiness.

You might recognize some of the following limiting beliefs:

- I am not smart enough.

- I don't have the ability to do that.

- My voice doesn't matter.

- I don't know enough of the right people.

- If I speak up, no one will like me or what I say.

- I am not important to my team.

- My coach and team don't care about me.

Underlying every limiting belief is the idea that we are not good enough. We must address our limiting beliefs because they are what limits us. You have the power right now in the present moment to change your limiting beliefs.

Break down those limiting beliefs that are holding you back.

You begin to fly when you address your limiting beliefs. You can move your vision for your future to new heights. As you change your beliefs, you change your experience and your future.

To address your limiting beliefs, follow these 5 steps:

1. First, ask yourself, "What are my limiting, or negative, beliefs about myself, what I can do, and the world?" Gently acknowledge what they are without judgment. Take time to evaluate if these beliefs are true or false.

2. Ask yourself, "Do I want to keep holding on to this limiting belief?" Consider what you're missing out on by holding onto them. Are you playing small? Are you holding yourself back? For example, the belief that your voice doesn't matter might mean you are not contributing ideas to your team.

3. Decide to conquer your limiting belief. Say out loud or in your head, "I no longer believe this to be true."

4. Without judgment, replace the belief. Ask yourself what belief would allow you to become all you could be?

5. Lastly, prove your new empowering beliefs true. Start noticing all the ways your new belief is proven true in your life.

As a high performer, you can't afford to let limiting beliefs become invisible barriers. When you limit yourself, others limit you, too. When you replace limiting beliefs, others will follow suit, doors will open, wrong doors will close, and you will attract the best that you deserve. You will begin to think more like the world's best. **Address those limiting beliefs to move toward your big vision and live your purpose.**

My High Performance Game Plan
DEFEATING YOUR LIMITING BELIEFS

1. Complete the following: I believe I cannot expand to my greater potential because _____ _____.

2. I commit to addressing my limiting beliefs on a daily basis.

3. This week, I'll notice the limiting beliefs that get in my way and know that I have the ability to overcome them.

4. I'll follow the 5-step model in this chapter to address one of my limiting beliefs this week.

My High Performance Power Phrase

I choose empowering beliefs so that I can reach my greater potential. I address my limiting beliefs as a daily practice. I choose empowering beliefs to stay gritty.

Practice 8
CONCLUDING THOUGHTS

Seriously, you are amazing! With each chapter you are getting mentally strong and gaining more useful strategies for your daily life. In Own Who You Are, you learned:

- You can "do you" and show up 100 percent authentically, guaranteed to find your next level.

- Let go of comparison because it is a trap—instead stay focused on being the best version of yourself.

- Your story creates your reality about life, and your destiny follows the story you create.

Now, take a moment to record the following on your Grit Board:

- 3 words that describe you when you're "doing you."

- A new empowering belief that you will begin to live by.

- A key phrase from this section such as "Do You," "Be the Best Version of Myself," or "Own My Story!"

Live and Let Go

MISTAKES

The world's best
know that people are not perfect.
They are kind to themselves, let go of
their mistakes quickly after learning from
them, and decide to live life full-out.

Chapter 43

Practice Self-Compassion

"A moment of self-compassion can change your entire day.
A string of such moments can change the course of your life."
—Christopher K. Germer

---

love watching Kerri Walsh Jennings compete. Kerri is confident, gritty, and authentic, all traits of high performers. Kerri is a three-time Olympic gold medalist in beach volleyball; she didn't lose a match in the 2004, 2008, and 2012 Olympics. In fact, she is one of the few athletes to have won three consecutive Olympic gold medals. At the 2016 Rio Olympics, however, she lost her first ever match to the second-ranked Brazilian team in three straight sets. It was a shocking loss for her and her partner, April Ross. Kerri placed the blame on herself and said on NBC, "I didn't show up. I wasn't passing the ball. . . . Tonight they rose to the occasion. I certainly did not, and there's no excuse for it."

The next day Kerri and April won the bronze medal match in four sets against the number one-ranked Brazilian team. At the end of the match, they were both emotional. The win meant a lot. That night I stayed up late watching their interview with Ryan Seacrest on NBC. In it, Kerri said something that I will never forget: "It was 24 hours of gnarly stuff. I thought, am I good enough? Do I have this? What did I do to my partner? It was gut-wrenching stuff [after losing the match]. To lose, and then to have to come back and win 24 hours later, that's why the tears after. I am so proud. . . . That bronze is right up there with my golds."

Kerri is one of the best beach volleyball players in the world, and even she sometimes questions if she still has it. It was nice to see that she is human like the rest of us. To come back and rebound the way she did to win bronze, however, Kerri had to show self-compassion. She had to be kind to herself as she was processing the loss. If she had continued to beat herself up all night and into the next day's match, things would have not turned out so positively. She would have likely been drained, lacking confidence, and unable to stay present during the match.

Do you ever find yourself questioning if you are good enough, just as Kerri did that night? Do you sometimes ruminate repeatedly over mistakes? Do you have a fear of failure that gets in your way of success? Have you ever beaten yourself up so much about a past performance that you can't perform better next time? If you are anything like me, you have.

The world's best have very high standards. They expect success. Along with high standards can come a difficulty letting go of mistakes. I've found that many elite athletes, talented coaches, and successful entrepreneurs have a hard time with self-compassion, or the practice of being kind to yourself. Often no one has taught them that such a practice is important. Instead they think that by beating themselves up, they are more likely to make the game-winning shot next time, complete that big project they are struggling to finish, or make it to the Pro Bowl. When I teach them about self-compassion, however, they play and perform more consistently even though they have already reached a high level of success. They tell me they are happier, less stressed, a better teammate, and treat their spouse in a kinder way.

The leading researcher on self-compassion, Dr. Kristen Neff, provides three elements of self-compassion in her book, *Self-Compassion: Stop Beating Yourself Up and Leave Insecurity Behind*. They are:

GET GRITTY

GET PURPOSE

MASTER THOUGHTS

KNOW SELF

DOMINATE CONTROLLABLES

OWN THE MOMENT

CHOOSE EMOTIONS

OWN WHO YOU ARE

LIVE AND LET GO

COURAGE ZONE

- Self-kindness – Being warm and kind to ourselves when we fail, make a mistake, or feel inadequate, rather than ignoring our pain or judging or criticizing ourselves.

- Common humanity – Acknowledging that suffering and feelings of personal inadequacy are part of the shared human experience rather than something that happens just only to one person.

- Mindfulness – Taking a balanced, nonjudgmental approach to observing our negative emotions so we don't suppress or exaggerate our feelings.

The practice of self-compassion is giving the same kindness to ourselves that we would give to others. It is about accepting yourself and recognizing you are not perfect. All humans are imperfect and mortal. Who ever said you needed to be perfect anyway? Likely no one! But we have this expectation in our mind that we need to be perfect.

Showing self-compassion means that you honor that you are human and accept that you are not perfect. When we don't practice self-compassion, we experience frustration, stress, suffering, and self-criticism, but when we accept our personal failures and mistakes we are more likely to take steps to improve ourselves. Staying gritty and reaching high performance requires adopting the mindset of constant and never-ending improvement. To reach your goals and to stay current and relevant, you need to constantly evolve your skills and mindset. Showing compassion to yourself is key.

Self-compassionate people can bounce back more easily from setbacks and are more likely to learn from their mistakes, a key factor in your high performance. Self-compassion is a powerful antidote to the perfectionistic thinking, stress, and anxiety that can lead to poor performance.

Self-compassion is not self-pity. That means that we don't get immersed in our mistakes, frustration, or suffering when we show self-compassion. There is no reason for drama; drama gets us further away from where we desire to go. Self-compassion also does not mean you are letting yourself get away with things. It doesn't mean you choose the ice cream instead of the fruit when you are trying to slim down, or you choose to watch a movie instead of train or study because you are being "kind to yourself." Self-compassion is not about making excuses for your bad choices. It means keeping your high standards, but being flexible and kind to yourself when you make mistakes.

Self-compassion is a practice; it is not a switch we can just flip on. Self-compassion is a habit we form by practicing kindness in the moment many times throughout our day. When you are kind to yourself, then you can be kind with others. As the Dalai Lama said, "One must be compassionate to one's self before external compassion."

Having compassion means that we gift others with our understanding and kindness when they fail or make a mistake. We avoid judging others harshly even though their mistake or shortcoming might impact our team's success or our family's opportunities. If we practice self-compassion, we are better able to forgive others, too.

Try the exercises below to increase your self-compassion.

Exercise: Increase Your Self-Compassion

1. *The Best-Friend Challenge:* A key in developing and practicing self-compassion is talking to yourself like you would talk to your best friend or family member. Take the Best Friend Challenge and each day this week make a commitment to be kind to yourself. Notice the tone of your self-talk and what you say to yourself. Make an effort to soften your self-critical voice and do so with compassion. You are always listening to yourself, so speak nicely!

2. *Self-Compassion Affirmation for High Performance:* To remind yourself to be kind and compassionate with yourself, read the following affirmation once a day:

I am kind to myself. I take a balanced approach when I make a mistake or experience a frustration or loss. I do not accept drama. Instead, I recognize that I am human and imperfect. I am doing the best I can. I accept myself as I am. I got it next time!

My High Performance Game Plan
PRACTICE SELF-COMPASSION

1. When I make a mistake or suffer a mishap this week, I'll remind myself to practice self-compassion.

2. I will share the science of self-compassion with others this week to encourage them to be kinder to themselves and others.

3. I can post the Self-Compassion Affirmation somewhere in my home or planner to remind myself to be more self-compassionate.

4. I commit to taking the Best-Friend Challenge and talking to myself like I would my best friend.

My High Performance Power Phrase
I am kind to myself. I am doing the best I can. I got it next time!

Chapter 44

Talk to Your Judge

"Every judgment blocks the light." —MARIANNE WILLIAMSON

A few years ago when I started working with a high-level lacrosse team, I could sense their negativity. Several of the team captains later told me, "We have the talent to win the state championship, but the culture is so negative. We are always getting on each other, judging each other and ourselves for not playing perfectly."

It took a deliberate shift in the culture by coaches, captains, and the team members to reduce the judgment and bring more positive energy. As we worked together, the athletes started taking better control of their thoughts, emotions, and actions. Using many of the tools in this book, they found their MVP level more consistently. They worked to stay more often in the present.

They started noticing and reducing the amount that they judged themselves and others. As a team, they developed the High Performance Mindset and the results were visibility noticeable. It was fun to watch them. They celebrated more on the field, brought more positive energy, and supported each other despite mistakes. The team started rolling and went all the way to the state championship—and they won! As the team captains predicted, they had the talent to do so, they just needed the mental attributes to make it happen.

Judgment is universal. It is a common ailment we all experience. We all judge ourselves and we experience the judgment of others, and it can be detrimental to our teams, our families, and ourselves. Judgment compels us to constantly find faults in and around us. When we judge, we think:

- What is wrong with me?

- What is wrong with you?

- What is wrong with things around me?

- What is wrong with my family?

- What is wrong with my team?

- What is wrong with this situation?

- What is wrong with this outcome?

- What is wrong with my ability?

We see things as bad rather than seeing them as a gift or opportunity. We focus on what is wrong instead of what is right. It may lead to thoughts like, "I'll be happy when . . ." The problem is that "when" is a moving target that is always changing.

Successful, high-achieving people are often especially tormented by their judge. They might appear happy and confident to the world, but many are privately tortured. This is rarely obvious to teammates, coaches, or others around them. I have seen this in all of my clients, including elite athletes, leaders, and entrepreneurs. We can all be sabotaged by this persistent judge.

Judgment impacts our success, happiness, confidence, and leadership. It generates anxiety, stress, anger, shame, and guilt. It causes issues with our relationships. Judgment plays a central role in team and professional conflicts, and we cannot lead effectively when we judge.

We don't see our worthiness and the worthiness of others when we judge. Our judge doesn't allow us to make the impact in the world that we were designed to make or to reach our greater potential. Our judge does not allow us to fully commit to our goals and dreams and become the best version of ourselves.

GET GRITTY

GET PURPOSE

MASTER THOUGHTS

KNOW SELF

DOMINATE CONTROLLABLES

OWN THE MOMENT

CHOOSE EMOTIONS

OWN WHO YOU ARE

LIVE AND LET GO

COURAGE ZONE

We think that without judgment, we would turn into lazy people and wouldn't achieve our goals and dreams. Without punishing ourselves for the mistakes we've made, we think we won't learn from them. If we don't feel bad, we will repeat them. We think that if we don't scare ourselves right now and make it worse than it is, we won't prevent the mistakes in the future.

But that is just plain wrong. In fact, it's just the opposite. Less judgment and more self-compassion make us feel alive. We are ready to go after our goals and dreams when we work to turn down or turn off the inner critic, our inner judge. The world's best work to reduce their judge.

This realization that we all have an internal judge had a profound impact on me. When I realized that we all have this judge, I became kinder to myself and to others. I still have high standards, but I have learned to recognize the judge in my own mind and when others are judging me. I can stay focused on being my best self every day, and comments from others roll off my back more often.

So, how do we address this judge? Use a version of the CAR Shift outlined in Chapter 16:

Catch it. Being aware that we all have a judge gives us permission to pay attention and helps us recognize that we are not suffering alone. When you notice and acknowledge your judge, you reduce the judge's power! A thought is just a thought, not a fact.

Address it. Look for ways to address your judge. Tell your judge why it is not accurate. We each tend to exaggerate the negative parts of a situation in our mind and make our judge bigger. Either talk back to your judge or decide to imagine it moving out of your mind like a cloud passing by. Start seeing the situation without your judge and ask yourself, "What is real here?"

Refocus it. Releasing your judge is essential. Instead of listening to your judge, get focused on the next step to reach your goals. Move on. Focus your attention elsewhere and decide to be kinder to yourself in the future.

Your judge can be overwhelming. It will take work and commitment to master your mindset. But it will be worth it! When your mind is working for you, you can reach higher levels of satisfaction, performance, and fulfillment in your life. You can go after your goals and dreams and make the impact you were designed to make. Notice your judge, talk to your judge, and ask yourself, "What is real here?"

GET GRITTY

GET PURPOSE

MASTER THOUGHTS

KNOW SELF

DOMINATE CONTROLLABLES

OWN THE MOMENT

CHOOSE EMOTIONS

OWN WHO YOU ARE

LIVE AND LET GO

COURAGE ZONE

My High Performance Game Plan
TALK TO YOUR JUDGE

1. I commit to judging myself and others less in order to connect at a deeper level.

2. Next time I notice my judge, I'll take a deep breath, talk to my judge, and ask myself, "What is real here?"

3. I will decide on a phrase I'll say in my head when I notice my judge. Try, "I see you, judge," and "Hi, judge. You won't get the best of me today!"

4. I can share with a good friend, teammate, or family member a time that I judged myself. What was the outcome?

My High Performance Power Phrase

I work to be kind to myself and reduce my judge. I see the good. I reduce my judge by noticing it and taking away its power.

Chapter 45

Foster a Growth Mindset

"I've missed more than 9,000 shots in my career. I've lost almost 300 games. 26 times I've been trusted to take the game-wining shot and missed. I've failed over and over and over again in my life. And that is why I succeed." —MICHAEL JORDAN

---

ow many times have you heard people say something like this?

Michael Jordan was a natural. He was born with talent.

Of course, Michael Jordan wasn't a natural and he was not born as the world's best. Instead, evidence suggests that he is the world's hardest-working basketball player.

It is well known that Michael was cut from his high school varsity team. The college team he wanted to play for, North Carolina State University, also didn't recruit him, and two of the first NBA teams that could have chosen Jordan in the draft did not. We laugh when we hear this. How could these coaches or an NBA team pass on one of the greatest?

What people don't pay attention to is the fact that while Jordan had talent, it was the real work he put in that made him one of the world's greatest. When he was cut by his varsity team, his mother told him, "Go back and discipline yourself." And he followed her advice! He started waking up at six a.m. to practice before school. His college coach said he was constantly working to improve his shooting and ball handling; his coach was floored by this work ethic. One year after his college team lost the final game of the season, he shot for several hours to get ready for next year. The former Bulls assistant coach, John Bach, said this about Jordan: "He is a genius who constantly wants to upgrade his genius."

The one time in which Jordan coasted was the year he returned to the Bulls after playing baseball. When the Bulls were eliminated in the playoffs, he knew he didn't give his all. He said, "You can't leave and think you can come back and dominate this game. I will be physically and mentally prepared from now on." And he was. For the next three years, the Bulls won the NBA title. He continued to out-work everyone, and as a result, he is a legend—one of the best to ever play the game. Jordan said, "The mental toughness and heart are a lot stronger than the physical advantages you might have. I've always said that and believed that."

Jordan embraced his failures and took a growth mindset approach to life and basketball. He saw every setback as a comeback and every difficulty as an opportunity to learn and grow.

According to over thirty years of research by Carol Dweck, a professor at Stanford University, we face challenges with either a "growth mindset" or "fixed mindset." When we adopt a fixed mindset, we see our ability, intelligence, and athletic talent as fixed at birth and unable to be changed. When we adopt a growth mindset, we believe we can grow and change for the better. We believe our ability is gained through hard work and dedication, and that natural-born talent is a starting point. We believe we can get better at something given the right opportunities, support, hard work, and belief.

When we adopt a growth mindset, we see challenges as exciting and find optimistic ways of explaining adversity. We focus on giving our best effort, and our attention is on how we can learn and grow instead of on our win-loss record. We continuously seek help from others because that is the way we learn and improve. We believe our qualities can improve with effort and constant learning. We can grow our talents, abilities, and intelligence. We learn from criticism and are open to information about ourselves, even if it isn't flattering. We find inspiration from the success of others.

When we adopt a fixed mindset, we avoid challenges and see them as threatening. Every situation is a test of whether we are good enough. We think that our qualities are just set in stone. We think we are stuck with the intelligence, personality traits, mental skills, and creative abilities we have now. We believe that failure is worse than trying at all. We focus on the outcome, and because of that, we fear screwing up and looking silly or like an idiot. We are crushed by mistakes and see them as an embarrassment. We see a missed shot, a loss at a championship, a C-, or a rejection letter as a setback, not a comeback.

When we adopt a fixed mindset, we take a pessimistic view of adversity and believe we don't have the right skills, that we are not enough. We give up easily, ignore criticism, and make excuses for our poor performance. We play the blame game and feel threatened by the success of others.

How can we accomplish our goals, stay gritty, and reach high performance if we are fixed where we are and adopt a fixed mindset?

We absolutely cannot.

The research confirms this. People with a growth mindset are significantly grittier than people with a fixed mindset. A growth mindset has been linked to achievement, more happiness, healthier relationships, and a higher motivation. Dweck's research confirmed that growth-minded athletes, CEOs, musicians, and scientists all loved what they did and got to the top as a by-product of their enthusiasm for it, whereas many of the fixed-minded people did not love what they did. Growth mindset leads us to focus on the process over the outcome and is one of the ways to get in our flow zone more often.

You might be thinking, "Of course, I have a growth mindset!" But I have found we easily default to a fixed mindset even if we believe we adopt a growth mindset. Our knee-jerk reaction to failure, challenges, and setbacks is to get frustrated and impatient. I've seen this in all my clients. Our set point may be to adopt the pessimistic fixed mindset, to judge the ability of ourselves and others. The key is to catch ourselves when we adopt the fixed mindset.

Here are three ways to help you develop a growth mindset:

1. Add the word "yet" to the end of your statement.

Fixed Mindset: "I don't get it . . . I can't do it . . . this doesn't work . . ."

Growth Mindset: "I don't get it . . . *yet.*" "I can't do it . . . *yet.*" "This doesn't work . . . *yet.*"

2. Catch yourself when you surrender to the pessimistic, fixed mindset, and change your thought to an optimist growth mindset.

Fixed Mindset: "She's a natural-born singer."

Growth Mindset: "She has worked hard to get to where she is."

Fixed Mindset: "This project is just too hard."

Growth Mindset: "I will conquer this project by staying relaxed and working hard."

Fixed Mindset: "I'm just no good at dancing."

Growth Mindset: "I can learn to be a great dancer with practice."

Fixed Mindset: "Coach/my boss is so rude to me.
                     He is always on my case."

Growth Mindset: "Coach gives me feedback so I can improve
                     and grow."

Fixed Mindset: "I am who I am."

Growth Mindset: "I can always improve and grow."

3. Commit to using at least one of the following Growth Mindset
    Phrases each day to stay gritty. Try these:

"Mistakes help me learn a lot about myself."

"I choose to challenge myself."

"I like to get out of my comfort zone."

"I am inspired by people who succeed."

"I can learn anything that I want to."

"I like to try new things."

"I embrace failure instead of fight it."

"I am always working to get better."

"Feedback is a great way to grow and learn."

GET GRITTY

GET PURPOSE

MASTER THOUGHTS

KNOW SELF

DOMINATE CONTROLLABLES

OWN THE MOMENT

CHOOSE EMOTIONS

OWN WHO YOU ARE

LIVE AND LET GO

COURAGE ZONE

FOSTER A GROWTH MINDSET

1. The next time I experience a setback like a poor game, a rejection letter, or an injury, I'll see it as a challenge to overcome.

2. When I catch myself using a fixed mindset, I'll change it to a growth mindset, adding "yet" to the end of my sentence.

3. When I try something new this week, I'll remind myself that doing new things is fun and exciting.

4. To begin to adopt a growth mindset more regularly, I'll write one of the Growth Mindset Phrases in a place where I will see it each day and stay focused on improvement.

My High Performance Power Phrase

I can learn anything with hard work and dedication. When I get frustrated with my progress, I will remind myself I just haven't done it yet.

Chapter 46

Strive for Excellence, Not Perfection

"Failure happens all the time. It happens every day in practice. What makes you better is how you react to it." —MIA HAMM

Mia Hamm is considered by many to be one of the greatest female soccer players to ever play the game. She won two Olympic gold medals, and was the World Player of the Year twice. Hamm held the record for the most international goals, male or female, in the history of soccer until 2013. She is legendary. She is also a great example of a person who works to keep her perfectionism in check.

Just prior to the 1999 World Cup, she failed to score in eight consecutive matches. The team lost to their rival, China, twice. Hamm was struggling. Her coach, Tony DiCicco, could tell. He said, "Mia, because she is so hypercritical, has always had to deal at times with less confidence than she wants. She puts so much demand on herself. It's why she's the greatest scorer in history. But those high standards are hard to reach on a consistent basis. If she doesn't feel she can reach those demands, she feels inadequate. It wears on her. I respect how she got through the year. It was a tremendous mental battle for her."

Hamm turned it around and played lights-out in the World Cup later that year. Reflecting on how perfectionism got the best of her, she said, "I want to do things as perfectly as I can. Obviously, it's not going to happen, but it's a good source of motivation. Sometimes it can work against me . . . I was worried about what people outside my support system were saying. I needed to go out and play for the reason I always played, because I loved what I do. I lost sight of that . . . I wasn't having any fun out there. I was critiquing every little thing I did."

When Hamm was asked, "What is the most important thing for a soccer player to have?" she said without hesitation, "Mental toughness. It is one of the most difficult aspects of soccer and one I struggle with every game and every practice."

One of the key characteristics that separate great athletes, entrepreneurs, and leaders from the rest is a burning desire to be at their best. High performers know they can be more than they already are. This desire, however, can result in negative tendencies that undermine performance, happiness, and grit. It can lead to an intense dissatisfaction with mistakes. This is what happened at times for Hamm.

Research by my performance psychology colleagues suggests that the best athletes in the world have perfectionistic tendencies. One study by Dan Gould and colleagues revealed that Olympians were moderately perfectionistic in a good way. They had high personal standards and levels of organization, but had low concern for mistakes, criticism, or self-doubt.

There are two types of perfectionism: adaptive and maladaptive, or positive and negative. The adaptive form of perfectionism can provide the drive that leads to great achievement and striving for excellence in sports, business, and life. People who are adaptively perfectionistic work with intense effort and drive to reach their high standards. They are highly motivated to be at their personal best, get pleasure from pursuing their goals, and are driven to succeed. They take their mistakes in stride, realizing no one is perfect. This good form of perfectionism can also result in outcomes that help performance, like low negativity, less self-criticism, and high self-esteem.

The maladaptive form of perfectionism can be damaging. This type of perfectionism is one of the most common psychological issues that I deal with as a sport and performance psychology specialist. This maladaptive form leads to procrastination, rumination over past events and mistakes, and avoidance of competition or practice. It can cut at our confidence and shred our self-esteem. We focus on avoiding failure instead of making things happen. We rarely feel good after a performance or at the end of our day even if we gave our best effort. The negative form can kill the fun that drew us to the activity, job, career, or sport in the first place, leading to burnout, anxiety, and avoiding pressure situations. These negative emotions prevent us from getting into their flow zone.

Nearly every high-level athlete, entrepreneur, and leader who I have worked with has perfectionistic tendencies. This can be a very good thing because they have high standards, continuously give their best effort, and are driven to succeed. Their perfectionism got them where they are. But often individuals come to me with many attributes of the negative perfectionism. For example, one NFL star continuously beat himself up over a dropped pass, poor block, or a missed assignment. He would ruminate over the mistake three or four days after the game. He expected himself to be perfect. This rumination led to a lack of confidence and hesitation at critical parts in the game. In our work together, we maintained the high standards he had for himself, but worked to modify his perfectionism. His consistency, happiness, and grit improved.

How do we keep perfectionism from sabotaging us, our grit, and consistently being at our best? Here are a few ideas to get you started:

- Have high standards and strive for excellence instead of believing you must always be perfect. Being perfect is impossible. Striving for excellence is achievable, believable,

GET GRITTY

GET PURPOSE

MASTER THOUGHTS

KNOW SELF

DOMINATE CONTROLLABLES

OWN THE MOMENT

CHOOSE EMOTIONS

OWN WHO YOU ARE

LIVE AND LET GO

COURAGE ZONE

and within your reach.

- Focus on why you do what you do. The maladaptive form of perfectionism can accompany an intense concern over what others like parents, bosses, coaches, or friends think. You may focus on letting them down. Instead, focus on why you love what you do to replace those worrisome thoughts.

It is good to have high expectations and strive for success. It keeps us going and energized. But perfection is unattainable. When we embrace our imperfections, we free ourselves of needless suffering. We come closer to thinking like the world's best. Instead of striving for perfection, work to see your imperfections as evidence that you are human.

My High Performance Game Plan

STRIVE FOR EXCELLENCE, NOT PERFECTION

1. I refuse to beat myself up for my shortcomings, mistakes, or failures.

2. The next time I ruminate over a mistake or a past event, I'll remind myself of what I learned and how much my effort matters.

3. I can give myself a gut-check and ask, "Am I striving for excellence?" If not, I should step up my standards.

4. Remind myself that it is irrational to believe that I can be perfect. Instead, I will focus on loving what I do, and keep learning and growing.

My High Performance Power Phrase

**I have a burning desire to be at my best.
I am driven to succeed. I focus on why
I love to do what I do.**

Chapter 47

Learn, Burn, and Return After Mistakes

"It is impossible to live without failing at something, unless you live so cautiously that you might as well not have lived at all. In which case, you fail by default." —J.K. ROWLING

When talking about how to handle mistakes, I always ask my clients, "Can you think of someone you know who made one mistake, and then that one mistake continued to snowball?" Recently when I ask that question, about nine out of ten times they say something like, "Yeah, remember Jordan Spieth at the 2016 Masters? Man, that was crazy!"

If you weren't watching the Masters, let me give you the short version. The 22-year-old Spieth was in prime position to win his second green jacket with nine holes to go. The year before he had won his first major, the 2015 Masters, and tied the 72-hole record making him the second youngest to win it (behind Tiger Woods). Spieth had a five-shot lead heading into the back nine and was looking like he might be the first player to win back-to-back Masters. On the 10th and 11th holes, he bogeyed (one stroke over par) both holes. Then, on hole 12, he fell apart. He said, "I didn't take that extra deep breath and really focus on my line on 12. Instead I went up and I just put a quick swing on it." He ended up hitting two balls in the water on a par-3 hole, recording a quadruple-bogey (that's four strokes over par!), dropping him to a tie for fourth, three shots back. He finished second in the tournament, losing to Danny Willett by three strokes. Writers called Spieth's performance the "The Ultimate Choke," "The Worst Master's Choke Ever," and "The Most Shocking in Golf History."

Spieth responded graciously and said just two weeks after the Masters, "I'm not taking it very hard. I laugh about it now. I really do. I've had ladies at grocery stores coming up and putting their hand on me and going, 'I'm really praying for you. How are you doing?' And I'm like, 'My dog didn't die. It happens!'"

In golf, it is easy to see mistakes snowball and spiral out of control. That is one of the reasons I love watching the sport. You can see clearly how the mind plays a role in performance.

As children, we failed many times. Think about how you mastered one of the most difficult skills, walking. You likely don't remember learning to walk, but your parents probably remember when you did. I remember watching my two boys learn to do it. They fell many times and I didn't think anything of it. I knew they needed to fall to learn. As we get older, we can forget to take this easy-going approach to failure. We forget to fail forward.

Failure is inevitable and essential for us to perform at our very best. We often think of failure as any time we don't meet our own expectations or reach our goals. But failure doesn't need to paralyze you. In fact, as a leader in your house, your team, your business, or of yourself, you can communicate to those around you that failure is a good thing, a learning tool. Failure isn't a reason to punish someone.

The world's best recognize that failures will occur and the real enemy is fear of failure.

The world's best have failed many times, and they view mistakes as mis-takes. Viewing failure as shameful creates anxiety, tension, and pain, emotions that do not support high performance. The mindset that you can fail forward will help you

GET GRITTY

GET PURPOSE

MASTER THOUGHTS

KNOW SELF

DOMINATE CONTROLLABLES

OWN THE MOMENT

CHOOSE EMOTIONS

OWN WHO YOU ARE

LIVE AND LET GO

COURAGE ZONE

relax, get in the flow zone, and improve your current performance.

There are four myths of failure that you might have learned at an early age. But these are myths, not truths. They are false beliefs, and you can change what you believe. These myths are:

- *Myth 1: I am my mistakes.* Some people internalize failure and see it as a reflection of themselves. They see their mistakes as validation of their negative self-talk. But you are not your mistakes! There is no reason to allow mistakes to negatively impact your self-worth.

- *Myth 2: I can avoid failure if I just work hard enough.* We all experience failure at some level. It is something that cannot be avoided unless we do nothing or be nothing. As Soichiro Honda, the CEO and Founder of Honda Motors, said, "Success is 99 percent failure."

- *Myth 3: Failure is useless.* Failure can teach you even more than success can. How we see failure can impact our wealth, according to a study presented by author Lewis Schiff. Only 17.5 percent of middle-class participants in his survey agreed with the statement, "Failure has taught me what I'm good at," whereas 78.1 percent of people described as high-net worth (between $10 million and $30 million) and 94.9 percent of individuals of ultra-high-net worth (defined as $30 million or more) agreed with the statement. The point? Those with high-net worth saw failure as a chance to fail-forward.

- *Myth 4: Failure is harmful.* It can be easy to exaggerate negative emotions when we fail. But failure is what you make of it. A mistake is only a mistake if you believe it is a mistake. We choose how we label something. Choose to view the mistake or failure as an opportunity forward.

When I teach elite athletes, entrepreneurs, and leaders how to let go of their mistakes, I talk about Learn, Burn, and Return, a catchy strategy for their High Performance Toolbox. You can use it anytime you are having difficulty letting go of a mistake or failure.

Learn, Burn, and Return goes like this:

Learn: Consider what you learned from the mistake objectively. While doing so, stay unemotional and focused on what you plan to do in the future instead of in the past. To do this, start a sentence with, "Next time I will . . ." Think of what you learned in an objective, factual way instead of a subjective, biased way, and avoid taking the mistake to heart.

Let's say you were unprepared for a big talk or presentation and as a result you didn't deliver your best performance. You could learn by thinking, "Next time I will make sure I devote one or two more hours to prepare for this type of presentation." Or, if you overslept for a meeting or appointment, you could learn by reflecting, "Next time I will go to bed on time." Or, if you were Jordan Spieth, you might learn by reflecting, "Next time I will take a deep breath before each and every hole to stay calm and relaxed."

Burn: The next step after learning from the mistake is to burn it. By this I mean let it go. This step is important because you cannot think about two things at once; you cannot think about the mistake in the past and what you need to do in the present moment at the same time. To burn the mistake, consider choosing one of these actions or phrases to use the next time you make a mistake:

Burn Phrases: "Let it go!" "Flush it." "Move on." "Burn it."

Burn Action: You could also choose an action to symbolize letting it go such as brushing down your arm with your hand as if you are brushing off the mistake, picking up a piece of grass and letting the mistake go when the blade of grass leaves your hand, or adjusting your headband or your socks to symbolize to yourself that you let the mistake go and are moving on. I find that if you use a phrase and an action, the impact is more powerful.

GET GRITTY

GET PURPOSE

MASTER THOUGHTS

KNOW SELF

DOMINATE CONTROLLABLES

OWN THE MOMENT

CHOOSE EMOTIONS

OWN WHO YOU ARE

LIVE AND LET GO

COURAGE ZONE

---

*What burn phrase or action do you want to choose
to let the mistake go?*

Return: After you have learned and burned, it's important to keep your self-talk and body language confident. You "return" to thinking and feeling confident despite the mistake. No one should know that you made a mistake from watching you. The mistake should not be evident on your face or reflected in your body language. If the mistake is apparent on your body, it will be more difficult to get back into your flow zone. Your self-talk should also remain confident. Repeat Power Phrases in your mind to ensure the mistake doesn't impact your confidence and belief in yourself (see Chapter 14). Remind yourself that you are ready!

You can use the Learn, Burn, and Return strategy anytime you make a mistake at work, in your business, with your family, or during a game or practice. If you are an athlete or coach, it may be difficult to use the strategy during the play of the game when it could take your attention away from the present moment. Wait until you have a break in the game (a timeout, between periods, or between plays) and then implement it.

My High Performance Game Plan
LEARN, BURN, RETURN AFTER MISTAKES

1. Next time I experience a mistake or failure, I'll remember that we all experience failure at some level.

2. I can bust through the Myths of Failure, reminding myself that my mistakes don't define me, failure is helpful, failure is inevitable, and I decide how to view failure.

3. I will use the Learn, Burn, and Return strategy regularly to let go of failure and mistakes so I can remain confident and at my best.

4. I can tell a friend, colleague, or family member about the Learn, Burn, and Return strategy to help them let go of mistakes and remain confident.

My High Performance Power Phrase

I see failure and mistakes as opportunity to learn and grow. I take an easy-going approach when I fail. I remember to learn, burn, and return.

Practice 9

CONCLUDING THOUGHTS

Almost to the finish line! In Live and Let Go, you learned:

- You can practice self-compassion by showing yourself kindness throughout your day and/or when you make a mistake.

- You can use the CAR shift to reduce your internal judge.

- You can adopt a growth mindset where you see challenges as exciting.

- And it's best to view the mistake as a mis-take and "learn, burn, and return" to bust through the myths of failure.

Now, take a moment to record the following on your Grit Board:

- A Growth Mindset Phrase to keep you focused on improvement.

- A key phrase from this section such as "Be Kind to Myself," "I Just Haven't Yet," or "Learn, Burn, Return!"

10

Choose Your Courage Zone

YOUR COMFORT ZONE

MAGIC

COURAGE ZONE

The world's best
feel uncomfortable regularly. When we stay
in our comfort zone, we don't grow.
High performers know that magic happens
in their courage zone.

Chapter 48

Find Your Magic

"If you are growing, you will always be out of your comfort zone." —JOHN MAXWELL

Afew years ago, I had the opportunity to get out of my comfort zone in a big way. I was asked to dance in a local version of the competition *Dancing with the Stars*. The competition was similar to the popular NBC show, but performed in my hometown to raise money for the American Red Cross.

Sounds easy enough, right? Local, not on TV . . . except that 3,000 people would be gathered to watch us dance. I was paired with Wade, a dubstep (hip-hop dance to electronic music) dancer. I felt fairly confident at first, until I searched for more information on dubstep dance, and I saw video after video of professional dancers crushing it.

Then anxiety took over.

I started learning dubstep and the anxiety didn't stop. "I am a runner, not a dancer," I thought. "Wade is so much better than me at this! I don't look like a dancer!" In a two-week span, we had only learned about ten seconds of our routine even though we practiced every day. I was stuck.

As I drove home from the dance studio after the tenth practice, I imagined getting halfway through the routine and freezing on stage.

"Geez, Cindra. This is what you do for a living. You help people get unstuck. You have to pull it together!" I thought. That's when I had an ah-ha moment. I realized I was stuck in my comfort zone: questioning if I had what it takes to do something new, afraid of trying new moves, thinking small, and believing that I wasn't a dancer.

I made a decision that very moment to take a big leap out of that zone. From that moment forward, each time that I felt that pit in my stomach while learning and performing the routine, I leaned in and worked to dance with passion, courage, and energy. I took a deep breath of confidence when I walked into practice and told myself, "I am a dancer." I started dressing like a dancer. I tried every move that Wade asked me to, believing I could master them all. "I am a dancer. I am a dancer. I am a dancer," I repeated in my head.

As a result, we performed an incredible dubstep routine and earned a second-place finish. And a cool and unintended benefit? My business grew 20 percent after that performance. More people knew who I was and what I did because of it. There is power in getting out of your comfort zone!

When we stay in our comfort zone, we do not grow. We play small and live small. We just survive, settle for less, and are okay with being like everyone else. We let fear, doubt, regret, and insecurity get the best of us when we live and work in our comfort zone, resulting in mediocrity. Our comfort zone is entirely of our own making. Many people live there—but not high performers or the world's best!

Growth happens outside of your comfort zone because you are developing and expanding yourself. You try new things, connect with new people, talk in front of large groups, and conquer your fears. You act with courage and bravery. You take calculated risks, turning "impossible" into "I'm possible," and pursue your dreams.

Welcome to your Courage Zone, where the results feel like magic! Yes, you will feel uncomfortable and experience failure, mistakes, and change in your Courage Zone. But it is the only place where you can reach your full

GET GRITTY

GET PURPOSE

MASTER THOUGHTS

KNOW SELF

DOMINATE CONTROLLABLES

OWN THE MOMENT

CHOOSE EMOTIONS

OWN WHO YOU ARE

LIVE AND LET GO

COURAGE ZONE

potential or high performance. It is the only place that true happiness occurs, because happiness doesn't occur when you wonder what you could have been; it happens when you are growing. High performance, happiness, and a life lived to your full potential begin at the end of your comfort zone. Your grit is begging you to live in your Courage Zone consistently.

In the field of performance psychology, we use often use the phrase **"Get Comfortable Being Uncomfortable,"** which I first heard repeated by Dr. Ken Ravizza. The phrase means to regularly move outside of your comfort zone by pushing past perceived barriers and limitations. Perceived barriers include emotional discomfort such as fear, doubt, and insecurity, as well as physical discomfort such as tiredness or soreness.

COMFORT ZONE

Safety and Security, Playing Small, Settling, Things I Usually Do, Just Surviving, Don't Stand Out, Doubt, Insecurity, Mediocrity, Fear, Depression

Most People Live Here.

COURAGE ZONE
WHERE MAGIC OCCURS

Courage and Bravery, Playing Big, Things I've Never Tried, Things I am Afraid Of, Opportunity, Hard and Difficult, Okay Standing Out, Risk, Fearlessness, No Regrets, Self-Discovery, Financial Freedom, Pursing Your Dreams, Grit, High Performance

Few People Live Here.

What does it mean to stay in your comfort zone? It might look like this:

- You want to run a 5K, but you stop running each time your legs feel fatigued.

- You want to move out of your parents' home, but "forget" to go apartment shopping.

- You say you want to stop smoking, but sneak cigarettes on the back patio when no one is watching.

- You say you want to be a state champion, but choose to party with your friends instead of working out.

- You say you want to lose weight, but can't stop eating chocolate before you go to bed.

- You say you want to get in shape, but oversleep each morning instead of going to the gym.

Think of how baby elephants are trained. From birth, they are confined to very small spaces; their trainer ties a rope around their leg and attaches the rope to a wooden post. The baby elephant isn't strong enough to snap the rope. It can try to day after day but won't be able to, so the baby elephant early on learns it can't break the rope. When the elephant grows to its adult size (typically five tons!), it is perfectly capable of breaking the rope. But the elephant doesn't even try. A puny rope confines the five-ton elephant. This is your comfort zone in action.

You only need a moment of courage to move out of your comfort zone and into Your Courage Zone. A moment is all it takes! Courage is not the absence of fear or doubt, but it *is* the ability to do something that is scary. We can train our minds to act more courageously every day. Commit to doing one thing that is uncomfortable or a little scary each day: call the person you need to, try that new play, or speak in front of that group. Small changes lead to big results. Don't settle for mediocre because you are scared to step out of your

GET GRITTY

GET PURPOSE

MASTER THOUGHTS

KNOW SELF

DOMINATE CONTROLLABLES

OWN THE MOMENT

CHOOSE EMOTIONS

OWN WHO YOU ARE

LIVE AND LET GO

COURAGE ZONE

comfort zone. See your step into your Courage Zone as adventurous and exciting, not scary or nerve-racking. As children, we are natural risk takers, but as we grow we hold back and attempt fewer things. Live life like a child and, as Nike says, "Just do it!"

When you step outside your comfort zone, you are creating who you will become. Take the leap and accept the 7-Day Challenge. To do so, each day this week, commit to doing something that is uncomfortable and scary. Do at least one thing each day in your Courage Zone to help create the life of your dreams! As Eleanor Roosevelt said, "Do one thing that scares you every day."

My High Performance Game Plan
FIND YOUR MAGIC

1. I will make a list of activities in both my comfort zone and my Courage Zone to understand how I am playing small.

2. When I encounter something that makes me uncomfortable this week, I'll go for it. I'll remind myself to choose courage and make it happen.

3. I will remember that in my Courage Zone, mistakes, failure, and change will take place. I'm going to embrace that.

4. I will complete the 7-Day Challenge this week and do one thing each day that is uncomfortable and scary. All it takes is a moment of courage!

My High Performance Power Phrase

I choose my Courage Zone over my Comfort Zone. I will play big, try new things, and act with courage and bravery. I get comfortable being uncomfortable.

Chapter 49

Choose Courage Over Fear

"Everything you want is on the other side of fear."
—JACK CANFIELD

In the last several years, my consulting practice has grown considerably. I attribute this growth to my ability to choose courage over fear on a daily basis. For many years, I was afraid to stand out. I let fear get the best of me. I wondered what people would think. I questioned if I could work big. I doubted if I could work with my dream clients. I thought too often, "I can't do that. I'm a woman." I delivered content and activities like others in my field. I played and lived small.

Magic started happening as I began studying fear and how to address it. I started to understand and live the four Fear Facts, which I'll share with you soon. Learning about fear was a game changer for me. I started reaching out to my dream clients, doing things differently than others in my field, and embracing standing out. I started playing and living bigger.

My biggest growth experience as a professional has involved my work with college, high school, and NFL football players and teams. While working with football teams, I stand out. I do not look like others in the room. I am usually the only woman in the room. I am also short (around 5' 2"), whereas most of the athletes on the football teams are around 6 feet tall!

Though I have studied and watched and mastered the mental game of football, I did not grow up playing football. I watched it often growing up (my most memorable experiences are watching it with my dad). There have been many times that my gender, size, and lack of on-field experience could have stopped me from making a difference and helping the athletes and teams I work with to master their mental game. In those times, if I listened to my fear, many successful athletes wouldn't have learned how to improve their mental game. Perhaps these athletes and teams wouldn't have had such successful careers or seasons.

But I didn't listen to fear. Instead, I began to see how being a woman was an advantage in the football space. I did this with the help of other professional women in performance psychology who work with male teams. They taught me to see how my demeanor and approach are valuable to football culture. This shift in my mindset allowed me to embrace my authenticity and to be more comfortable standing out. It has helped me live and play even bigger. It has helped me choose courage daily.

So what are the Fear Facts that I worked to embrace? They are:

FEAR FACT 1: Fear lives in the future. Everything you fear is self-created. You are fantasizing about your future in a negative way. What you fear is not real; it is in your imagination. You are likely imagining the worst-case scenario instead of the best-case scenario or my-scenario. We experience these three types of fears most often.

- *We fear pain.* What if I try something new and fail? What if I go for that national championship and don't even get close? What if I go after the job of my dreams, position of my dreams, or my dream clients and fail? What if I lose money, status in my community, or the confidence that I have what it takes? We ask a lot of "what if?" questions when we dwell in the future. *Instead of fearing pain, think courageously: "I can do anything I want in the present moment."*

GET GRITTY

GET PURPOSE

MASTER THOUGHTS

KNOW SELF

DOMINATE CONTROLLABLES

OWN THE MOMENT

CHOOSE EMOTIONS

OWN WHO YOU ARE

LIVE AND LET GO

COURAGE ZONE

- *We fear difficulty.* We fear that it is going to be hard. We make up stories in our mind about how difficult it will be. We fear the hours, days, or years of hard work we will have to put in. We don't own our goals and dreams. We think things are impossible. *Instead of fearing difficulty, think courageously: "I can handle anything that comes my way."*

- *We fear the result.* We can become fully focused on the result or outcome. We become consumed by things we can't control such as winning, other people, or the economy. We question if we have what it takes to achieve the result or outcome we want in the future. We think about how our failure will continue in the future. *Instead of fearing the results, think courageously about the one action you can take in the present moment.*

To address your fear, think and act courageously in the present moment. Remember, you only need a moment of courage to do so. Accept the past, live and play in the moment, and look forward to the future with courage instead.

FEAR FACT 2: Choosing courage will feel better than denying your fear. As Nelson Mandela said, "Courage is not the absence of fear." Courage is feeling the fear and choosing to act bravely instead. There is no need for courage if you aren't scared of something. As my friend and fellow mental coach for high-performing athletes JF Menard told me when he visited the *High Performance Mindset Podcast*, "The best in the world are not fearless, they just fear less." See? You need fear or you can't act in a courageous way.

You will feel better acting courageously and staring fear in the face than refusing to take risks and living with the feeling of dread. Addressing your fear is less frightening than feeling helpless, powerless, or regretful. If you resist or deny fear, you are just keeping fear alive. And that can have a lasting impact on your grit, happiness, and performance.

FEAR FACT 3: Fear will always be there when you are trying something new and growing. Fear applies to everyone. In fact, whenever you are trying something new, taking on a new project, going after a new goal, or stretching yourself emotionally or physically in some way, you will experience fear. You might fear asking your boss for a raise or making the call that can change your business. The very thing that you fear can provide you with your greatest growth experience. Doing what is scary will allow you to address your fear.

One of my clients—let's call him Kevin—wanted to start competing in triathlons, but feared the swim. He didn't see himself as a swimmer, and worried that he would drown. He knew his fear was irrational. He could swim well—it was just an excuse. His courage moment took place when he registered for an adult swim class. When he stopped making excuses and acted courageously in the moment, he gifted himself with an opportunity to gain more confidence and skill. Those twenty seconds of courage made a difference.

FEAR FACT 4: To reach high performance, you must do what scares you. Fear can paralyze you if you let it. It is a four-letter word that can be harmful to our grit, happiness, and performance. Some people let the fear stop them from taking the necessary steps to achieve their goals and dreams. They worry about their performance and worry if they will win or lose. They worry about their business, their future, or their families, and the fear they feel stops them from reaching their full potential.

The world's best choose courage instead of fear. They feel the fear, but don't let it keep them from doing what they want to, have to, or were designed to do. High performers know that the fear means they are doing something important and meaningful. To reach their goals and dreams requires a risk. As Jimmy Johnson, the coach who led the Dallas Cowboys to two consecutive Super Bowls, once said, "Do you want to be safe and good, or do you want to take a chance and be great?"

High performers choose courage words such as "I know . . ." instead

GET GRITTY

GET PURPOSE

MASTER THOUGHTS

KNOW SELF

DOMINATE CONTROLLABLES

OWN THE MOMENT

CHOOSE EMOTIONS

OWN WHO YOU ARE

LIVE AND LET GO

COURAGE ZONE

of "I hope . . ." in order to remain confident and excited in the future. "I know . . ." statements give us the courage to do what is scary.

"I hope I can be successful" becomes "I know I can be successful."

"I hope I play well today" becomes "I know I will play well today."

"I hope my day goes great" becomes "I know my day will go great."

Exercise: Awareness of Fear

To bring awareness to your fear, make a list of things that you fear or are afraid to do. Start each statement beginning with *"If I wasn't afraid, I would . . ."* For example, a list like this might include statements such as: "If I wasn't afraid, I would compete in an Ironman, ask Samantha on a date, and submit my resume for a new job."

Then, turn these fears into "I know" statements. Then your list might become, "I know I can compete in an Ironman, I know I can ask Samantha on a date, and I know I can submit my resume for a new job." Post your new list of "I knows" where you can see it daily to remind yourself of what you know.

My High Performance Game Plan
CHOOSE COURAGE OVER FEAR

1. This week when I feel fear, I'll remember that everyone experiences fear when they are growing and learning. It simply means that I am doing something important and meaningful.

2. When I experience fear, I'll remind myself that the very thing I fear will provide me with a great growth experience.

3. I commit this week to building awareness about my fears. I'll complete the Awareness of Fear Exercise and change my fears into "I know" statements.

4. I'm going to decide to choose courage over fear. I'll flex my courage muscle and remind myself that I can do anything in the present moment.

My High Performance Power Phrase

I choose courage over fear. I flex my courage muscle, take a deep breath in, and go for it.

Chapter 50

Turn Impossible to "I'm Possible"

"Nothing is impossible...the word itself says 'I'm possible.'"
—AUDREY HEPBURN

On May 25, 1961, then-U.S. President John F. Kennedy stood before Congress and requested an additional seven billion dollars for the space program. Seven billion dollars is a lot of money! His request was to support landing a man on the moon over the next five years. He said,

> "I believe that this nation should commit itself to achieving the goal, before this decade is out, of landing a man on the moon and returning him safely to the earth. No single space project in this period will be more impressive to mankind, or more important."

To put his request into perspective, the U.S. was far from a leader in space exploration and was miles behind the Soviets in developing a program. Skeptics questioned the ability of the National Aeronautics and Space Administration (NASA) to put a person on the moon. Naysayers said it was simply impossible, even if they had all the money requested.

Despite all those doubts, on July 20, 1969, two U.S. Apollo 11 astronauts, Neil Armstrong and Edwin "Buzz" Aldrin, Jr., became the first two individuals to ever land on the moon. Six hours after landing on the moon, Neil Armstrong became the first person to step onto the lunar surface. On live television with a worldwide audience, he said that landing on the moon was, "One small step for man, one giant leap for mankind."

Kennedy started with a vision of what many thought was impossible. He believed and led the quest toward the goal. That's a familiar story. Nothing legendary has ever happened without someone believing the impossible could be made possible. Consider these examples:

- In 1903, Orville and Wilbur Wright piloted the first powered airplane 20 feet above the beach in Kitty Hawk, North Carolina. "Flying? That is impossible!" people thought.

- Matt Stutzman hit a long-distance target at 930.04 feet to own a new world record on December 10, 2015. Matt, known as the "Armless Archer," was born without arms. He expertly used his bow and arrow using only his feet and shoulders, and broke a record previously held by an able-bodied person. People thought, "Break an archery world record without arms? That is impossible!"

- Misty Copeland became the first African-American female principal dancer with the prestigious American Ballet Theatre. *Time Magazine* reported that she "changed the face of ballet." "An African American principal dancer? That is impossible!" people thought.

- Sara Blakely, founder of Spanx, was getting ready for a party in 1996 when she realized she didn't have the right garment to provide a smooth look under her white pants. She cut off the feet of her control top pantyhose and got the idea behind Spanx. Sara was named the world's youngest self-made female billionaire by *Forbes Magazine* and one of *TIME*'s 100 Most Influential People. "Sara, a billionaire because of spandex? That's impossible!" people thought.

GET GRITTY

GET PURPOSE

MASTER THOUGHTS

KNOW SELF

DOMINATE CONTROLLABLES

OWN THE MOMENT

CHOOSE EMOTIONS

OWN WHO YOU ARE

LIVE AND LET GO

COURAGE ZONE

As is evident in these examples, impossible is temporary. Impossible is brief. Impossible is short-lived. Impossible is not permanent. As Muhammad Ali said, "Impossible is not a fact. It is an opinion. It is not a declaration. It is a dare!"

The world's best view the impossible as a challenge or dare. When people say, "That's impossible!" they say, "Watch me do it!" They do not put limits on their ability or achievements. They defy limits. They move boundaries. They push past other people's restrictions. They consider all of the ways they can make it happen.

Many of the elite individuals who I have worked with use critics and naysayers as fuel. They wake up and work harder because of them. They use other people's comments and limitations as motivation to stay gritty. They do not give in to what other people think; they rise above their own limitations and the restrictions of others. There was a time in Muhammad Ali's career when everyone around him doubted him—the media, his friends, and even his family. Ali didn't ignore their criticism; he used it as fuel to become the champion of the world. As Aristotle said, "Criticism is something you can avoid easily—by saying nothing, doing nothing, and being nothing."

You see, people rarely outperform their goals or dreams. They rarely achieve more then they set out to. Pushing past your own limitations and the restrictions that others may try to place on you is key in reaching high performance. Restrictions can even unintentionally come from people we love— our parents, siblings, aunts, uncles, cousins, and friends. Pay close attention to the limitations that others try to place on you and break free from those boundaries!

To do so, take a few minutes to reflect on these questions. Dive deep and consider:

- What critics or naysayers do you need to stop listening to?

- Have you given up on a previous dream or goal because

someone believed it was impossible? Have you given up on a previous dream or goal because you thought it was impossible?

- What impossible feat, goal, or dream do you need to reconnect to today?

Exercise: Turn Impossible to I'm Possible

1. First, consider what you think is impossible for you to accomplish. Then, write these impossibles into "What if . . ." questions. For example, perhaps you think it is impossible for you to get into the best shape of your life, make a million dollars, or run an ultramarathon. Put those things into questions like, "What if I got in the best shape of my life?" and "What if I made a million dollars?" and "What if I ran an ultramarathon?" Continue until you have at least ten questions.

2. Next, consider what you have already accomplished that you once thought was impossible. My guess is that you have done the impossible many times in your life! Make a list of your impossibles and read it when you feel tempted to give up or listen to your critics!

GET GRITTY

GET PURPOSE

MASTER THOUGHTS

KNOW SELF

DOMINATE CONTROLLABLES

OWN THE MOMENT

CHOOSE EMOTIONS

OWN WHO YOU ARE

LIVE AND LET GO

COURAGE ZONE

My High Performance Game Plan

TURN IMPOSSIBLE TO I'M POSSIBLE

1. I will complete the Turn Impossible to I'm Possible Exercise to remind myself that I have already done the impossible!

2. When I think, "That's impossible," I will remember that nothing legendary has ever happened without someone believing it was once impossible.

3. When critics or naysayers tell me, "That's impossible," I'll think like the world's best and use those words as fuel and motivation.

4. I will keep in mind examples of those who have done the impossible to remind myself that I can do the same.

My High Performance Power Phrase

I defy limitations. I move boundaries. I push past other people's restrictions. I do the impossible because I'm possible!

Chapter 51

Use the 40 Percent Rule to Find Your Reserve Tank

"When your brain says that you're done, you're only 40 percent done." —DAVID GOGGINS, NAVY SEAL AND ULTRAMARATHONER

You are more capable than you realize. You can run faster, lift more, or work harder. You have a reserve tank that you haven't even tapped. When you feel like giving in, you probably have 60 percent left. You can move to the next level.

David Goggins, a Navy SEAL and ultramarathoner, popularized the Navy SEAL's 40 percent rule. The 40 percent rule states that when you feel like giving in and giving up, you have only used 40 percent of your effort and potential because your reserve tank has 60 percent remaining. Jesse Itzler, co-owner of the NBA's Atlanta Hawks and co-founder of Marquis Jet, one of the world's largest private jet companies, recently wrote the book *Living with a SEAL*. In it, he described his experience hiring Goggins to live with him and his wife Sara Blakely (the founder of Spanx) for 31 days. Itzler saw David running all by himself at a race that was intended for a six-person relay team. He said "I knew he had something I wanted. . . . He was locked in. He was on a personal mission."

On the first day at Itzler's home, Goggins asked him, "How many pull-ups can you do?" He did eight. Then he told him to take thirty seconds and do it again. Itzler described that he did six more, struggling. "We are not leaving here until you do 100," Goggins told him. One at a time, Itzler completed 100 pull-ups. He later reflected, "[Goggins] proved to me right there that there was so much more. We're all capable of so much more than we think we are. It was just a great lesson."

How much more are you capable of? What more can you do when you truly tap into the remaining 60 percent that you have in your reserve tank?

Itzler learned important SEAL training principles from Goggins. He learned that you can train yourself to get past the initial thought, "I'm done." When you appreciate the difficulty, you can embrace the discomfort. The harder the training, the more courage you take from it and the more satisfaction you get when things are difficult or hard. When you dig deep, you feel alive.

My friends, to stay gritty and accomplish our goals and dreams, we have to do the things that don't always feel good. We can't avoid the things we don't like or are not happy about. When we embrace everything in our lives, business, sport, team, or families, we can move easily through them. We realize life is not perfect and never will be. The world's best don't distract themselves from or numb themselves to the discomfort. They don't disconnect, ignore, or procrastinate when they feel discomfort. High performers embrace the uncomfortable, work hard, and stay gritty.

High performers learn to embrace the discomfort so that they continue to learn and grow. They are ready and plan for it. Amateurs dread when the discomfort sets in and wonder if they can handle it.

To be clear, I don't mean embracing and pushing past physical pain. Some of my clients, especially the gritty ones, struggle with when to quit or take a break. I struggle with this sometimes, too, when I am training for a marathon and want to run a personal best, or am so involved in a big project that I don't know when to stop. (Just ask my husband!)

As a general rule, we should embrace discomfort, not pain. There is a distinct difference between these things. Discomfort is duller and generalized, like an aching feeling all over your legs when you run, or an ache in your arms when you are lifting weights. When we embrace discomfort, we realize it helps us accomplish a meaningful goal and doing so will be a source of satisfaction for us. Discomfort happens as you continue to develop yourself. Pain, however, is severe, localized, and persists after you push yourself in that moment. You experience a loss of confidence and motivation when you push through pain. Physical pain is a signal you need to stop or take a break.

Discomfort – When to Push	Pain – When Not to Push
Dull and generalized	Severe and localized to a specific area
Goes away after pushing yourself	Persists after pushing yourself
Under your control	Signals danger to your body and health
Source of satisfaction and inspiration	Can cause loss of confidence and motivation

What can you do to embrace the suck or discomfort (not pain)? Plan for it. Planning for the discomfort allows me to feel more confident in the present moment, and it is something that my clients have found useful, as well. I write out a discomfort plan before each marathon and identify tools from my High Performance Toolbox that I can use while I race. I write out Power Phrases I plan to say during the race, commit to imagining myself finishing in my goal time, and plan to change my stride slightly if my quads get tired. The same kind of planning can be done for the emotional discomfort that comes from pushing yourself and learning new things.

GET GRITTY

GET PURPOSE

MASTER THOUGHTS

KNOW SELF

DOMINATE CONTROLLABLES

OWN THE MOMENT

CHOOSE EMOTIONS

OWN WHO YOU ARE

LIVE AND LET GO

COURAGE ZONE

My High Performance Game Plan

USE THE 40 PERCENT RULE TO FIND YOUR RESERVE TANK

1. When I feel like giving in or giving up, I'll remember the 40 percent rule and how much more I have to give—perhaps up to 60 percent more!

2. When I feel emotional or physical discomfort this week, I'll remember that discomfort is an ally, not an enemy.

3. I commit to distinguishing between discomfort and physical pain. When I feel pain, I'll stop and take a break.

4. To embrace my discomfort, I will write out a discomfort plan so I am ready and can stay gritty.

My High Performance Power Phrase

I have a reserve tank that hasn't even been tapped. I work hard, stay the course, and remain gritty.

Chapter 52

Go for the Gold

"Once you make a 100 percent commitment to something, there are no exceptions. It's a done deal. Nonnegotiable. Case closed!" —JACK CANFIELD

Joseph Schooling, then a thirteen-year-old boy from Singapore, first met Michael Phelps just before he won eight gold medals at the Beijing Olympics. Schooling said, "I wanted to be just like him." The picture of the two shows a world-recognizable Phelps with Schooling, a small boy with glasses.

Eight years later, they were racing head-to-head at the Rio Olympics in Phelps' second-to-last career race. It was the 100-meter butterfly, a race Phelps won in the previous three Olympic Games. Schooling led at the half, and as Phelps turned, he had to push to try to catch up to him. Phelps couldn't do it, and finished just behind Schooling by about three-fourths of a second.

Schooling finished with the gold—the first gold medal ever for Singapore—clocking 50.39 seconds in a new Olympic record, faster than Phelps swam any of his previous three Olympic victories in that event.

After the race, Schooling remarked, "It's crazy to think of what happens in eight years. A lot of this is because of Michael. He's the reason I wanted to be a better swimmer." He continued, "I really can't describe how this moment feels. All the adrenaline is running through my veins right now. It's a dream come true."

Schooling, just like every Olympic medalist and just like his idol Phelps, gave everything he had to becoming a world-class swimmer. He was 100 percent committed. To be world-class at anything, you must be or it won't happen.

When it comes to commitment, 99 percent is hard, 100 percent is easy.

Let me explain.

When you are 100 percent committed, you don't let excuses get in the way. The 100 percent commitment keeps you focused. It frees up energy so you don't have to decide in the moment. Your decision is already made, no matter what. You give it your all. You reduce the excuses and keep them out of your mind. You don't play mind games, and you don't go halfway. You are all in.

Your 100 percent commitment could mean earning a gold medal at a major championship, buying the home of your dreams, losing 20 pounds, getting the job you always wanted, or winning the Super Bowl.

If you do something only at 99 percent commitment, you might not make it to the major championships or Super Bowl, not earn enough to buy the home of your dreams, stay at the same weight even though you know losing weight is necessary, or keep a job that is not fulfilling you. Your 99 percent commitment opens the door to wavering on your dedication. Before you know it, that 1 percent becomes 2, 4, or 10 percent of the time when you are not committed.

If you are 100 percent committed to something—working out, for example—you will do it regardless of how you feel. You will work out even though you went to bed late the night before or you have five million other things to do.

As Ken Blanchard, the author of over thirty books including *The One Minute Manager*, said, "There is a difference between interest and commitment. When you're interested in doing something, you do it only when it's convenient. When you're committed to something, you accept no excuses, only results."

Let's get clear on your commitment with the 100 Percent Committed Exercise:

1. First, write down the "gold medal" you want to be 100 percent committed to. What is worthy of your 100 percent commitment? What deserves your time and attention? Pick one thing and make a commitment by writing it down. It's now a nonnegotiable.

2. Now, make a list of the habits and daily disciplines necessary to ensure you are 100 percent committed to your "gold medal." What must you adhere to every day? Perhaps it's 100 sit-ups every day, running five miles, calling two new potential clients, meditating each morning, shooting two hundred free throws each day, or reading for 1 hour a day.

3. Then, write down what you need to start, stop, and continue to do to reach the 100 percent commitment.

    START: What are the habits you need to start to be 100 percent all-in? Have you listed all of them?

    STOP: What do you need to stop so you avoid the 99 percent commitment?

    CONTINUE: What do you need to continue so you are 100 percent all-in?

At some point, you will likely wake up and not want to take the necessary steps to reach your "gold medal." You will have to fight with yourself to have daily discipline. You will experience ANTs that you must address. You will get in your own way.

When you do, focus less on how you feel and more on the feeling you will get from accomplishing your goal or dream. Stay focused on

GET GRITTY

GET PURPOSE

MASTER THOUGHTS

KNOW SELF

DOMINATE CONTROLLABLES

OWN THE MOMENT

CHOOSE EMOTIONS

OWN WHO YOU ARE

LIVE AND LET GO

COURAGE ZONE

the process and the daily disciplines that you committed to. Follow through with them whether you feel like it or not.

The distance between your dreams and reality is commitment. Daily commitment develops your grit on purpose and in an intentional way.

Are you 100 percent committed to your future? Are you all-in?

The next level is calling you.

My High Performance Game Plan
GO FOR THE GOLD

1. I'll consider what is worthy of my 100 percent commitment. I'll write it out to make my commitment clear.

2. Then, I'll write down the daily disciplines that are necessary to ensure I am 100 percent committed. What do I need to do daily?

3. I'll reflect on what I need to start, stop, and continue to do to reach my "gold medal." I'll write it down to help make it stick.

4. Next time I don't feel like following through with one of my daily disciplines I've outlined, I will remind myself to focus on my commitment, 100 percent.

My High Performance Power Phrase

**I am 100 percent committed and all-in.
I don't make excuses. The next level is
calling me and I hear it.**

Practice 10

CONCLUDING THOUGHTS

Here you are: at the end of this book, with 10 new practices and 52 new strategies to support them. Here in Choose Your Courage Zone, you learned:

- You can choose your Courage Zone over your Comfort Zone by acting with a moment of courage.

- By understanding the Four Fear Facts, you can address your fear and choose courage instead.

- You can change "impossible" to "I'm possible" like the world's best.

- And you can go for your "gold medal" goal by being 100 percent committed and following through with the daily discipline needed to get there.

Now, take a moment to record the following on your Grit Board:

- Your new list of "I knows . . ."

- Your "gold medal" you are 100 percent committed to.

- A key phrase from this section such as "Choose My Courage Zone," "Impossible = I'm Possible!" or "Go for the Gold!"

Free Resources to Go Beyond Grit

This book provides strategies and tools to help you develop a High Performance Mindset to reach new levels of your potential. To help you apply the information provided, I've created bonuses for you at beyondgrit.com/bonus. You can take the Beyond Grit Questionnaire to find out how you score on the Top 10 Practices of the World's Best. You can find more information about the *Beyond Grit Workbook* at beyondgrit.com.

If you want to get an automatic e-mail when my next book is released, you can sign up at cindrakamphoff.com. Your email address will never be shared and you can unsubscribe at any time.

Word-of-mouth is crucial for any author to succeed. If you enjoyed the book, please consider leaving an online review, even if it's just a line or two. Your review would make all the difference in the world! I am grateful for you!

Finally, I am here to help. If you'd like me to come speak, work with your team/group, or work with you individually, you can reach me at (507) 327-9193 or cindra@cindrakamphoff.com. Please share your ideas, feedback, and questions by emailing me or finding me on Twitter @Mentally_Strong. Add #beyondgrit to your tweet or share a picture of your Grit Board.

The next level is calling you. Stay gritty and mentally strong, my friend!

Book's website: beyondgrit.com

Author's website: cindrakamphoff.com

Twitter: @Mentally_Strong

Facebook: facebook.com/drcindrakamphoff

Instagram: instagram.com/cindrakamphoff

Email: cindra@cindrakamphoff.com

Podcast: cindrakamphoff.com/podcast

Acknowledgements

Thank you for your patience, Dara Beevas and Amy Quale, my publishers at Wise Ink Creative Publishing. Dara, you helped me get unstuck many times. Thank you from the bottom of my heart!

Thank you to my designers, Nupoor Gordon and Dan Pitts—your work is top-notch and I love it. Thank you to Nicole Mueller for your sweet illustrations.

Kris Woll, you are a masterful editor! Thank you for helping my voice shine through.

Thank you to Jeff Locke, Cassie Weaver, and Kate Johnson for reading a draft early on. Our conversations were invaluable and shaped the final product!

Many thanks to my personal coach, Su Thomas. My business and this book would not be thriving without your support. Thank you for pushing me!

Thank you to my academic mentors, Dr. Diane Gill, Dr. Dan Gould, and Dr. Shannon Huddleston. You are the world's best!

Big thank you to my sport psychology mastermind peeps: Angie Fifer, Ian Connole, Carrie Cheadle, Josh Lifrak, Bernie Holliday, and JF Menard. You push me outside my comfort zone in each conversation.

Much gratitude to my current, past, and future graduate students in sport psychology. You help me stay fresh and creative! Special thanks to Dave Williams, Jed Clay, Kelsey Timm, Alex Russell, Sophie Kaeter, Eydie Kramer, and Ryan Olson for helping some of these ideas take shape.

Thanks to Faryn Wirkus for helping make my podcast so awesome.

Big thanks to my track and field coaches Dale Clefish, Jim DeJong, John Doely, and Lea Ann Shaddox. You supported me when I needed it the most!

Thank you to all of my clients, who helped me learn about how performance psychology happens in the real world and provided me the trust to teach these principles.

Gratitude to Les Pico and Don Patterson with the Minnesota Vikings. Your support and wisdom are invaluable.

Thank you to everyone at Minnesota State University who support the book and our work in sport and performance psychology.

Much love and gratitude to my parents, Hank and Bev Schelling, who provided me with unconditional love and support. Thank you for always pushing me to be my best!

Thank you to my sisters, Crystal and Chasitie; your conversations and support mean the world to me.

Most importantly, thank you to my soul mate, Dan, who supports me in my passion. Without you, this book would not be possible!

And, Carter and Blake—this book is for you! I love you.

References

Chapter 1

Duckworth, Angela. *Grit: The Power of Passion and Perseverance*. New York: Simon & Schuster, 2016.

Duckworth, Angela. Grit: The Power of Passion and Perseverance. TEDtalk. Accessed May 1, 2017: https://www.ted.com/talks/angela_lee_duckworth_grit_the_power_of_passion_and_perseverance

Eskreis-Winkler, Lauren, Elizabeth P. Shulman, Scott A. Beal, and Angela L. Duckworth, "The grit effect: Predicting retention in the military, the workplace, school and marriage." *Frontier Psychology* (2014), accessed May 1, 2017, doi: 10.3389/fpsyg.2014.00036

Martin, Jeffrey J. , Brigid Byrd, Michele Lewis Watts, and Maana Dent "Gritty, hardy, and resilient: Predictors of sport engagement and life satisfaction in wheelchair basketball players." *Journal of Clinical Sport Psychology* 9 (2015): 345-359.

Chapter 2

Ericsson, K. Anders and Robert Pool. *Peak: Secrets from the New Science of Expertise*. New York: Houghton Mifflin, 2016.

Ericsson, K. Anders, Michael J. Prietula, and Edward T. Cokely. "The making of an expert." *Harvard Business Review*, 2007. Accessed May 1, 2017, https://hbr.org/2007/07/the-making-of-an-expert.

Malcolm Gladwell. *Outliers: The Story of Success*. New York: Back Bay Books, 2011.

Chapter 3

Gillett, Rachel. "How Walt Disney, Oprah Winfrey, and 19 Other Successful People Rebounded After Getting Fired." *Business Insider.* Accessed May 1, 2017: https://www.inc.com.

Katie, Byron. *Loving What Is: Four Questions That Can Change Your Life.* New York: Three Rivers Press, 2003

Katie, Byron with Stephen Mitchell. *A Thousand Names for Joy: Living in Harmony with the Way Things Are.* Easton, PA: Harmony Press, 2008.

Oettingen, Gabriele. "Future thought and behaviour change." *European Review of Social Psychology* 23 (2012): 1-63.

Chapter 4

What Oprah Learned from Jim Carrey. Accessed May 1, 2017: http://www.oprah.com/oprahs-lifeclass/what-oprah-learned-from-jim-carrey-video

Canfield, Jack. *The Success Principles: How to Get from Where You Are to Where You Want to Be.* New York: HarperCollins, 2005.

Chapter 5

Getting After It with Olympian, Entrepreneur, and ESPN2 Analyst Carrie Tollefson, Episode 3. Accessed May 2, 2017: https://itunes.apple.com/us/podcast/high-performance-mindset-i/id1034819901

Locke, Edwin A. and Gary P. Latham. "Building a practically useful theory of goal setting and task motivation: A 35-year odyssey." *American Psychologist*, 57 (2002), 705–717.

Locke, Edwin A. and Gary P. Latham. "New directions in goal-setting theory." *Current Directions in Psychological Science, 2006.* doi: 1467-8721. Accessed May 2, 20017: http://journals.sagepub.com/doi/abs/10.1111/j.1467-8721.2006.00449.x

Weinberg, Robert and Daniel Gould. *Foundations of Sport and Exercise Psychology*, 6th edition. Champaign, IL: Human Kinetics, 2014.

Williams, Jean (ed.). *Applied Sport Psychology: Personal Growth to Peak Performance*, 7th edition. New York: McGraw-Hill, 2014.

Chapter 6

Bolt, Usain. *Faster than Lightning: My Autobiography*. New York: HarperSport, 2014.

Mischel, Walter. *The Marshmallow Test: Why Self-Control is the Engine of Success*. New York: Back Bay Books, 2015.

Chapter 7

Sinek, Simon. *Start with Why: How Great Leaders Inspire Everyone to Take Action*. New York: Portfolio, 2011.

Chapter 8

Jobs, Steve. "You've Got to Find What You Love." Last modified June 15, 2005, http://news.stanford.edu/news/2005/june15/jobs-061505.html

Chapter 9

Canfield, Jack. *The Success Principles: How to Get from Where You Are to Where You Want to Be*. New York: HarperCollins, 2005.

Leider, Richard. *The Power of Purpose: Find Meaning, Live Longer, Better.* San Francisco, CA: Berrett-Koehler, 2010.

Maslow, Abraham H. *Motivation and Personality*, 3rd edition. London, England: Longman, 1987.

(Note: There are lots of ways to define your purpose. The purpose statement exercise I presented in this chapter has been informed by Jack Canfield and Tony Robbins).

Chapter 10

Hendricks, Gay. *The Big Leap: Conquer Your Hidden Fear and Take Life to the Next Level*. New York: Harper Collins, 2009.

Chapter 11

Seligman, Martin. *Learned Optimism: How to Change Your Mind and Your Life*. New York: Random House, 2006.

Chapter 12

Amen, Daniel. *Change Your Brain, Change Your Life: The Breakthrough Program for Conquering Anxiety, Depression, Obsessiveness, Anger, and Impulsiveness*. New York: Three Rivers, 1998.

Leaf, Caroline. *Switch on Your Brain: The Key to Peak Happiness, Thinking and Health*. Grand Rapids, MI: Baker Books, 2013.

Chapter 13

Afremow, Jim. *The Champion's Mind: How Great Athletes Think, Train, and Thrive*. New York: Rodale.

Vealey, Robin. *Coaching for the Inner Edge*. Morgantown, WV: Fitness Information Technology, 2005.

(Note: Robin Vealey talks about P3 Thinking in her book which inspired me to create my own way of understanding self-talk included in this chapter. Jim Afremow also talks about Power Phrases in his book).

Chapter 16

Nolen-Hoeksema, Susan. *Women Who Think Too Much: How to Break Free or Overthinking and Reclaim Your Life*. New York: Holt, 2004.

Chapter 17

Take What the Defense Gives You with Cancer Survivor Jonathan Zierdt, Episode 57. Accessed May 2, 2017: https://itunes.apple.com/us/podcast/high-performance-mindset-i/id1034819901

Bradberry, Travis and Jean Greaves. *Emotional Intelligence 2.0. San Diego:* TalentSmart, 2009.

Chapter 18

Frankl, Victor. *Man's Search for Meaning* Boston: Beacon Press, 2006.

Chapter 19

Brooks, Alison Wood. "Get Excited: Reappraising Pre-Performance Anxiety as Excitement." *Journal of Experimental Psychology 143* (2014): 1144-1158.

Hanin, Yuri. *Emotions in Sport*. Champaign, IL: Human Kinetics, 1999.

Williams, Jean and Vikki Krane. *Applied Sport Psychology: Personal Growth to Peak Performance*, 7th edition. New York: McGraw-Hill, 2014.

Chapter 20

Csikszentmihalyi, Mihaly. *Flow: The Psychology of Optimal Experience*. New York: Harper Collins, 1990.

Kotler, Steven. *The Rise of the Superman: Decoding the Science of Ultimate Human Performance*. New York: Houghlin Mifflin, 2014.

Chapter 21

Ravissa, Ken and Tom Hanson. *Heads Up Baseball: Playing the Game One Pitch at a Time*. New

York: McGraw-Hill, 1998.

Selk, Jason. *10-Minute Mental Toughness: The Mental Training Program for Winning Before the Game Begins*. New York: McGraw-Hill, 2008.

Chapter 22

Mack, Gary with David Casstevens. *Mind Gym: An Athlete's Guide to Inner Excellence*. New York: McGraw-Hill, 2001.

Chapter 23

Cain, Brian. *The Daily Dominator*. Brian Cain Peak Performance Publishing, 2013.

Chapter 24

Downing, Skip. *On Course: Strategies for Creating Success in College and in Life, 4th edition*. New York: Houghton Mifflin, 2005.

Holiday, Ryan. *The Obstacle is the Way. The Timeless Art of Turning Trials into Triumph*. New York: Penguin, 2014.

Chapter 25

Love, Resilience and Thriving in Difficulties with WYSIWYG Juice Founder, Kristi Schuck, Episode 42. Accessed May 2, 2017: https://itunes.apple.com/us/podcast/high-performance-mindset-i/id1034819901

Canfield, Jack. *Success Principles: How to Get from Where You are to Where You Want to Be*. New York: Harper Collins, 2005.

Chapter 26

Gould, Daniel, Diane Guinan, Christy Greenleaf, Russ Medbery, and Kirsten Peterson. "Factors affecting Olympic performance: Perceptions of athletes and coaches from more and less successful teams." *Journal of Applied Sport Psychology, 13* (2002): 371-394.

Gould, Daniel , Kristen Dieffenbach and Aaron Moffett. "Psychological Characteristics and Their Development in Olympic Champions." *Journal of Applied Sport Psychology 14* (2002): 172-204.

Chapter 27

Ruiz, Don Miguel. *The Four Agreements: A Practical Guide to Personal Freedom*. San Rafael, CA: Amber-Allen Publishing, 1997.

Chapter 28

Kabat-Zinn, Jon. *Full Catastrophe Living: Using the Wisdom of Your Body and Mind to Face Stress, Pain, and Illness*. New York: Bantam Dell, 1990.

Mumford, George. *The Mindful Athlete: Secrets to Pure Performance*. Berkeley, CA: Parallax, 2015.

Roenigk, Alyssa. "Lotus Pose on Two." *ESPN the Magazine*. Aug 21, 2013. Retrieved on May 1, 2017: http://www.espn.com/nfl/story/_/id/9581925/seattle-seahawks-use-unusual-techniques-practice-espn-magazine

Chapter 29

Saban, Nick and Brian Curtis. *How Good Do You Want to Be? A Champion's Tips on How to Lead and Succeed.* New York: Ballantine Book, 2007.

Stulberg, Brad. *Big Goals Can Backfire. Olympians Show Us What to Focus on Instead.* August 3, 2016. Retrieved on May 1, 2017 from http://nymag.com/scienceofus/2016/08/why-having-big-goals-can-backfire.html

Chapter 30

One Play at a Time with Minnesota Vikings Wide Receiver, Adam Thielen. Episode 64. Accessed May 1, 2017: https://itunes.apple.com/us/podcast/high-performance-mindset-i/id1034819901

Chapter 31

Weisinger, Hendrie and J. P. Pawliw-Fry. *Performing under Pressure: The Science of Doing Your Best When it Matters Most.* New York: Crown Publishing, 2015.

Chapter 32

Achor, Shawn. *The Happiness Advantage: The Seven Principles of Positive Psychology That Fuel Success and Performance at Work.* New York: Crown Business, 2010.

Ben-Shahar, Tal. *Happier: Learn the Secrets to Daily Joy and Lasting Fulfillment.* New York: McGraw Hill, 2007.

Fredrickson, Barbara. *Positivity: Top-Notch Research Reveals the 3-to-1 Ratio That Will Change Your Life.* New York: Random House, 2009.

Gladwell, Malcolm. *Blink: The Power of Thinking Without Thinking.* New York: Back Bay Books. 2007.

Losada, Marcial and Emily Heaphy. "The Role of Positivity and Connectivity in the Performance of Business Teams." *American Behavioral Scientist, 47* (2004), 740-765. doi:10.1177/0002764203260208

Seligman, Martin E. P. *Flourish: A Visionary New Understanding of Happiness and Well-being.* New York: Free Press, 2011.

Chapter 33

Cuddy, Amy. *Presence: Bringing Your Boldest Self to Your Biggest Challenges.* New York: Little, Brown and Company, 2015.

Vealey, Robin. *Coaching for the Inner Edge.* Morgantown, WV: Fitness Information Technology, 2005.

Chapter 34

Ferguson, Yuna L. and Kennon M. Sheldon. "Trying to be happier really can work: Two experimental studies." *Journal of Positive Psychology, 8* (2013): 23-33.

Hsieh, Tony. *Delivering Happiness: A Path to Profits, Passion and Purpose.* New York: Grand Central

Publishing, 2013.

Lyubomirsky, Sonja. *The How of Happiness: A New Approach to Getting the Life You Want.* New York: Penguin Books, 2008.

Chapter 35

Olympic Hopeful & 2-Time Cancer Survivor Talks Resilience, Gabe Grunewald. Episode 15. Accessed May 1, 2017: https://itunes.apple.com/us/podcast/high-performance-mindset-i/id1034819901

Chen, Lung Hung and Chia-Huei Wu. "Gratitude Enhances Change in Athletes' Self-Esteem: The Moderating Role of Trust in Coach.*" Journal of Applied Sport Psychology* 26 (2014): 349-362.

Chapter 36

Selk, Jason. *10-Minute Mental Toughness: The Mental Training Program for Winning Before the Game Begins.* New York: McGraw-Hill, 2008.

Williams, Jean and Vikki Krane. *Applied Sport Psychology: Personal Growth to Peak Performance,* 7th edition. New York: McGraw-Hill, 2014.

(Note: I first read about the Centering Breath in Jason Selk's book which I discuss in the chapter. I'd like to thank Jeb Clay, former graduate student, for taking time to brainstorm the VICE acronym together).

Chapter 37

Cornelius, Allen, John M. Silva, David E. Conroy, and Greg Petersen. "The Projected Performance Model: Relating Cognitive and Performance Antecedents of Psychological Momentum." *Perceptual Motor Skills, 84* (1997). Retrieved May 1, 2017: http://journals.sagepub.com/doi/pdf/10.2466/pms.1997.84.2.475

Gordon, Jon. *Energy Bus: 10 Rules to Fuel Your Life, Work, and Team with Positive Energy.* New York: Wiley, 2007.

Meyers, Chris. *The Top 3 Entrepreneurial Lessons Learned from Watching Football.* Retrieved May 1, 2017 from https://www.forbes.com/sites/chrismyers/2016/01/24/the-top-3-entrepreneurial-lessons-learned-from-watching-football/#6cda2fb65b56

Chapter 38

Kiyosaki, Robert T. *Rich Dad, Poor Dad: What the Rich Teach Their Kids About Money That the Poor and Middle Class Do Not!* Scottsdale, AR: Plata Publishing, 2011.

Chapter 39

Brown, Brene'. *The Gifts of Imperfection: Let Go of Who You Think You're Suppose to Be and Embrace Who You Are.* Center City, MN: Hazelden Publishing, 2010.

Chapter 40

Eker, T. Harv. *The Secrets of the Millionaire Mind: Mastering the Inner Game of Wealth.* New York: Harper Business, 2005.

Kamphoff, Cindra S. Diane L. Gill, and Sharon Huddleston. "Jealousy in Sport: Exploring Jealousy's Relationship to Cohesion." *Journal of Applied Sport Psychology,* 17 (2005): 209-305.

Chapter 41

Brown, Brene'. *Daring Greatly: How the Courage to Be Vulnerable Transforms the Way We Live, Love, Parent and Lead.* New York: Penguin, 2012.

Loehr, Jim. *The Power of Story: Change Your Story, Change Your Destiny in Business and in Life.* New York: Free Press, 2008.

Sandberg, Sheryl. *Lean In: Women, Work, and the Will to Lead.* New York: Knopf Publishing, 2013.

Sandberg, Sheryl and Adam Grant. *Option B: Facing Adversity, Building Resilience and Finding Joy.* New York: Knopf Publishing, 2017.

Chapter 43

Neff, Kristen. *Self-Compassion: Stop Beating Yourself Up and Leave Insecurity Behind.* New York: William Morrow, 2010.

Chapter 45

Dweck, Carol. *Mindset: The New Psychology of Success.* New York: Ballantine Books, 2006.

Chapter 46

Gould, Daniel, Kristen Dieffenbach and Aaron Moffett. "Psychological Characteristics and Their Development in Olympic Champions." *Journal of Applied Sport Psychology 14* (2002): 172-204.

Chapter 47

Schiff, Lewis. *Business Brilliant: Surprising Lessons from the Greatest Self-Made Business Icons.* New York: Harper Business, 2013.

(Note: I'd like to thank Dave Williams, a former graduate student, for contributing the start of the concept Learn, Burn, Return to the Center of Sport and Performance Psychology's curriculum).

Chapter 51

Itzler, Jesse. *Living with a SEAL: 31 Days Training with the Toughest Man on the Planet.* New York: Center Street, 2016.

Chapter 52

Blanchard, Ken and Spencer Johnson. *The One Minute Manager.* New York: William Morrow, 2003.

Canfield, Jack. *The Success Principles: How to Get from Where You Are to Where You Want to Be.* New York: HarperCollins, 2005.